# WASTED GENIUS

## How IQ & SAT Tests Are Hurting Our Kids

### and Crippling America

## Other Books by the Author

### Common Genius
**Guts, Grit and Common Sense**
**How Ordinary People Create Prosperous Societies**
**and How Intellectuals Make them Collapse**

Amazon Book Reviewers wrote:

> "Simply superb. It was hard for me to believe that there could be a totally new theory of history.... But Mr. Greene ties a myriad of sources together and draws the only possible (and startlingly simple) conclusions. Kudos. Don't miss this."

> "The GENIUS of this book is that it provides a compelling framework for the interpretation of history: ECONOMIC FREEDOM allows the COMMON GENIUS of millions of men and women to spark the human progress we all desire."

### Stories for Kids
**A collection of outdoor stories for youngsters 4–12**

# WASTED GENIUS

## How IQ & SAT Tests Are Hurting Our Kids

### and Crippling America

## by Bill Greene

### Illustrations by Bruce Greene

### Introduction by
### Kathleen J. Wikstrom

**LOST NATION BOOKS**

LANCASTER, NEW HAMPSHIRE
WWW.LOSTNATIONBOOKS.COM

ISBN-13: 978-1453896372
ISBN-10: 1453896376

Library of Congress Control Number: 2011900255


Printed in the United States of America

To Our Children:
Bill, Bruce, Josie, Winnie, Amy, Leo, Jill, Jeff, Whitney

To Our Grandchildren:
Emily, Alex, Rosie, Sam, Abby, Annie, Peter,
Abby, Katie, Leo, Mark, Brian, Carissa, Nathanael, Theo

And The Angels:
Alyssa Faith, Timothy Robert,
Jared William, and Christina Hope

# Table of Contents

# Preface

> "I dream fondly but futilely of my own 1950s
> childhood, when by far the commonest words I heard
> from my parents were 'Go out and play. Make sure
> you're back in time for supper.' How on earth did
> civilization survive?"
>
> —John Derbyshire

WRITING A BOOK CAN BE an educational experience, not so much
from the research required, but more significantly from the challenge
of marshalling the insights gained from all the random material
gathered into some ordered form. It is not enough to know everything
ever written or thought on a subject—that is the hallmark of "experts"
who try to dazzle you with their accumulated knowledge. What
matters, and adds to a reader's understanding, can only come from a
synthesis of everything discovered into meaningful patterns and conclusions.

In the case of *Wasted Genius*, the writing process forced me to
draw some overarching conclusions based upon my own experience,
the history of education and the theories put forth by scholars in the
field, and from correlating such knowledge with recent findings in
neurology that reveal how our brains and personalities develop and
function. I discovered that the "theories" of most current scholars on
the subject are the least instructive, but their diverse opinions do
illustrate the vast number of wrong answers that come from most
experts. (When most experts disagree with each other, shouldn't we
assume that most of them have to be wrong?)

"Experts" in soft sciences such as politics, economics, climatol-
ogy, psychology, anthropology, and education usually lack the objectivity found among experts in the hard sciences. The rigors of the
scientific method—observation, measurement, and the requirement
of consistency of results—are not part of the soft-scientists' tool kits.

Their deficiencies stem from trying to emulate the physical scientists, an effort that requires them to treat human behavior as if it obeyed some absolute physical laws such as gravity, momentum, evolution, or could be mapped like the celestial orbits of inanimate planets. That, of course, is impossible, humans being such independent and ornery creatures, so their findings end too often in the speculative, philosophical, often utopian arena of recurring fads, fancies, and follies that have so often throughout history held up mankind's progress. The recent hundred- year love affair with IQ tests is one such fancy that should be unmasked.

I have for years had a vague uneasiness with the undue emphasis placed on tests and school grades. But it still came as a surprise to discover that such fears are fully justified. There have been a few vocal and authoritative critics of IQ tests during the past thirty years, and in the following pages, their warnings are summarized. But such criticism of IQ tests is not new. They were anticipated by J. P. Guilford fifty years ago, when he asserted the idea of "multiple independent mental abilities." And more than seventy-five years ago, L. L. Thurstone tried to warn us about the complexity of measuring anyone's full capabilities with a single yardstick.

Jean Piaget, a pioneer creator of IQ tests, indicated one hundred years ago that there could be no single test of a student's abilities and that the tests were only useful to measure a teacher's progress in instructing students. In spite of such warnings, the entrenched educational and testing interests have promoted the tests far beyond their relevance—with dire consequences for both our children and our country. The voices of reason were drowned out by the self-aggrandizing ambitions and greed of the teaching and testing industry. This history illustrates a common feature of soft-science intellectuals: that they will drown out all opposition to their pet theories, not with logic or conclusive facts, but with what Thomas Sowell describes as their "verbal virtuosity."

A related "blind spot" that has been perpetuated by soft scientists comes from numerous fallacies based on Darwinian evolutionary theories—that humans are just big apes, ruled by atavistic passions, and incapable of either controlling themselves or rising above raw instinctual behavior. This view, with its exaggerated application of the "survival of the fittest" mentality, and an excessive regard for "human nature," gave added credence to the notion that intelligence is a fixed-at-birth biological fact. That recently discredited notion has allowed the academics and intelligentsia to assert that intelligence varies by race and class, and that some people are "better" than others. It does not take a genius to see that these insidious concepts have been advanced by those who want to elevate themselves by denigrating everyone else.

Because abstract thinkers score higher on IQ and SAT tests, we have gradually become burdened by a new elite leadership that is long on theory and short on common sense. What's worse, their influence has permeated the "approved" methods used for both parenting and schooling our youth. In the following pages, we will examine the results, focusing on the question of whether these new theories have resulted in any gains for our children compared to the children of our recent ancestors.

Two important elements of the nature-nurture debate that have been ignored by most writers on the subject are the importance of a *balanced* cognitive capability and the necessity to concede that there is a vast array of multiple capabilities that need balancing. Mitchell Estaphan teaches psychology at a nearby community college, and he has a theory about every human's need for "balance." His ideas are founded on an understanding of how different people's brains work. The Left and Right sides contribute differing amounts of input to different individuals. The Left mode tends to supply a rational, emotionally controlled, and logical approach, usually based on observations of the real world and drawing on accumulated information. The Right side of the brain leans to intuitive, subjective judgments, with a more open expression of feelings. The Left is more concrete and "masculine"; the right more abstract and "feminine." Since everyone has a mix of these quadrants, their abilities are founded on a number of different forms of intelligence, all of which contribute to success, and relegates the ability to nail IQ tests to being just one of their "multiple intelligences."

Mitch's research supports the belief that slightly under one-half of students are abstract learners, who can readily learn from merely reading, while slightly more than half are applied learners, who learn best by seeing and doing real-life tasks. Because our schools teach a one-size fits all pedagogy, some students benefit while others fall behind. And yet all methods of learning are beneficial. My studies of history show that it has been the concrete thinkers, far more than the abstract thinkers, who have achieved the innovations and discoveries that have advanced societies. However, it is no secret that IQ tests reward the conceptual abilities of abstract thinkers and penalize the capabilities of practical doers.

Today's teaching establishment, which has made a fetish of multiculturalism, claiming that all cultures are equally praiseworthy, reveals its hypocrisy by failing to accept and cultivate the diversity of our students' learning styles. There are many equally valuable ways of learning and different personal bases for knowing. We must accept the idea of multiple intelligences and the need to understand the many elements that make up an individual's total mental capability. Estaphan points out that those individuals with skills across three or four quadrants gain an advantage from such "whole brained" flexibility and power that allows them to work with many groups and assume leadership roles and executive functions. A high IQ by itself offers no evidence of such capability.

This significant variability in the way our brains work reveals a few things about the history of human advances. If classic Darwinian theory applied to humans, the "survival of the fittest" concept would suggest that those with the greatest survival and reproductive skills would have passed on their genes to most of today's peoples. In most of the animal kingdoms, the strongest males control their harems and pass on their aggressive natures and vigorous bodies. Quite differently, when the earliest humans adopted monogamy, they established a pattern where a much greater diversity of genetic types was perpetuated. Almost all males succeeded at reproduction, and the resulting multi-faceted gene pool created a greater probability for innovative and creative genius to emerge. And when our ancestors discovered fire, built shelters, and donned fur clothing, they largely escaped the harsh laws of survival of the fittest. And that was tens of thousands of years ago!

With shelter, heat, and monogamy, the human race has been able to sustain a broad ranger of capabilities, unavailable to all other living things. The occasional innovative tinkerers that emerged from that large and varied gene pool were the scientists, engineers and mechanics that powered civilization's advances. Unfortunately, for the past fifty years, our colleges have rejected diversity of mental style and instead have selected the tiny percentage of students who display the highest abstract and intuitive thinking revealed by IQ tests. Those are the people being advanced more and more into leadership positions, representing a new elite with a fondness for abstract concepts, an out of touch elite that harbors a contempt for the practical and traditional ways of thinking, a dangerous group that exposes us all to the folly of their ideologies, their speculative financial dealings, and their corrupt politics.

It is worth noting that few individuals being "produced" today are the equal in wisdom, maturity, and value to their country as the historic leaders that built and sustained us: Adams, Franklin, Carnegie, Washington, Lincoln, Reagan, Abigail Adams, Edison, or Harriet Beecher Stowe. The differences are not of a genetic or cognitive nature. On average, Americans today have the same cognitive powers that our ancestors did one hundred and two hundred years ago. The differences are of an environmental nature, a difference in attitude, a difference in initiative and self-reliance. There was some such "X factor" in the earlier Americans' childhoods that is missing today. If there are ways to isolate that crucial influence—and we could thereby help our children grow, while simultaneously enhancing our winning national character—we would do well to find that principle and use it.

Any search for the secret ingredient that made America great must include the cumulative knowledge we have from the physical sciences of biology and psychology, as well as from the lessons to be derived from history.

Science tells us three things:

1. Children's brains are not fully developed until their mid-20s.
2. There is no way to predict which child will accomplish great things.
3. Test scores miss most of the vital traits that make for success.

History tells us three things:

1. Great people make great nations
2. Empowering and ennobling cultures help people attain their full potential.
3. Parents, families, and schools are the bedrock of culture, and can be supported or undermined by community organizations, churches, and the media/entertainment industry.

The related historical truth that conspicuously applies to America is that our nation was made by its people—the various enterprising immigrants who settled the land. They left behind their homelands, their Kings and pompous aristocracies, and the closed economies that offered little opportunity to the poor or disadvantaged. They brought with them their love of freedom, their many spiritual Faiths, and their fierce independence and self-reliance. And those people, along with the hordes that followed, built America.

America did not become great because of its climate, geography, natural resources, or lady luck. Most of the European countries along with much of Asia and South America, North Africa, and the Far East had similar natural advantages. But the people inhabiting those other equally "blessed" regions never found a way to do what the Americans did. That failure to keep up was not because they were inferior in any way, but simply because their political systems, cultural mores, and autocratic leadership obstructed individual initiative. The ordinary people in those lands lost out simply because they never had the freedom or opportunity that was available in America.

America's growth in population and affluence was explosive! Starting in 1620 as a few small outposts, the new arrivals spread up and down the coast, into the mountains, and beyond to the Pacific ocean. There was no infrastructure waiting them, no docks, no bridges, no shelter or farms. With hand tools, they cut the forests, dug out the rocks and roots, plowed the soil, and grew their food. Within two hundred years, these first eight generations of Americans built a democratic nation of unheard of prosperity and power.

Within 150 years of the landing at Plymouth Rock, six generations of Americans had challenged—and then beaten—the most powerful nation in the world, claiming and winning liberty from their mother country. There were dozens of nations from China to Persia to France, spanning most of the globe, that had been building their cities, roads, and businesses for more than a thousand years, and yet not one could match the extraordinary and rapid progress achieved by those American pioneer generations. A marathon runner would have to give all his competitors a twenty-mile head start, then sprint to the finish line before all of them, to match the enormity and rapidity of America's achievement, an achievement fueled by our past generations, generations that were fueled by a different psychology than the one being taught in today's schools and colleges.

That explosion of progress from 1620–1870 occurred with no aristocracy, virtually no government, no large organizations, no stultifying Faith, no taxes, and no intellectual class. It is the author's contention that it was the absence of those impediments that allowed American individuals to attain such extraordinary progress. The common people of most any other society in the rest of the world could have done the same—if they had been free of such restraining and repressive influences.

Ralph Waldo Emerson has been called America's first intellectual, and his first published book was issued in 1836, more than two hundred years after the first settlers had arrived. Many intellectuals followed, and after 250 years of unparalleled progress, the common people—the concrete thinkers—started to be pushed aside by those who pretended to be smarter, more sophisticated, and better educated. That was the beginning of our national decline. The momentum and vigor of practical people is still carrying us forward, but slower and slower, as the obstacles to their efforts multiply. It is worth asking why members of our "Ruling Class"—with their years and years of schooling, advanced primarily because of their high IQ and SAT test scores, and employing all the advances science has offered—have somehow managed to reverse three centuries of progress. But reverse it they have, and one of the objects of this book is to explain how such an anomaly has occurred.

America is Broken. There were early signs in the 1960s, when a Harvard professor received favorable media coverage when he urged students to "light up, turn off, and drop out." Later, we saw Presidents John F. Kennedy and Bill Clinton turn the oval office into a Hugh Hefner playhouse. Just recently, the breakage became significant, unprecedented, and unmistakable; the financial collapse of 2009 revealed the corrupt conspiracy between Congress, the Treasury Department, Federal Reserve officials, Fannie Mae, and the most speculative trading divisions of our largest and once respected financial banks and insurance companies.

Corruption is not new. Politicians have always wasted or "redirected" billions of dollars to cronies and special interest groups; that is what government officials do. In the past, we were not crippled by a billion dollars of fraud here and a billion there. However, today's leadership elites have escalated the cost of their greed and incompetence. We are talking in the trillions of dollars, and our ballooning national debt threatens the future of America.

This book is not political, but it does call for fiscal prudence—which might be called a form of "conservative" financial management. But the alternative—liberal spending in excess of one's income—is a violation of every sound financial planning rule and should not even be considered a debatable political issue. There are many social issues where one can debate liberal-conservative positions, but in financial matters the need to minimize debt, eliminate deficits, maintain a strong currency and banking system, and establish transparency and honesty, are simple time-tested principles.

While deficits will eventually bankrupt the country, they have an added perverse effect: The growing acceptance that deficits can be tolerated is bankrupting the fiscal common sense of the American people. We are told that the deficit and national debt are not problems. We are told that each of us should also use credit to live the good life. Our governments at all levels sell us lottery tickets so we can hope to hit it big without the pain of saving or thrift. And yet we know that our children must be taught to save, to defer gratification of some impulses and desires, and to possess the character to be honorable in their personal and financial dealings. Those values are three of the most important things they need to learn.

But look at the bad examples rampant around us! The politician-demagogues deliberately create deficits to pay for the promises they made to keep getting elected. They lie. They steal. They cheat, and some demean the office they sit in. In this book we will examine how we got to be burdened by this new elite class in Washington and Wall Street that is destroying our country. We will reveal the impact they have on us, the citizens, on our children, and on American character. If we don't throw the rascals out, these demagogues will surely bring on the decline of America and the end of our power and prosperity. Then what will happen to this sweet land of liberty?

Because the "best and brightest" as measured today by our left-leaning academics have few practical skills—and are predisposed against concrete thinking—their primary employment opportunities are in government-planning roles, complex financial manipulations, and in the proliferating special advocacy organizations and foundations that seek to change America. As a group, they have become parasites feeding on the productive fruits of the working people. Until we get our schools to nurture the practical abilities of "average" students and encourage the high IQ types to enter the hard-physical-sciences, we are doomed to keep producing a harmful crop of unreasoning graduates hell-bent on assuming power-based positions in government and think-tanks. And all because we have been hoodwinked into an incorrect understanding of who's smart and who isn't!

We must look beyond both IQ and EQ to a new concept of TCQ—a person's total competency quotient. All kids can be inculcated with the values and attitudes that make for successful lives. The average ones are frequently the most valuable to the nation, and the "brightest," except for their efforts in the physical sciences, should not get preferential treatment. We must recognize the great variety of attributes that make up a person's "intelligence." Only then can we gain an understanding of whether such qualities as integrity, rational decision-making, and initiative, are inborn or learned—and how these components affect the destiny of children and the country.

In short, we will examine just what "intelligence" represents, what makes a person an intellectual, and just what makes an individual and a nation successful. The good news is that parents and schools can once again raise the kinds of people that made America great. We will show that it has been our false notion of intelligence and expertise that has caused our growing national dysfunction. And curiously, it all gets back to the problems caused by overemphasis on IQ and SAT scores, school grades, and current theories on schooling and parenting. We will show how practical thinking trumps abstract thinking and how our nation's future is dependent not on the most intelligent but on the most balanced, the most pragmatic, and those with the highest integrity.

# Introduction

As President of Laissez Faire Books from 2004 to 2007, I received a lot of manuscripts from hopeful authors. Ninety-nine percent of these were rejected, so I was excited to read one from Bill Greene that was truly insightful and offered unique conclusions about how the "common man" has created prosperous societies and how the "intellectual class" has so often caused them to crumble. I was pleased to have the opportunity to publish that book, *Common Genius*, in 2007.

But I was even more excited when he sent me an early draft of *Wasted Genius*. Here, Bill has taken the important ideas presented in *Common Genius* and applied them to the subjects of education and childrearing, two subjects of particular interest to me. As a parent and long-time homeschooler, I have put a lot of thought and personal research into how children learn, what keeps them from achieving their potential, and what leads them to success. And Bill Greene has hit the nail on the head in this impressive book.

*Wasted Genius* is one of the first serious attempts to define all the various capabilities that define a mature adult. It establishes that characteristics such as persistence, imagination, and emotional restraint are no less important than IQ (and probably more important). Placing IQ and EQ alongside the other equally important personal characteristics that make an adult successful, contented, and complete, Bill Greene has come up with a much more meaningful scale for intelligence, which he calls Total Competency Quotient (TCQ).

Bill Greene shows that most of the great inventors and most successful entrepreneurs were empowered more by these kinds of practical and personal abilities than by mere memorization and arithmetic skills. And these conclusions force us to recognize the possibilities of every child and to better understand the value of concrete pragmatic thinking over the abstract thinking found in the academic elites.

For ten years, I ran a children's theatre for the homeschooling community, first in Northern Virginia and later in Arkansas. I can't tell you the number of parents that have told me they were totally shocked at what their children where able to do on the stage. And it wasn't because I was able to identify the most talented young actors around. We normally found a part for every child who auditioned. What I did do was let them know that I expected them to work hard, attend every rehearsal, and give it their all. I had high expectations for them, and they nearly always came through to exceed them.

My experience with my theatre students confirmed the idea presented in this book that it is more important to motivate and inspire children than to teach them a canned curriculum, that their success will depend upon, first, their learning to work hard at some task; secondly, finding an area where their capabilities can flourish; and, finally, applying themselves to that field of work. And less-than-superb grades and test scores don't have to hold them back. Parents and school can provide guidance, encouragement, and a foundation for successful effort, but children must understand early that the rest is up to them and the sky is the limit—if they are willing to work for it.

Parents needn't buy into the current emphasis on mere academic skills—what Bill Greene calls "A Conspiracy of the Egg Heads," because it seeks to fill all leadership positions in America with abstract thinkers who will parrot the grand schemes of those who seek to rule, while ignoring the significant contributions of the less intellectual and more practical among us. Rather than worry if their children will get into the best colleges, parents can once again focus on encouraging their children to be the best they can be in whatever field they choose.

*Wasted Genius* gives parents and teachers a wonderful guide for helping children reach their potential and to put them on the road to happiness and success as an adult. If you're concerned about building your child's self-esteem in a meaningful way, imagine the effect when children are taught to understand that they truly can do just about anything they put their minds to (and effort behind). And no IQ or SAT test can tell them they can't!

You will probably learn a bit about how human beings are wired while reading this book. The new knowledge will be valuable in understanding just how much potential exists—and how you and your children can reach it. To me, the most exciting research shared in *Wasted Genius* concerns the unique human ability to choose what one wants to be best at by simply working at the "talent" that one wishes to develop (see the section in Chapter 5 subtitled "How Malleable Is Intelligence? Developing Talents"). The implications open an incredible number of possibilities and can't help but inspire young people to be the best they can be.

Our children and our society suffer from the failure to help all our kids reach their full potential, a totally avoidable gap that the author appropriately calls "Wasted Genius," a loss primarily attributable to the current obsession with SAT scores and the overvaluation of abstract thinking.

I hope every parent and every teacher reads this book. The future of our children—and our society—may depend on it.

*Kathleen J. Wikstrom*
*President,*
*Center for Libertarian Thought, Inc.*

# Chapter 1
# How Much Can Parents Do?

 *"A child born into roughly the bottom sixth of the SES distribution will have an IQ 12 to 18 points higher if raised by parents from roughly the top quarter of the SES distribution.... Certainly much if not most of the 10 points separating the average of the children of the lower third and the average of the upper third is environmental in origin."*
—Richard E. Nisbett

Most EXPLANATIONS FOR HOW our children grow into adulthood revolve around the nature/nurture debate and its unsolved question: How much of us is "fixed" by our genetic makeup, and how much does the environment contribute. The issue is thus framed in a deterministic manner—that we all are simply the product of either our genes or culture, or both.

The writers who have sought to resolve the debate have generally failed because they assume for themselves a personal exemption from such deterministic limitations. Thus, one group concludes, like B. F. Skinner, that humans can be trained like hunting dogs, are for the most part defective and in serious need of behavioral modification, but that they themselves are superior and should be in charge of that training.

Other "experts" claim that we are all pre-wired, our future conduct determined by our genetic makeup, that animal passions dictate our behavior, and that they, being somehow exempt, must oversee our every move. If we look through these elaborate explanations their self-interest and bias becomes quite transparent—Facts and logic don't matter as long as they end up in charge.

Of course, in case you didn't notice, the experts have framed the argument so they can't lose. Whether we are shaped by nature, heads, or nurture, tails, the self anointed experts win a place at the top to take care of us. They choose to ignore free will—the ability of every individual to overcome both cultural and genetic disadvantages, a uniquely human capability that has always allowed men and women to shape their own destiny, and to rise above "human nature."

In order to understand how children grow and develop you must put aside all the experts' political and personal agendas and accept the complex mixture of genes, human nature, environment and free will that in combination play a role in everyone's development. The process is not a scientific puzzle that lends itself to precise measurement, like the orbits of planets that can be measured mathematically and precisely, but there is a lot we do know, and much to be gained by providing every child with the support needed to reach his or her full potential.

The extraordinary genius within human beings lies in their varied and unpredictable hopes and dreams; and sorting out the best ways of nurturing those possibilities is the subject of this book. But right here at the beginning, suffice it to state the obvious—all factors play a role: genes, culture, family, schools, environments, peer groups, media, and so forth and so on. And, so what if the child possesses some fixed characteristics that can not be significantly changed? Isn't that reason to be even more concerned about those elements that do lend them-selves to positive encouragement? And isn't it abundantly clear that such encouragement must start with parents and in the home?

### Culture, Family, and Peer Pressure

There is no doubt that young children form very strong emotional attachments to their parents. The significant difference between a happy child in a stable family with strong bonds to its parents and one without such support has been confirmed by many studies. Among the professionals, there is a special field called "attachment theory," and it has become a core idea behind child development. Good attachments pay off. Children from dysfunctional homes or those who have been neglected, or moved about between foster parents, gener-ally have less successful outcomes. This fact is obvious—simple common sense—but it is ignored by some "experts." It may be that their desire to denigrate traditional family structure encourages an inflated belief in the role of nature over nurture. Parents should understand that such biases run throughout the debate over genes versus environment.

The idea that nurturing families offer the best environment for children suffered an attack in the 1970s from feminism. The more radical feminists did not like the idea that women were expected to stay at home rearing children instead of pursuing career goals outside of the home. The dispute was over traditional family structure versus emancipated career women and single moms. The elites in the media, Hollywood, and radical political action groups ridiculed stay-at-home moms. First Lady Hillary Clinton jeered at the suggestion she stay home and make cookies. Hollywood celebrities ridiculed Vice President Dan Quayle for suggesting that children benefited from two-parent homes. Women's Lib won the media battle, but attachment theory remains the bedrock of child development courses. And yet, there are still many unanswered questions: Many full-time moms do not make the necessary connection with their children, and some career women do. The answers may depend not so much upon how much time one spends with children, or who spends it, but how the time is spent. This dispute reveals a new divide in American thought.

The nurturing a child benefits from need not come from parents. A good coach, a concerned teacher, an uncle, or a grandparent can do the job. But *someone* is vitally needed. From the child's point of view, how many people do you know who will say their childhood could have been improved, if only they had been give certain opportunities, or certain counseling, or more love, or better role models, or whatever is thought to have been missing in their own childhood? And, on the opposite side, we hear of children achieving great success in spite of what seems like very damaging childhood environments. How do we make sense of all this?

There is no general agreement on what the answers are, but it seems clear that humans are influenced by both their genes and their environment. And it is a fact that, regardless of their genes, parents can shape their children's environment. That is all the parents can do, but when done properly, it is of tremendous importance.

In her book, *The Nurturing Assumption*, Judith R. Harris provides immense detail on scientific studies that show that parents play a small role in shaping their children.[1] But surprisingly, it is not because she believes genetics are more important than nurture. Her provocative point is that, sure, environment plays an important role, but it is the peer environment, not the family influence, that shapes the child. To the extent that Harris is right, her message underscores the need for a new approach to child rearing, because most of what a child needs is definitely not available from his or her peers.

Of course Harris' theory can be shattered by the fact that parents have the power to control whom their children's peers will be, and to regulate other outside influences their children may be subjected to— if they choose to use that power. Unfortunately, many parents choose not to. It is only when parents provide little direction or a damaging environment that peer pressures can be overwhelming. So once again, we see that it is up to the parents!

Many homeschoolers would agree at least partially with Harris, but they have chosen to do something about it: They home school their children. They quite properly fear the influence of not only the other students but the public school curriculum as well! And why else do so many inner-city parents move to suburban schools districts? By selecting the better schools and neighborhoods, they determine their children's environment and schoolmates. The obvious desirability of giving parents a choice is one of the powerful arguments for school vouchers and a free market in education.

In earlier times, America possessed a somewhat monolithic character. It was peopled by a variety of ethnic groups, but they almost all shared a European and Judeo-Christian heritage, and they were united by the fact that they had all been motivated to migrate here to gain freedom, opportunity, and independence. Due to that commonality of background and nature, subsequent generations were reared within a common culture with little variation between family, school, and the culture. All three were united as one with a desire to continue the "American" character within each new generation. New arrivals wanted to quickly conform to the model.

Now, almost four hundred years later, with new more diverse immigrants and a different elite leading the nation, there is not the same commonality to what children are exposed to. Many traditional institutions are breaking down, and many influential people actually promote anti-American criticisms of the most basic parts of our history. In many ways, this is the undoing of American character and requires parents to make the effort to support those parts of the traditional American character that will help put their children on a successful path.

**Accepting the Inherited Blueprint**

Any parent seeking to be successful at transforming their toddler into a responsible and reasonably competent adult must recognize and accept the different traits that make each child unique and special. The varied traits of personality, intelligence, and disposition are to a large extent inherited from one's parents and grandparents. These traits have to do with whether a person is by nature reflective, aggressive, nimble, sociable, outgoing, or reserved. Those inherited traits are then modified as a growing child is subjected to the people, places, and conditions of his environment. Obviously, to the extent to which parents can shape that final whole person, they seek to produce a healthy and happy self-confident adult.

Many twin and adoption studies demonstrate the inheritability of personality, physical, and mental traits. Identical twins share 100 percent of the same genes. Fraternal twins and ordinary brothers and sisters share 50 percent of the same genes. Adopted children share no genes with the siblings they may be raised with. If genes determine some part of a person's traits, then identical twins should be twice as similar to each other as are fraternal twins or ordinary siblings.

Studies have confirmed that identical twins separated at birth and raised in different homes will end up being very similar to each other in physical, behavioral, and mental traits. For example, fingerprints came out to be 97% heritable, IQ was 70% inherited, personality 50%, and social attitudes were 40% inherited. Studies have indicated that aggression and criminal behavior are 50% inherited: About 50% of identical twins with criminal records have twins with criminal records, while only 25% of fraternal twins with records have twins with records. Apparently, a close genetic relationship with a criminal can make a person twice as likely to exhibit criminal behavior himself.

Thus, it seems clear that temperament and personality are primarily inherited. However, it does not follow that one's inherited personality is the key to becoming a productive and happy adult. The underlying bone of contention may be how important is personality in defining what a mature adult represents? After all, the main impact of nurturing is to civilize the raw bundle of genetic mishmash that makes up each newborn child. That civilizing process helps them to grow into competent and successful adults regardless of their personality. And it should be obvious that the learning process works better when coming from an inspiring mentor than from their peer group. That parent or mentor's task is simply to teach each of their charges how to make the best use of their God-given talents and personality. Whatever was inherited, that is only a starting point. What counts is what is made from that beginning.

> **Inborn Temperament at Four Months of Age[2]**
>
> 20% of kids—Inhibited, fearful
> 40% of kids—Bold, fearless
> 40% of kids—Moderate, in the middle

## Can Manners, Culture and/or Religion Trump Human Nature?

In recent years many writers have made the case against any cultural or family role in shaping children and argued that we are all pre-wired at birth by a fixed never-changing human nature. This is the type of genetic "determinism" displayed in ant and bee colonies. It is partly true even for humans, but far from the whole truth. Such an exaggerated role of genetics is the opposite of the idea that people are born as blank slates, malleable, and receptive subjects for the social engineering schemes of utopian dreamers. The genetic determinists are also realistic enough to argue against the proposition that "every person, given the chance, could do most anything." These genetic determinists are correct in opposing social engineering, massive government planning, and naive schooling objectives "to leave no child behind" on the grounds that such programs deny human nature. But they don't have to go all the way *for* genetics and deny the equally or more important roles of culture, family and religion. We can all rise above human nature, at least to some degree.

One such pessimistic and determinist writer, John Derbyshire, seems to be opposed to culture as a determinant, because he rejects the idea of human perfectibility as well as the idea of cultural relativism. Thus, he concludes that on the nature-nurture war, "Nature is the clear winner. Name any universal characteristic of human nature including cognitive and personality characteristics. Of all the observed variation in that characteristic, very roughly half—from a quarter to three-quarters—is caused by biological differences."[3] But, hold on— is that really "a clear win" for nature over nurture? Fifty-fifty sounds like a draw.

Derbyshire does add that those numbers present "only a half victory for the Biologians, but it is a complete shattering of the Cultural absolutism that ruled in the human sciences forty years ago, and that is still the approved dogma in polite society, including polite political society, today."[4] The problem with almost all such analyses is the idea of "absolutism." There is nothing absolute about human beings, who are all, like Cleopatra, infinite in their variety.

We will in this book be more subtle and show where each element of our being comes from and how the relative importance of each source can vary between individuals. And we will emphasize that while some characteristics of a person seem to be cast in stone, that fact of life only gives added reason to work on the parts that can be perfected.

The distinction must also be made that while an individual, working with his family, friends, or coach, can perfect his skills, it does not therefore follow that any government should try and socially engineer the nature of their citizens. That is Derbyshire's prime fear, although he is also very pessimistic about the ability of an individual to improve him or herself. By overemphasizing the role of nature, he thus minimizes free will and ignores the potential for each child to strive to be the best that he can be. He likens self-improvement to "only walking north on the deck of a southbound ship".[5]

Derbyshire's fears of cultural relativism are also misplaced. If you look at the varying success rate of the hundred-plus nations in the United Nations, it becomes very clear that culture is a vital factor. The danger Derbyshire correctly refers to is that today's academics incorrectly preach that all cultures are equally praiseworthy. In fact, some cultures produce extraordinarily better results for their members than others. Indeed, we will show that the ennobling cultures, institutions, and attitudes that empower individuals are superior to those that stifle human freedom, initiative, and self-reliance. That is why culture counts. That is why those who would destroy America's foundational institutions and attitudes are so dangerous. And that is why your children must be exposed to the essential cultural principles that have made America great.

## Personality Versus Ways of Thinking and Doing

Parents often have problems with their kids, because they expect them to be like themselves. But each person's personality is unique, and parents do well to accept the fact that their child's inborn personality is not going to change a lot as they grow up. It helps if you recognize the fact that "it takes all types," and there is no perfect personality. They all have their pluses and minuses.

There is good reason to recognize and accept the differences in children. By accepting what is given, parents can avoid giving negative messages that impair a child's self-image. Such messages arise from misguided parental efforts to change the way the child is built.

Children, like all people, have to be loved for who they are and praised for whatever good they do. Child psychologists stress the need to accept these inborn tendencies. "A person doesn't choose to be an Extravert, nor can we change any of our Type preferences. We're born with a (personality) type and stay that type our whole lives."[6]

There are two features about all human beings that are largely inherited: the instinctive elements of human nature and the varied personal traits. The remaining bulk of characteristics that distinguish individuals are learned—and that learning is primarily shaped by their family and culture.

Steven Pinker has set forth the importance of one of these: human nature. He writes, "The denial of human nature has not just corrupted the world of critics and intellectuals but has done harm to the lives of real

> **The 3 Elements of Every Person**
>
> 1. Instinctive Human Nature (inherited needs for survival, self preservation, reproduction, and social contact).
>
> 2. Personal traits (Largely inherited but subject to modification)
>
> 3. Behavioral Traits (partially inborn but largely learned from family, culture, and self imposed effort)

people. The theory that parents can mold their children like clay has inflicted childrearing regimes on parents that are unnatural and sometimes cruel."[7] He goes on to criticize the intellectuals of today as being improperly convinced that children are "blank slates," and that "the human mind has no inherent structure and can be inscribed at will by society or ourselves."[8] This is a wonderful recognition that those who would "engineer" citizens along some utopian paths are in for a fruitless battle against human nature. When it comes to changing human nature, we are as stubborn as mules.

Pinker thus underlines the importance of the "selfish gene" that lies at the root of the problem between socialists and those who advocate free enterprise: Communism and socialism rely on an incorrect notion of human nature. They assume that "the butcher, the brewer, and the baker will provide us with dinner out of benevolence or self-actualization—for why else would they cheerfully exert themselves according to their abilities and not according to their needs?"[9] Ant colonies and honey bees are the only creatures that appear to survive on that type of a communist/socialist system. It could only work for humans if we all became masochists or saints. As some wise man said about Marxism: "Great theory, wrong species."

Pinker is quite correct in arguing that self-interest and the instinct for survival are among the basic inborn human needs—such as the need for food, water, sex, and companionship. However, these factors are all so obvious that it does not enlighten us much to assert that all humans are pre-programmed in those areas. It's comparable to stating that cars all have four wheels and a steering wheel—those distinctions do not help choose between cars. They represent simply a starting point to build upon.

In addition to basic human nature, there are two other groups of characteristics that do vary and create important distinctions between individuals: their personal traits and their learned behavioral habits. A major confusion in all Nature/Nurture studies comes from the failure to separate these three elements that define each of us as individuals. The first element is the "instinctive human nature" mentioned above that Pinker emphasizes. The second group is largely inherited and includes personality, physique, skin color, and, to some extent, different cognitive capabilities. Most writers concentrate on this second group and, within it, on differences in personality and cognitive skills. (Physique and skin color are rather obvious, largely inherited, but irrelevant in evaluating people unless, like the Tar Heels' Coach Smith, you quite realistically recognize that you can't teach height.)

The Tiegers have written extensively on personality and correctly point out that certain personality types are not better than others—each has strengths and weaknesses. They outline four "continuums," or elements to personality: Extraversion vs. introversion, sensing vs. intuition, thinking vs. feeling, and judging vs. perceiving. They define sixteen combinations of these four characteristics.[10] Most people are somewhere in the middle of these various combinations. Obviously it is good to think rationally *and* feel emotionally, and to be at least somewhat sociable. But each person is what they are, and the Tiegers' book makes clear how parents can and must understand and accept where their child is coming from.

Another area of inherited aptitudes lies in physical or athletic fields. There are natural athletes and many levels and types of athletic skills. Most of these inborn skills can be improved, if not made perfect, by practice and good training. One of my granddaughters is working hard to develop her basketball skills and part of her regimen is to develop a left hand lay-up that will be as good as her "natural" right hand shot. By such conscious *willed* effort, she will advance beyond her "native" ability.

Just as physical skills can be improved by practice, various personality traits can be modified by concentrated effort. An introvert by nature should be encouraged to learn social skills, although they will never equal those of a natural "schmoozer." And my granddaughter's left-hand shot may never be the equal of her right-handed one, but working on it will help make it more functional than it is by nature. The point for parents is to accept what *is*, praise *its* proper application, and encourage efforts to create balance.

There is a danger, however, in all this understanding and accepting. It is never wise to over-do the acceptance of personality differences as an excuse for bad behavior or limited effort. The trend toward "individualized parenting" results in some parents giving too much time to coddling small personality differences. The outside world that children will encounter when away from mom and dad does not blindly accept all types.

While a genetic disposition may never weaken, everyone can shape their public persona—hide their worst natures and present their best. This third area—our learned behavioral habits and capabilities—is the most important of all. Therein lies the secret of how people can rise above their inherited human nature and their genetic endowment. After all, all human groups are basically equal at birth in

their basic nature and genetic endowment. It is their learned behavioral
attitudes and cultural institutions
that have created the huge national
and ethnic differences we see
around the world. America's success rests on how its culture and
institutions empowered its people
and provided opportunity for their
enterprise.

It appears reasonable to believe
that four infant boys born today in
Uganda, the Australian outback,
Iran, and Bronxville, New York, all
have the same human potential.
Their innate personalities may differ, but those differences are incon-
sequential compared to the "civilizing" culture they will be reared in.

While it is very possible the
Bronxville boy will end up as an MIT
Ph.D. and move on to win a Nobel
Prize in science, there is almost no
chance the other three will. And, if

*Isaac Newton, a quiet and serious student, always spoke of his being self-taught. A practical inventor, when creating the first reflecting telescope, he built the body, ground the glass, and built his own tools to do the work. By the age of twenty three he had determined that the same force that made an apple fall governed the motion of the moon! His personality and temperament have never been deemed important.*

they were girls, the first three won't even get a chance at any school.
Plus, the MIT grad will probably have learned to fit in socially at the
country club, give a good speech, or lead a major corporation. Almost
all of the most important characteristics that distinguish these four
individuals at maturity will be based on their environments and
upbringing.

The key role of such learned behavior is evident to anyone who
has studied history. Societies that have prospered have been powered
by a citizenry possessing very specific attributes that created progress.
And, these attributes had little to do with mere personality. Luther,

Cromwell, Adams, Newton, Jefferson, Coke, and Blackstone played vital roles for their nations and in history's advances, but who knows or cares about their personalities? Weren't Ben Franklin and John Adams equally important to America—even though one was fun-loving and popular and the other dour, sour, and given to narrow-minded introspection?

The following traits, which may well affect an individual's chances of success, may be primarily genetically-based, but they can also be influenced by nurturing and experience:

1. Ingenuity and an experimental mind—A person with an un-imaginative, accepting-without-question mindset does not re-ally care much why something works and will tend to go along with existing or traditional methods. Inherited traits affecting how people approach problems and seek solutions may be hard to overcome, but training in simple logic and creative brainstorming may close the differences. And more hands-on practice at building and creating things can ignite the confi-dence and desire to construct and innovate.

2. Managing emotions and interpersonal skills—Self-awareness and understanding other peoples' needs creates the ability to handle relationships well, to regulate extreme emotions, and provide equanimity under duress.

3. Self-restraint and impulse control—Basic drives and selfish traits are a fact of life. Babies are notoriously self-centered and demand instant gratification. These are among the most in-grained traits that must be softened for a civilized society to exist. Their intensity varies initially based on genetics, but they can be subjected to self-control by training and discipline. We do have free will, and a key part of growing up is to learn personal responsibility and self-control. A parent's most diffi-cult task lies in this area, with the need to balance tender nurturing with tough love.

4. Intelligence—Although genes are a significant factor in IQ, the brain has the potential to improve or deteriorate in response to

empowering environments and exercise. Such improvement is most apt to happen during teen years, but changes caused by the environment can arise, for the better or worse, from pre-conception to old age.

5. Leadership skills and charisma—The power of charm and persuasion is an extremely valuable asset. In spite of personal differences, if you were coached to act in a play—to be Charlton Heston's adaptation of Moses, for example—you could learn to come close. Professor Ericsson, for one, has helped business executives make "remarkable improvement" in how they display leadership strength.[11]

6. Long-Term Planning—Patience is a virtue when it comes to meeting goals. Persistent effort guided by a personal plan will more likely lead to success than an unstructured lifestyle. Children must learn the value of thrift, regular saving, the power of compound interest, and the need to go up a ladder one rung at a time.

7. Independence and self-reliance—Aside from your mother, no one will look after your best interests better than yourself. Children should not look to others—especially the government—to help them. When someone tells your kids: "I'm here from the government to help you," they should be prepared to run for their lives!

In the course of this book, these several truths about building strong individuals will come up again and again. It will become clear that cultivating such virtues in your children will prove to be much more important in their lives than their IQ scores or which "prestige" schools they attend.

**SUMMARY**

A. A baby born today anywhere on earth has approximately the same ability and potential as any other baby born anywhere on earth during the past 50,000 years. Within each locale, babies may differ in competency based on a normal distribution range, but on average, they are all truly equal genetically.

B. The "experts" who advise us on the nature-nurture debate are mostly "intellectuals" so their logic—and conclusions—are often manipulated in order to support their political and social theories. If in doubt, trust your own common sense!

C. Personal liberty is essential for human happiness. Human nature demands the opportunity to act individually, to enjoy the fruits of one's labor, and to be free from undue interference. Regulation of human behavior and excessive redistribution of wealth runs contrary to normal human motivation and has never produced an affluent or happy population.

D. Appearances and personality take a back seat to character, initiative, learning, and persistence. Shy and unattractive people can succeed. Barring bigotry and discrimination, a person's physique, race, and personal idiosyncracies do not prevent a successful and happy life. What counts most is what the individual does for him or her self.

E. Human nature represents the fairly universal and foundational instincts that most humans share. It is a given, and the extraordinary accomplishments of many individuals are based on that foundation. Nevertheless, as Katherine Hepburn informed Bogart in *The African Queen,* "Human nature is something you are supposed to rise above."

# Chapter 2
## The IQ Sham: Shortchanging Our Children

 *"If the intelligence test proved scientifically that the majority of children were doomed to failure, not through any fault of the schools but because of bad genes, so much the better for school administrators... the useful test not only categorized and filtered but also absolved."*
—Steven R. Quartz

In the previous chapter, we outlined some of the character traits that make each person unique. IQ was not one of the most important. Indeed, the qualities evaluated on IQ and SAT tests represent a small fraction (perhaps 20 percent) of a person's total competency.[1] That is why such tests should not be used to segregate children in a way that determines their training or future lives. What we must do is identify the other 80 percent of traits that shape every individual's competency, so those essential characteristics can be nurtured as much as the traditional academic skills.

The reliance on IQ and SAT tests to identify America's "best and brightest" has led to the preferential elevation of high IQ types. These people's minds are then encouraged to emphasize abstract and theoretical thinking at the expense of practical reasoning. This selection for abstract thinking, devoid of balanced ability, has deformed the nature of our leadership, and the harm caused is evident in the recurring economic crises, bailouts, and the increased burden of taxes, regulation, and debt.

### The History of IQ Testing

Like most harmful abstract notions, theories about the inheritance of intelligence—and the consequent need to sort humans by their innate abilities—was the brainchild and darling of intellectuals.

It started with Darwin and his aristocratic cousin Francis Galton in the mid- to late-1800s. By 1900, a number of tests to quantify "brains" were put forth, but it was a Frenchman, Alfred Binet, who designed the winner—a test that would measure differences in the use of language, abstract thinking, and complex cognitive capacity.

The belief was that by measuring that group of mental abilities, they could come up with an overall measure of "general intelligence," which came to be known as "g." This concept of measuring general intelligence has dominated psychology and mental testing ever since, and remarkably, today's tests have not changed much from those developed one hundred years ago. The SAT tests are based primarily on the IQ test model and measure the same type of intelligence-memory and the ability to deal quickly with numbers and language.

In the United States, the use of IQ tests became popular at the beginning of World War I, as a way of helping build up the armed forces. In 1917, the U.S. Army totaled less than 200,000 men, and by the end of 1918, it had to induct and train about 3.5 million men to fight in Europe for President Wilson's "war to end all wars." Professors of psychology were at that time developing their new academic specialty, IQ tests—and seeing the opportunities and funds involved, they volunteered to help the military. They claimed they could sort the new recruits into classes to help fill the varied positions needed to run a force of 3.5 million men. Seven leading psychologists worked together to test almost half of the Army inductees and sort them by their most suitable roles. Although Army officers were not enthusiastic over their advice, the psychologists amassed reams of data they are still using.

Of the seven professors, Louis Terman emerged after the war as the leading exponent of IQ tests. Stephen Murdock writes in his book, *IQ*, that the biggest accomplishment of these professors was not convincing the army to test one-half of their recruits but convincing America's educational establishment of the importance and success of the army tests.[2] Funded by the Rockefeller Foundation, Terman led the movement, using a multiple-choice test that excited educators. It was easy to use, simple to grade, and reeked of modernity and scientific precision. Educators loved it. And the concept of a fixed IQ absolved them of responsibility for charges that they failed to teach. Like many ideas of the intellectuals, it may have done more harm than good in the hundred years since its "discovery."

**What Is IQ?**

There are many types of human ability, and standard IQ tests only test one set of mental abilities. Several researchers in this subject have written of the wider diversity of mental skills, many of which are not measured by the IQ test.

Critics of IQ tests assert that the test does not indicate the actual real intelligence of a person. Instead, they believe that high scores simply go to those who have accumulated extra knowledge from a more sophisticated environment, better schooling, and lots of practice at taking tests. Thus people from higher SEC levels will provide their children such an environmental and educational advantage, allowing them to outscore children from less nourishing environs.

Recent studies by Professor James R. Flynn have lent support to the critics' charges.[3] His observation that IQ scores have been steadily rising for decades suggests that either (1) each generation has been getting "smarter" than the one before, (2) the tests measure only one small part of total intelligence, or (3) the tests do not supply any useful measurement of intelligence. The steady increase in scores has been dubbed "The Flynn Effect" and suggests that each new generation is not "smarter" than the ones before—except at memorizing, taking tests, and debating abstract concepts.

Flynn discovered the rise in scores by simply understanding how the test-takers calculate their scores: Each year they simply average the scores of all takers and give the midpoint grade a value of 100 and scale all the others around that base point. That way each year's final scores reflect 100 as the median. But tests are not updated that often.

When the same test was used over a ten-year period, Flynn noted that each year the average raw score would be higher, but once scaled to 100, this would not be readily evident except to those doing the scoring. It is providential that Flynn "discovered" this, but it makes one wonder about the brilliant test designers' intelligence and why it took so long for the discovery to be reported!

Experts in the field suggest that IQ tests measure two types of intelligence: crystalline intelligence, a measure of accumulated learning, and fluid intelligence, a measure of one's innate cognitive capability and abstract problem-solving ability. In response to the critics, newer IQ tests attempt to remove acquired knowledge and capture solely fluid intelligence.

The Raven matrices test is based on geometric patterns that may reduce the impact of acquired knowledge or cultural differences on the score. However, practice at taking Raven tests must help one student over another who has never seen one before. It should be rather obvious to anyone who has played checkers or chess or done crossword puzzles or Sudokus that practice makes one better at it. The argument that these tests measure innate intelligence is also belied by the Testing Preparation Schools, which have shown they can raise scores on IQ tests, as well as SAT and GRE tests, by proper coaching and practice. No wonder that the well-prepared higher-SEC children have an advantage over others not getting the coaching!

Clearly, there is considerable ambiguity over what "intelligence" is made up of, and the alleged difference between fluid and crystalline elements of intelligence may just be the tip of the iceberg. If one can improve the score by coaching, the result is not a measure of innate ability. And, even to the extent that it may be accurate, we are not sure just what portion of mental ability is being measured. Alfred Binet, the originator, believed his tests should only be used to see which students needed more teaching in the basic skills—the Three Rs.

Almost everyone can become literate and able at basic reading, writing, and arithmetic, given enough coaching and instruction. This is (or should be) one of the basic tasks of the schools, which are, as everyone knows, failing miserably at it. It would be well for teachers to concentrate on achieving that basic mastery for every child before moving them on to all the other "subjects" such as diversity, gender studies, and multiculturalism. After all, we know that many of the slow and average learners will become the workers, entrepreneurs, and innovators who may do more for the country than many of their "smarter" classmates.

## The Cultural Destruction Caused by Reliance on IQ and SAT Tests

In this book, we will make numerous references to the work of six major critics of IQ as a standard of measurement. They are John Mayer, Peter Salovey, Howard Gardner, Thomas Stanley, Daniel Goleman, Robert Sternberg, and Keith Stanovich. They have, as a group, built a powerful case that exposes the limitations of IQ type tests. They have confirmed what one of the originators of the tests, Jean Piaget, declared one hundred years ago—that the tests are designed to measure achievement so that more schooling in areas of low scores can be applied. As an absolute measure, the tests only reveal one small portion of what constitutes human intelligence.

These researchers have attempted to identify the other elements of human mental abilities that are not adequately measured at present by any tests. These new findings are important for several reasons:

1. The emphasis on high IQ students neglects the others, many of whom may rank higher in total human capability.
2. The unmeasured competencies may represent a more valuable set of talents than the "book smarts" of the high-IQ students.
3. The existing process may unfairly and unwisely give a preference to the high-IQ students: First, they receive advanced training in school, then admittance to the "best" colleges, and finally employment in the top professions and job opportunities. This flawed selection system distorts the nature of our

leading citizens by allowing a disproportionate number of abstract thinkers to dominate our institutions and government.

4. Conversely, our government and think-tanks are denied the more practical and competent aptitudes of those who may be average in IQ but superior in all other measures of rationality and decision-making aptitude.

Unfortunately, because of the single-mindedness of school admission officials and educators, it is the high-IQ individuals who get selected and steered into leading roles in society. And yet it is the very love and knack for abstractions that makes them somewhat dangerous to society, compared to individuals with a more practical and character-driven persona. We will see in later chapters that the Western democracies have been hurt by their new overeducated elites, who have stressed abstract utopian ideas and the love of centralized government and human engineering. These unsound notions have been laid on the backs of the practical-minded people, who pay the taxes that subsidize all the social experiments and programs dreamed up by the heavily "g" loaded elites that run the country. It is time for the real producers to say "Enough!"

**SUMMARY**

A. Because the qualities that constitute IQ as tested on IQ and SAT tests represent only a small fraction (estimated at 20 percent) of a person's total competency, they should not be used to segregate children in such a way that determines their training or future lives.

B. The preferential elevation of high IQ types distorts a nation's leadership by emphasizing abstract and theoretical thinking at the expense of practical reasoning.

C. What we must do is identify the other 80 percent of traits that shape every individual's competency so those essential characteristics can be nurtured just as much as the traditional academic skills.

D. Every child should be encouraged equally, because there is no accurate way to separate the winners from the losers until it is too late.

# Chapter 3
## Is IQ an Accurate Predictor of Success?

*"If you have leadership qualities and tenacity you may eventually outpace all the whiz kids in your class. That is exactly what many millionaire respondents have actually accomplished."*
—Thomas J. Stanley

THE MYSTERY OF HUMAN INITIATIVE, motivation, and imagination may be too subtle and ever-changing to be reduced to a test. However, we now know that there are important forms of intelligence that are not measured by IQ tests and that those qualities play a major role in a person's success in life.

Simple observation of friends and family members confirms the many forms of ability: We all know of people without high IQs who outperform those with higher IQs. And there are many very high IQ people that never achieve more than average success in life. Concentrating on IQ—which is limited to a narrow subset of cognitive intelligence—gives a false indication of a person's ability, since there are so many other abilities that are essential for success. The irrational focus on IQ scores has led educational programs to be designed to teach to the IQ test, where the "successful" are best suited to be college professors, Wall Street speculators, or political spin-masters. There are, of course, many successful lawyers, mechanics, and business people who survive the current academic requirements, but there is a great cost in the huge numbers of students who are left adrift, often with considerable talent, and given little encouragement or direction.

We should recognize that with the right instruction and encouragement, every student can find his sweet spot, where he can capitalize on his strengths. Instead of grooming Ivy League candidates who will rule from the brain, there would be a greater societal gain from making the most of everyone.

## SATs and the New Meritocracy

Prior to World War II, the most selective colleges catered to the sons and daughters of the rich Brahmin class of old families. Those children were sent to the best private "finishing" schools and then to Ivy League colleges. Academic qualifications were hardly examined if the family's social standing was strictly "upper crust." The graduates went on to take the best jobs in legal firms and in financial and manufacturing corporations.

Meanwhile, because the economy was open with few barriers to starting a business, the children of ordinary folk found whatever employment they could or started a business of their own. Although they were denied opportunity in the prestige companies and occupations, there was still opportunity, but only if they worked harder and more persistently than everyone else. And that's what they did. Andrew Carnegie, an uneducated immigrant, had the practical smarts to create one of the nation's leading manufacturing companies.

In the 1930s, the president of Harvard University decided to change things. He wanted to admit more educationally gifted students even if they were without social connections. James Bryant Conant and his associate Henry Chauncy began the shake-up of prestige colleges by opening Harvard to a more diverse student body. What's more, Conant adopted the SAT test and used it to select children who demonstrated academic excellence. This test had been created in the 1920s by Carl Brigham and was based on the same principles as the Army IQ tests that Lewis Terman had used to screen Army recruits during World War I.

Brigham had developed an interest in IQ tests as a result of his interest in eugenics. His interest in the SAT tests may have been increased by its supposed scientific objectivity, as well as the fact that it supported prevailing bias against blacks, Jews, and Mediterranean people, all of whom generally scored low on such tests. Ironically, the use of SATs by college admissions people resulted in giving more places in the freshman classes for just those kinds of the "wrong" people—as long as they scored high on the test. And, many of them did just that! This result suited Conant, who believed in a "natural aristocracy of educational talent."

*"Intellectual morons are the cognitive Elite who champion idiotic ideas and theories. They are the 'smart' people that fall for stupid ideas. Ph.D.'s high IQs, and intellectual honors are not antidotes to thick-headedness."*

—Daniel J. Flynn

The test gradually became widely used and, by the 1970s, was the standard to qualify for application to almost all the top colleges and universities in America. And, as Conant had hoped, many of these "bright" graduates went into law and government. However, his hopes that this new meritocracy would act like a moral elite and reform society has, like most dreams, had its unintended consequences. And, most certainly, recent events in Washington and Wall Street have shown that there has been little if any improvement in the character and integrity displayed by the supposed moral elites.

Nicholas Lemann wrote about Conant's new academic meritocracy in his book, *The Big Test*, in which he criticizes the SATs and argues that they mismeasure students. Lemann describes how three different types of students are impacted by the SAT:[1]

1. "Mandarins" are those with the high test-scores that currently get into the best schools and then get the best jobs that most influence modern America.

2. "Lifers" are the competent individuals who, because they lack a high IQ, have to slowly but doggedly prove themselves and may eventually work their way up to top spots in American businesses and institutions.

3. "Talents" are the innovative individuals who find ways to bypass the customary organizational careers by starting businesses of their own.

Lemann hints at the fact that the Lifers and Talents actually play a more positive role for the country than do the Mandarins. However, because the Mandarins lead most financial, academic, and government institutions, they have the greatest influence in shaping the youth of America. Lemann's point supports the idea that there has been a gradual shift in America's leadership from the practical thinkers to the abstract thinkers. Thus, it is the new "Mandarins" that have brought a new ideology-based approach to American politics, and the continued upward flow of these types of minds via prestige colleges is being fed by the excess reliance on IQ and SAT test scores.

Lemann makes it clear that the Mandarins are the least socially or economically valuable class and that those with lower IQs are the ones that make the country work. It is no coincidence that Theodore Dalrymple's latest book is subtitled "The Mandarins and the Masses."[2] Dr. Dalrymple, who has worked around the world treating the denizens of the urban underclass, is an exceptional commentator on the plight of the modern Western democracies. He attributes much of the cultural breakdown in England and America and the abject misery of those "at the bottom" to the abstract and hedonistic ideas of Western intellectuals, or in other words, "the Mandarins" at the top.

The irony of all this history is that the "blue blooded" aristocracy that had enjoyed preference before Conant's revolution has been effectively replaced by an IQ meritocracy. It is not clear that any improvement in the conduct of the nation's affairs resulted. What is clear is that before, during, and after that shift in leadership positions, the country was being carried forward primarily by the hard work and ingenuity of the common people—the lifers and talents. And because the increased number of nonproductive jobs in governmental, academic, and nonprofit organizations has been filled mostly by mandarins, there has been a reduction in the common sense intelligence of the leadership.

By using the term "Mandarins," both Lemann and Dalrymple are comparing our intellectual elites to the effete members of classical Chinese Emperors' courts, who lived in opulence on the backs of the

Chinese peasants. And that is what the modern intelligentsias do. They produce no product, provide no service, but, in Thomas Sowell's words, they are merely dealers in secondhand ideas—schemes they want to administer that will control our lives, all at our expense. You do not want your children to be part of that class. And you do want to warn them about the mischief such people promote.

**The Canadian Mistake**

An odd thing happened in the mid 1980s when the Canadian psychologist, Roger Barnsley, and his wife attended a hockey game in Alberta. It was his wife, Paula, who made the discovery: She noticed in the program that most of the players had been born in January, February, or March. Her husband's curiosity was whetted, and he went home and checked the birth dates of more professional hockey players. The same pattern emerged. By an overwhelming margin, more players were born in January than any other month.

What the Barnsleys had noticed was what came to be known as "The Matthew Effect." When they checked other top teams in Canada and Europe, whether it was football, soccer, or hockey, they found an enormously large percentage of high-level players who were born in the same few months. It became clear that this was not an isolated finding, but holds true for many sports. It's all a matter of relative age and the common mistake of coaches to confuse ability with maturity. When children are grouped by the calendar year in which they were born, ten months difference in age can make a major difference in ability. Even the Gospels acknowledge this inequity in life.

Geoff Colvin and Malcolm Gladwell have both written about how this distorted selection process impacts those who succeed and those who are held back, through no fault of their own. Gladwell writes, "In any elite group of hockey players 40% of the players will have been born between January and March, 30 percent between April and June, 20 percent between July and September, and 10 percent between October and December."[3]

Now we all know that being born in the winter or spring should not make you a better player—that is, unless the coaches select their players for the all-Star teams each year with a January first cutoff date for eligibility. Each year's crop of nine- to ten-year-old youngsters compete with others born in the same calendar year. The biggest and most mature kids usually perform better than those ten months younger. The older ones get selected for the All Star teams, and the rest is history. Once the favored group gains the advantage, that advantage accumulates from the extra training and experience they receive. Those excluded tend to stagnate in relative obscurity, unless through extraordinary talent and effort they find a way to catch up.

This process illustrates the fallacy of self-fulfilling prophecies. By giving the oldest members of each year's group a ticket into specialized training and advanced opportunities, the coaches are creating an elite based on a flawed assumption. By the time the kids are eighteen, the older ones selected "as the best" turn out to be actually better simply because they got the extra attention. Some of the babies born late in the year may have had more potential, but the selection process relegated them to second-class citizenship.

Barnsley's curiosity led him to examine the effect of birth-month on other competitive situations. His research has shown that the same effect is found when you compare academic achievement. Children entering grade one at a relatively young age have difficulty keeping up with those who are older. That disadvantage, and the resulting poorer performance, often leads to disappointment and frustration. Barnsley found that for those younger children there was a resulting reduction in self-confidence and self-esteem, an increase in drop out

> **The Matthew Effect**
>
> *"For unto everyone that has, more shall be given and he shall have abundance; but for him that hath not, even that which he has shall be taken."*
>
> —Matthew 13:12

rates, and a higher frequency of eventual suicide. This irrational process that elevates some youths at the expense of other equally deserving youths is cited in many psychological works to reveal the damage done by the wisest experts even when they are trying to be completely impartial. It is a lesson to be applied to today's theories on tests, schooling, and the cultivation of talent within our very valuable youth.

## Why Teachers Cannot Predict Success

It has been said that teachers are not very good at predicting which students will succeed, because they themselves know so little about success. But there is another reason that is explained by Benjamin Bloom, based on his study of 120 of the top achievers in several highly competitive fields of work. His study of the childhoods of these "wunderkinds" showed that even when they were twelve to fourteen years of age, no one had any reason to believe they would be great at anything.[4] Bloom found no early factors that would predict their great success. There was no correlation between IQ and their ultimate great

*Cajal wrote in disdain about intellectual "thinkers" who preferred constructing audacious theories to discovering facts by precise observation. "It matters very little (to them) whether the concept itself is based on thin air, so long as it is beautiful."*

performance. And these individuals gained world renown in music, sports, mathematics, chess, science, and medicine.

One youngster very much underestimated by his teachers was Santiago Ramon y Cajal (1852–1934). He was considered a problem student but became a Nobel Prize winner and the "father of neuroscience" with his discoveries of how neurons function within the brain. As a child, he was transferred from one school to another because of poor behavior and a pugnacious attitude. An innate rebelliousness resulted in his imprisonment at the age of eleven for blowing up the town gate with a homemade cannon. In desperation, his father apprenticed him out, first as barber, then as a cobbler, but Santiago's chief desire was to be an artist.[5]

Even in his twenties, no one could have foreseen his great future successes. However, after his mandated service in the Spanish army, he applied his drawing skills to an interest in biology and eventually obtained a medical degree. His talent for creating detailed anatomical drawings then played a major role in building his future scientific renown.

What made such people excel was not their innate ability or their knack for getting good grades but the other 80 percent of cognitive capabilities we discuss in this book. And for Bloom's subjects, those qualities had been developed in three ways: they had the support of enthusiastic parents, they practiced and worked intensively to gain their skills, and they received good coaching. Bloom's conclusions were that, overwhelmingly, true experts are made, not born.

And the route they took to their ultimate success was often circuitous and counterintuitive. The beginnings of their ascent seemed to have little to do with the eventual skill involved. At an early age, parents stressed the work ethic, the family responsibility, and the importance of working toward distant goals. The children were expected to do family chores and to do them well. Their work was to be finished before they went out to play. The parents created an atmosphere not unlike our grandparents' era, when children were required to contribute a lot of effort to the family workload.

One of the best compliments I ever received was from a son who, when asked how he got so distinguished in his career, replied that his father had taught him how to work hard. Now, the work I gave him was mostly digging fence posts and cutting brush, which would seem to have no place in his more aesthetic adult vocation. But the hardnosed determination to pick-axe his way through hardpan and cut through tangled brush apparently helped provide the foundation for a lifetime of overcoming obstacles and reaching desired goals.

Many teachers are not aware of these homely virtues, but learning how to apply themselves and to accomplish a task will frequently lay the basis for a child's future success. And that success cannot be foreseen, often coming long after they have left the public school system. Jonas Salk entered college intending to be a lawyer! And by the time he became a doctor, he had made no conscious effort to become an immunologist. No one could have ever predicted during his school and college years that he would develop one of the world's greatest medical vaccines.

**Wisdom and Common Sense**

One of the strengths of American democracy is the ingrained belief by most Americans that they may not be as smart, good looking, or experienced as someone else, but damn it, their ideas and decisions are just as good if not better than anyone else's. And this belief in "the wisdom of crowds" and the irreplaceable common sense of ordinary people has in fact been established as superior to the wisdom of experts—even when the experts have more experience, higher IQs, and are better talkers. This confident, self-reliant, and independent attitude is essential to make a democracy work well. And Americans have it. Or, at least, they used to.

Teaching common sense and a respect for simple moral truths is a great way for parents to give their children the kinds of traits that make for success and help avoid mistakes of youth. George Will's admonishment remains valid: If you want to avoid being in the lowest socioeconomic class, simply follow three rules: finish high school, avoid teenage pregnancy, and stay off drugs. Attentive families, especially in upper SECs, will generally instill such valuable habits of behavior in their children. In the United States, anyone of any culture or race has a fair chance to attain some degree of success by following those three rules and applying themselves to their work in a consistent and attentive manner.

Those rules require little IQ but a lot of nurturing in the arts of self-control, hard work, and persistence. The fact that upward mobility is alive and well in America indicates that statistical correlations of IQ scores with socioeconomic classes may not be telling the whole story. If there is a constant upward flow from lower to upper economic classes, one should expect the upper layers at any point in time to test better. But, how do all those "dummies" at the bottom keep coming upward? Evidence shows that someone in their families not only passed on some brains but, maybe more importantly, taught them the skills and self-discipline to make that journey.

The fable of the tortoise and the hare used to be a standard for American children and illustrated the traditional and sentimental support for the slow and steady underdog. The biblical theme of a David over a Goliath was taught to all school children. Given a level playing field, in America, a David will still slay the Goliath. The issue for today's parents is whether we still have a level playing field or whether there is a new form of discrimination in the land.

James R. Flynn writes in *What Is Intelligence?* that, throughout the world, there is a positive correlation between IQ and success. There is little doubt of this fact: Individuals with higher IQs tend to be among the higher SEC of every society. This remains true even in African countries, where almost everyone is of one race, discounting racial bias as a factor. People with higher IQs enjoy higher standards of living. But this correlation could be coincidental. Correlation does not equate to causation, so what other explanations could there be?

## Separating Cause from Effect

Most people have been led to believe that a person's IQ is an unchanging genetic fact that is determined at conception and determines their future. That was the common belief until a few decades ago. Now we know that IQ scores are not fixed but can vary up or down depending on environment and age.

It could be that successful people develop higher IQs as a part of their personal growth. The very fact that a person has become successful means he has worked harder and been exposed to a wider involvement with the world and has had to practice his literacy and mathematical skills. Thus, a successful person's IQ would be higher as a *result* of the individual's success. And the kids growing up around such a person would be expected to absorb much of that advantage and thereby score higher on tests.

I haven't seen a study on peoples' clothing, but I suspect those in the higher SECs are better dressed than those in the lower SECs. Can we assume the better clothes made one group more successful than the other, or are the better clothes simply a financial and cultural result of being successful? Successful people tend to drive more BMWs than unsuccessful people, but most would agree the BMW is only a badge for those who have already succeeded. I can't just go out and get a Beamer and expect it to make me successful. Or can I?

Some people might argue that dressing well and driving an impressive vehicle can help a person succeed. And that is to some degree true, but note that it is only true because the image of the well-dressed individual in a fancy car might gain him an easier contact with customers or financiers. The clothes would not make him any more competent. Indeed, he may just be what is referred to as "an empty suit." This analogy might reveal exactly what high IQ scores do: They gain a person preferred entry to colleges and jobs—not because he is necessarily more competent, but because he appears to be successful and smart by virtue of his high scores.

There is little doubt that test scores play a big part in determining a child's future. Those who do well get into the best colleges, and they in turn get into the biggest and best companies as executives and professionals. In the process, they become more sophisticated and learned than those left behind. And they end up earning more than everyone else! Could there be a self-perpetuating fallacy here? Could there be an injustice here?

Is it possible that we are testing for the wrong thing? By advancing those with good test-taking skills, are we missing out on the talents of many who could fill those top jobs as well or better? Are these tests a self-fulfilling system of advancing certain types of minds over other kinds of minds? Is it all a conspiracy of the eggheads?

A simple comparison of average SAT scores for the entering freshman class at different universities reveals this skewing or grouping of students into strict levels of prestige: In the competition to get into the best colleges, most high IQ applicants seek admittance to top-ranked colleges such as MIT, Cal Tech, Princeton, Harvard, and Stanford. These schools have the advantage of placing their graduates into the most competitive jobs after graduation. This process selects a certain type of person for eventual leadership posts. In the hard sciences, at MIT and Cal Tech, such high IQ types make some sense, but do they for other occupations?

Let's assume that SAT scores are not an indication of one's ability to function in the business world. Would not most businesses still struggle to hire the graduates of MIT and Princeton? And then would not those so favored get better jobs and eventually score high on the SEC levels? Just as the well-dressed person in a new car gains respect and an advantage by appearing successful, so does a high-grade scorer get an advantage by appearing smart and successful. The appearance creates an illusion that leads to success, just as the size of spring-born hockey players gives the illusion of being better than those six to ten months younger. Is it possible that the wrong people are being advanced within the educational-business world to eventual positions of great power?

### Motivation, Nurturing Its Source, and Igniting Effort

A patient came to us a few years back that appeared at first look to be timid and insecure. She complained of her fear of social situations and her inability to interact with people and wanted help overcoming those fears. "I am just so afraid when I meet new people," she explained. On further investigation, it came out that Jane held several degrees in computer science and was employed at a very good salary as a program evaluator at a well-known company. In fact, she was second in command of a ten-person department that tested all new programs that the company developed. Their job was to break the system, find flaws, and suggest corrections.

Jane lived alone in a rented apartment near her place of employment. She had turned down promotion to head her department, because she was not able to see herself being the boss. Although she had been a very bright student with top grades, she was being held back by a lack of confidence, which, in turn, produced low expectations. This client needed training on how to hone her social and leadership skills, but there was no question of her motivation. Jane had clearly spent the 10,000 hours to become very skilled in her vocational specialty. But there was something lacking: self-confidence. She had demonstrated the motivation to work hard and develop the skills needed for her high paying job. It had not been easy, since she had had to pay her own way through school by working and attending school at the same time. It had taken twice as long as a conventional college program. She apparently had the energy and commitment to develop her skills. She had what Daniel Coyle calls the "motivational fuel," the major element of what is needed to develop talent.[6]

Coyle cites the breakthrough situations that spark such motivation among the world's superstars. He visited and studied the people at the world's top training centers. He calls them talent hotbeds, because they impose a concerted training process on aspiring stars. Coyle studied why the people at these training centers had such a passion to learn and perfect their skills. He found that, for each individual, some moment had occurred when his motivation was "ignited." For South Korean golfers, it was May 18, 1998, when a twenty-year-old Se Ri Pak won the McDonald's LPGA Championship. Many young Korean girls were suddenly empowered and eager to follow in Se Ri's footsteps. "If she can do it, I can," they thought.[7] There had never been a Korean woman champion before. Popular belief was that PGA Championships were for others, so no one tried. But, ten years after Pak's win, her countrywomen were major factors in the LPGA tour, with forty-five players who collectively won about one-third of the events.

In the same summer of 1998, Russian women were ignited by Anna Kournikova, who reached the semifinals at Wimbledon. It motivated many young girls in Russia to try to do what she had done. By 2007, they occupied five of the top ten rankings. Coyle describes "ignition" as a hot, mysterious burst, an awakening, a sudden awareness that "that is what I want to be." The spark comes from seemingly insignificant cues that over time create huge differences in skill. The process is enabled by a recognition that "it can be done." Many people never try, because they have been taught that they couldn't do it.

The initial spark that Coyle talks about can start an individual onto a path of rigorous training, but once started, what makes a person keep trying? They usually are met by frustrations along the way and have to devote large amounts of their time to practicing. Being motivated and remaining so verges on masochism, all for a barely possible reward somewhere out in the future. But if there is an image of your goal firmly planted in your mind, the objective may become worth the effort.

Stephen R. Covey suggests the need for a personal mission statement—to focus on what you want to be (character), what you want to do (accomplishments), and on how you will do it (the values and principles upon which your being and doing will be based).[8] Coach John Wooden suggests beginning with what his father taught him: "Never lie, never cheat, never steal." And what's more: "don't whine, don't complain, don't make excuses."[9] When I first read these six admonishments from Wooden's dad they made a lot of sense but seemed perhaps simplistic. Later, in reading George E. Vaillant's scholarly tome on the importance of a person's finding the right ways to adapt to the difficulties we all face in life, these simple rules appeared both wise and succinct.

Vaillant studied the different ways people deal with life's stresses. Some cope much better than others, and the distinction has to do with their ability to progress through stages of ego maturity and attain "mature defenses." Successful adaptive mechanisms mark the mature individuals who are comfortable with themselves, oriented toward the future, invested in life, autonomous, and able to deal with situations with humor, tolerance, and kindness.

On the other hand, there are those who never grow up beyond a self-centeredness and acting out, with the immature defenses of protesting and blaming others. The mature are capable of love, sound decision-making, and gain the mental and physical health that comes from inner satisfaction.[10] Such maturity also comes from following coach Wooden's six rules. Kids have to go through the usual stages of growth, but the last three rules are especially great starting points for even five-year-olds. It is never too early to learn not to whine, complain or make excuses for your failings.

Wooden offers a seventeen-point pyramid of success for older children. But all his lessons call for self-discipline and a goal-oriented life, regulated by integrity, loyalty, and cooperation. It is hard to believe that such training cannot improve almost any genetic endowment.

What kinds of people look at things this way, to see a goal and be ready to work enough to attain it? They must be optimistic to see the possibilities of success. A pessimist would weigh the odds, look at the 10,000 hours of work, and decide it's not worth the effort. A person who is predisposed to a short-term view, who prefers instant gratification, will not undertake a long-term effort for eventual possible success. A person with little impulse control will get sidetracked. But a person who looks to the future with hope and optimism and has some inner confidence will make the gamble. Hulk Hogan has written a compelling story of how his success and glamorous career was actually based on many ups and downs and the need to keep getting back up and starting over. Late in life, he relied on a positive-thinking form of Christianity to see him through severe depression. He believes it's up to you to choose your destination in life. You can't always choose the path, but you can strive for the goal.[11]

Coyle suggests that the signals that ignite serious effort are often based on a desire for future belonging.[12] Humans have been called social animals, and the need to belong is strong in many people. There is a growing group of psychologists that study the unconscious mechanisms that influence human decision-making and goals, seeking to understand the hidden connections between our environment and motivation. Such behavioral causes are based in our motivational circuits in a section of our brains (the reptilian brain) and go back millions of years.

When all the studies are looked at en masse, they become frustrating, because they seem so anecdotal, even though they were all scientifically conducted with control groups, carefully recorded observations, and statistical results. We learn that parental triggers can be vital. A child watching his parent work at some creative task can trigger a desire to emulate the parent's passion. We learn that loss of a parent can trigger the desire to work harder to be safe and gain access to some future group of secure achievers. We learn that practicing in a dingy environment creates the motivation to get to a comfortable lifestyle. But many educators today believe that having excellent modern facilities helps one study or practice. So what does a good parent do? Nurture the child or desert him so he can trigger his energy himself? It is a delicate balancing act, as Dr. Carol Dweck shows with her studies of the relationship between motivation and language.

One of her studies selected four hundred New York fifth-graders and gave them an easy test. When she told each of them their scores, she added a single six-word sentence of praise: Half were told, "You must be smart at this." The other half were told, "You must have worked very hard."[13]

Then she tested them again, telling them they could choose either a harder test or an easier test. Ninety percent of those who had been praised for their effort chose the harder test, and a majority of the kids praised for being smart chose the easier test. Dweck concluded, when we praise kids for being smart, they assume that simply being "smart" is important, so they choose an easy hurdle in order to look smart. She then gave them all a very hard test, and no one did well; however, the kids who had been praised for effort worked hard and said they liked the test. The others hated the test, because it indicated they might not be smart.

For the fourth round, Dweck gave them all a final test—with the same difficulty as the first. The praised-for-effort group scored 30% higher than the first time, and the smart group's score was 20% lower. It seems that praise for effort works better than praise for being talented, smart, or gifted. Praise can reduce motivation as well as increase it. It has to be done the right way, at the right time, and with the right message. The current fad in our public schools that seeks to build self-esteem by finding ways to praise failing students is undoubtedly the wrong way. Coaches like John Wooden knew all this from years of coaching. Public school teachers might do well to study the books by successful coaches instead of taking all those educational courses their union certification requires.

## The Supremacy of IQ in the Hard Sciences

I had a roommate in college who illustrated the importance of IQ in the physical sciences. Bill graduated from a public high school in upstate New York with school grades and a SAT score that would have gotten him into just about any college in the country. He worked harder than myself and our other roommates, probably because he knew exactly what he wanted to become: a research professor in biochemistry at a top college. In the spring of our senior year, he was admitted to Phi Beta Kappa, graduated summa cum laude, won the Chemistry Prize, and ranked seventh in a class of about 750. After graduating, he went to Germany on a series of Fulbright Fellowships, married a German lass, came back to get his doctorate at Harvard, and went on to become a distinguished professor at the University of Texas. Because of his extensive travel delivering papers at international scientific conclaves, he became very well known in his field. We stayed in close touch, and one evening about twenty years after we had graduated, he called to let me know he was taking a sabbatical and would be at the Max Planck Institute in Heidelberg for the coming winter. It sounded impressive—and contrasted sharply with my evening's work helping my daughter with her long-division homework. But tearing myself away from my humdrum interests, I asked what kind of stuff he would be doing in Heidelberg. He said it was actually very simple: The award from the German government merely stated that during his one-year stay, he was to study the origin of life. Wow! That takes a high IQ and "school boy smarts." Bill was born and raised to do what he did—conduct extraordinarily complicated scientific inquiries into the nature of the most minute biochemical phenomenon.

The kinds of minds that Bill exemplified are rare and valuable to the scientific community and the country. That is why intelligence testing that reveals and encourages such youngsters is an important function of our schools. But their success at test-taking should not in any way relegate others with different types of minds to any lesser measure of approval and encouragement. In most schools, the various IQ and aptitude tests that are administered to children play too big a role in determining the classes the child will be put in, the classmates selected to be his peers, his application to college and post-graduate programs, and the jobs he may apply for. My roommate Bill's scientific skills were impressive, but they are only one of many skills needed to maintain the American success story.

## Even Geniuses Need Concrete Thinking

The great scientist Nicola Tesla exemplified the broad type of mental ability needed to conceptualize new scientific advances. Tesla would visualize an invention in his head with exactness, including all dimensions, and then use that "drawing" to construct his new machine. He typically did not make drawings by hand, instead just conceiving them in his mind. He had an intuitive way of perfecting his hypotheses. After watching a demonstration of an electrical producing machine, he visual-

> ### On "Thinking" Deeply
>
> *The scientists of today think deeply instead of clearly. One must be sane to think clearly, but one can think deeply and be quite insane.*
>
> —Nikola Tesla

ized a new approach for a rotating magnetic field and designed an induction motor that led him to one of his greatest inventions—alternating current. He never stopped with just an idea; he had to build and prove his hypotheses. He explained his mental process this way:

> Before I put a sketch on paper, the whole idea is worked out mentally. In my mind I change the construction, make improvements, and even operate the device. Without ever having drawn a sketch, I can give the measurements of all parts to workmen, and when completed, all these parts will fit, just as certainly as though I had made the actual drawings. It is immaterial to me whether I run my machine in my mind or test it in my shop. The inventions I have conceived in this way have always worked. In thirty years, there has not been a single exception. My first electric motor, the vacuum wireless light, my turbine engine, and many other devices have all been developed in exactly this way.[14]

Thus, hard scientists may use abstract conceptions to visualize possibilities, but unlike soft-science theorists, they go on to physically build and demonstrate the practical significance of their concept. That way of thinking would never visualize some utopian communist system of government, ignore its failings and terror for seventy years, and then begrudgingly argue that the three generation experiment wasn't done right. The true innovative geniuses had a lot of both the theoretical and pragmatic parts of their brain in full gear!

To keep things in perspective, it is helpful to remember that useful science only developed in nations where ordinary people had already created, through their enterprise and initiative, a general prosperity that allowed investment in universities and research organizations. Without that security and affluence, there would never have been a place for hard scientists to conduct their experiments and studies. Without a stout defense from enemies and an orderly law-abiding citizenry, no progress is possible. That is why ordinary patriotic soldiers are the first requirement for human progress. That is also why Madame Curie's lab was not housed in a grass hut, an adobe structure, a Masai manyatta, or under a tent!

While IQ may play a minor role in determining the overall ability of individuals, it is obviously more important in some fields of study and work than in others. In the soft sciences, the types of intelligence not revealed by today's IQ tests are probably more important than they are for hard scientists. The need for abstract and theoretical thinking is important in hard sciences like chemistry and physics. The need is much less important, and perhaps detrimental, in management fields and entrepreneurial situations, where people skills, emotional control, and practical decision-making abilities are more vital for success. By overemphasizing just one measure of a student's competency, we may be mismeasuring and misdirecting the students that are needed to become our nation's future leaders.

David Brooks has written about the Obama administration's education initiatives: Teaching to the test and tough measures to ensure the right educational results are fine, but what if the "right" results are incorrectly defined. Teaching to the test may be useful if

*"It is the soldier, not the reporter, who has given us freedom of the press. It is the soldier, not the poet, who has given us freedom of speech. It is the Soldier, not the campus organizer who has given us freedom to protest."*

—Charles M. Province

selecting for hard sciences, but not for other subjects. He warns that we must be careful not to get so enamored with reform and improved achievement that we misdirect our children into the wrong pathways.

This concept of "teaching to the test" requires more subtlety than it has received. There is every reason to make sure every elementary student masters basic reading, writing, and arithmetic. These are life skills that will pay dividends regardless of the career path chosen, and achievement tests that measure progress on those skills are useful. Achieving a minimal level of competency should be the primary focus of elementary grades, and training should continue until competency is achieved. Beware the educational establishment's complaint that such work leaves little time "for all the other subjects." The other major subjects, such as science and history, are best learned after a child can do the basics. How can you teach a kid science if he can't read, write, or do simple arithmetic? If there is a need to measure high school students, we need to find more meaningful standards than currently used in IQ and SAT tests.

## SUMMARY

A. IQ and SAT tests predict school grades very well, but being only a small part of total human capability, they do not predict success in life. There are other measures we will look at that provide a clearer prediction of success.

B. When it comes to great innovative genius, there are no predictors, even for ten- to fourteen-year-olds, to indicate the extraordinary possibilities of some youngsters.

C. Most of history's great innovators and scientists were not intellectuals but came from the ranks of pragmatic mechanics, engineers, and technicians, who combined a hands-on genius with curiosity, imagination, and persistence to create breakthroughs in science and technology.

D. Pure high-IQ speculative philosophers such as Rousseau, Hegel, and Marx never invented anything except abstract ideas that, for the most part, did more harm than good.

E. Confusing "high IQ scores" with "intellect" has allowed many impractical theorists to gain important social roles, where they prove unable to fashion improvements in the affairs of their nations. In the next chapter, we will investigate the varied elements of a person's total competency and reveal how they trump IQ.

# Chapter 4
# What Is "Real" Intelligence?

 *"The academic achievement and occupational attainment of Asian Americans exceed by a great amount what they 'should' be accomplishing given their IQs. The explanation for the Asian/Western gap lies in hard work and persistence."*
—Richard E. Nisbett

SOME YEARS AGO WHEN I was acting as a financial consultant to individuals, I was both surprised and pleased to see that many of the most successful individuals had not gone to college. One of them came to me by a mutual friend's reference and brought his wife to seek my advice on a rather simple matter: how to safely set aside and invest a half-million dollars of extra cash they had just "come into." They were about forty years old and were shy and serious, because they were not used to talking finances, investments, and taxes.

The husband, who we can call Jim, told me that six years ago, he had been laid off for eight months from a stockroom job. He was to be rehired, but in the meantime he was getting a modest union stipend. Not wanting to be idle, he decided to build a ten-unit apartment building. He had once helped a buddy on such a project and believed he could get a construction mortgage to build one in his hometown. It was successfully rented a year and a half later, so he built another bigger one. He hired the subcontractors, and his wife was always at his side keeping track, summarizing costs, making suggestions, and, most importantly, encouraging him.

When Jim and his wife had completed construction and filled the larger apartment house, they showed their banker the cost figures, the rent income, and the operating expenses. They had constructed the building so efficiently that the banker looked at the figures and told them they could justify a much bigger mortgage, so they rewrote the mortgage, and obtained almost a million dollars in cash. They set aside half to build another building and came to me to see where they could "salt away" the other half-million. As Jim said, "You never know what can happen, so we want this kept separate and safe for the kids." My job was simple: I helped them buy U.S. Bonds directly from the Federal Reserve and we put them in a trust for the kids.

Now, Jim's wife might have been a good student. She was certainly good with her checkbook and monitoring expenses, but Jim was the ultimate "concrete thinker." Over the ensuing years, I got to know them both very well, because they kept coming up with "problems" about how to safeguard their surplus cash and how to pass it on to their kids. It became clear that Jim had no use for abstractions, and his thinking and speech were always deliberate, hesitant, and careful. But in a slow and steady way, he gathered information, made good decisions, maintained prudent and logical control over his actions, was considerate and generous with others, worked well with his wife, and became extremely successful.

Jim and his wife obviously had all the non-IQ talent and probably less of the algorithmic and memorization skills required to ace the IQ and SAT tests. They were not the exceptions. I had many blue collar, small business, and tradesmen clients that were very successful in spite of less than stellar educational pedigrees. One of my wealthiest clients was a logger from Nova Scotia who had come to America, gotten a plumber's license, and saved regularly at the local Cooperative Bank. These are the kinds of people that possessed an abundance of the non-IQ smarts that create success.

The original proponents of EQ, Mayer and Salovey, would agree that Jim the apartment builder was strong in terms of the five key emotional intelligences: Knowing one's own emotions, managing emotions, motivating oneself, recognizing emotions in others, and handling relationships.[1] These emotional intelligences are quite different from IQ intelligence, but whatever they are, they clearly are very important in determining who succeeds and who doesn't.

Daniel Goleman suggests it is good to have all types of intelligence and that there are only rare situations where people are extremely strong in one area and terrible at the other, with a varying mix often found. "The high-IQ pure type (that is, setting aside emotional intelligence) is almost a caricature of the intellectual, adept in the realm of the mind but inept in the personal world."[2]

Goleman adds that there is only a slight correlation between IQ and some aspects of emotional intelligence. The correlation is "small enough to make clear these are largely independent entities."[3] The real burden of teachers' concentration on grades and tests scores is that no one is nurturing the other 80 percent of our children's capabilities, which provide the real positive forces in our economy. Instead, the entire educational establishment is concentrating on the few students who possess the least valuable cognitive traits: the high IQ types who, outside of the physical sciences, are of dubious value and who often do more harm than good.

### Emotional, Practical, and Social Intelligence

In the preceding section, we mentioned some of the critics of IQ tests. They have urged consideration be given to a number of other independent elements that make up the whole person. Thus, an individual might score poorly on IQ, be a poor athlete, and have a tin ear but still be a magnificent architect, provided he had spatial and aesthetic talents. But such a person would probably get passed over in the competitive scramble for schooling and training, due to his average or low IQ. That exclusion could in turn eliminate his chance to become an architect, even though it is a field that he has a real talent for. There are many important talents other than those involved with having top school grades.

Goleman points to the need to measure three things: acuity, acumen, and wisdom.[4] We all know very smart people with poor judgment and questionable wisdom, while there are very simple folks wiser than many college graduates. The acumen and wisdom Goleman looks for are ignored when we look just at a person's IQ scores.

This call for more emphasis on people skills, leadership, and sound decision-making ability is further developed by Robert Sternberg, who underscores the need to get away from present IQ tests that overemphasize abstract thinking at the expense of concrete or practical thinking. The "g" factor of IQ tests simply tests the schoolbook academic form of intelligence. It is affected by the environment's impact on its subjects, who will do well if they have had an enriched environment but will do poorly if they come from a less privileged background. He suggests we go to a three-headed analysis of intelligence:

1. "Analytic intelligence" is similar to existing IQ tests of fluid intelligence solving abstract problems.
2. "Creative intelligence" would try to evaluate creativity of a practical or useful kind.
3. "Practical intelligence" would test the ability to apply solutions to practical issues in a real-world environment.[5]

Some other writers have called for evaluation of the ability to make good decisions under uncertainty, which might fall within Sternberg's third category of practical intelligence. Two of Gardner's eight forms of intelligence deal with self-control, personal awareness, empathy, awareness of others, and social skills. These are comparable to the "emotional" intelligences that Mayer and Salovey identified. They are also the nearest thing to Goleman's idea of EQ, or people and social skills. In discussing them, Goleman refers to the need for people to work together cooperatively and to understand what others are thinking—the "I hear what you're saying and I know where you're coming from" type of interpersonal understanding that makes effective leaders and workers.

Goleman also emphasizes the need for a willingness to work hard. He suggests this trait is especially important in music and sports, where he refers to the 10,000-hours theory regarding the need for very diligent practice to make perfect. However, the 10,000-hour rule does not just apply to sports and the performing arts. That same type of persistence can be effective in most occupations and can dwarf the contribution of IQ alone. In *The Millionaire Mind*, Dr. Stanley reports that most of the self-made individuals he studied emphasized the importance of tenacity over IQ. As Thomas Edison quipped, "Genius is 99 percent perspiration and 1 percent inspiration."

In addition, there are specific mental attitudes that can trump IQ. In this regard, consider resisting impulse, self-control, and "The Marshmallow Test" for deferred gratification. Goleman tells of Dr. Walter Mischel's test with four-year-olds at a Stanford preschool. The kids were shown a batch of marshmallows and told that they could have one now, but if they waited until he ran an errand and came back, they could have two. Some managed to wait "but others, more impulsive, grabbed the one marshmallow, almost within seconds of the experimenter's leaving the room on his 'errand.'"[6] Twelve years later, the emotional and social difference between the two groups was dramatic. Those who had resisted temptation at four became more confident adolescents, socially competent, self-reliant, dependable, and better able to cope with the frustrations of life. Those who had grabbed the marshmallows tended to be mistrustful, resentful, jealous, and short-tempered. The children who exercised restraint became better students and displayed a greater ability to make plans and see them through to completion than the other group.

Such emotional control is one of the best predictors of success. Goleman calls it "a meta-ability, determining how well or how poorly people are able to use their other mental capacities." [7]

Some people have a long-term frame of mind, and others live in the present. Goleman suggests that this is a trait, like reading a social situation or listening attentively to others, that can be learned. "There is perhaps no psychological skill more fundamental than resisting impulse. It is the root of all emotional self-control, since all emotions, by their very nature, lead to one or another impulse to act." [8] There is no doubt that all these forms of human competency should be valued and that we should get away from the simple mindedness of just looking at IQs.

**Practical Intelligence**

Robert J. Sternberg has been among those who believe that intelligence as evaluated by IQ tests represents only a small portion of a person's cognitive skills. Like Gardner and Goleman, he seeks to broaden the term "intelligence" to include other important abilities, whether they represent musical aptitude, athleticism, logic, or common sense. Sternberg believes that IQ tests measure only "inert intelligence," processing speed, memory, and accumulated academic knowledge. He rightly points out that the academic skills that earn high SAT scores do not necessarily lead to goal-directed action or effective real-world problem-solving.[9]

Sternberg, a professor of psychology at Yale, also stresses the need for mental flexibility, the ease with which one can adapt to new situations and to question established wisdom, which seems to be a combination of the second and third. It might be noted that "intellectuals" of the high IQ type, are, once they have established a theory they like, among the least able to maintain flexibility or question their own established wisdom. (This inflexibility may be attributable to the arrogance that sometimes is created in the minds of those who gain high test-scores, some of whom actually but erroneously believe they are smarter than everyone else).

The importance of creative and practical thinking was demonstrated when John Harrison solved one of the greatest technical problems of his age. Born in 1693, the son of a poor carpenter in Yorkshire, Harrison received very little schooling. As a teenager, he learned his father's trade, and his skill at woodworking led him to repair clocks, which in those times were constructed with mostly wooden parts. By the time he was twenty, he was able to keep busy full time building and repairing clocks.

Because the young woodworker was self-taught, he looked beyond the confines of established clock mechanics and soon made many important mechanical innovations that improved the accuracy and durability of pendulum clocks. When Parliament announced a handsome prize to the first person to solve the problem of determining longitude with a sea-going time-piece, he tried his hand. The leading scientists of that era were stumped, but Harrison made a breakthrough with a spring-powered watch and kept modifying it until it attained the needed accuracy for oceanic voyages. This carpenter's son, an uneducated wooden clock repairman, had the practical and creative "smarts" to do what all the brilliant scientists at Cambridge and Oxford could not do. His talents also included, we should note, the tenacity and persistence to devote twenty years to the fine-tun-

*John Harrison—A working class carpenter and clock repairman with no formal education, he solved the problem that had stumped all the King's astronomers*

ing of his successive innovations until his goal was attained.

Sternberg explains that such creative and practical types of brainpower represent "successful intelligence." Their presence determines one's ability to do well in both career and in life. "Successfully intelligent" people take advantage of their strengths and compensate for their weaknesses. Their unique cognitive style allows them to be flexible in their approach to work and to maintain the drive to complete tasks undertaken. Being pragmatic, they create their own opportunities, recognize and correctly define problems, and know when to persevere and when to quit.[10]

These aptitudes are similar to the ones that Dr. Thomas J. Stanley found common in the self-made millionaires that he studied. These skills, which are probably in part a genetic inheritance, can be enhanced in our homes and schools by providing instruction that will teach logic, build recognition of rational thinking, and grant common sense the respect that it deserves.

## Terman's Termites

In the days leading up to World War I, the U.S. Army had to create an immense fighting force from scratch, and several academic volunteers offered to help solve the problem. Lewis Terman, a psychology professor from Stanford University, had already developed such a test, called the Stanford-Binet, based on an earlier one that had been developed by the pioneering work of Alfred Binet. That is how Professor Terman and several other psychologists made the first massive use of IQ tests in America. Their well-publicized work established IQ tests and their administrators as "experts" in evaluating human competence.

After World War I, in the course of his academic work, Terman noticed a few people who were employed in menial jobs, even though they possessed special talents such as a great facility with numbers, an unusually retentive memory, or above-normal musical and artistic ability. He decided to find such gifted individuals while they were still young and provide guidance and support. He contacted hundreds of California's elementary schools and selected the brightest children by having them take his IQ test. He accepted only the top 1,500 scores out of a quarter-million tested, selecting only those above the 99.5 percentile!

This select group had scored IQs between 140 and 200 and had been born between 1903 and 1917. They came to be known as "Terman's Termites," and their lives were carefully chartered and analyzed ever after. Professor Terman took a strong interest in these geniuses, provided them with support and wrote glowingly about how such great minds would contribute greatly to America's future. "There is nothing about an individual as important as his IQ, except possibly his morals."[11] He saw them as an elite that should lead the nation.

Malcolm Gladwell tells the story of these termites in his book, *Outliers*, to illustrate that IQ alone does not determine the great success of individuals. The brilliant termites proved that point: Although Terman worshipped their intellects, the termites did not live up to his expectations. There were some successes—a couple authors, a few judges, a few state legislators—and, on average, they earned good incomes. However, the majority, Gladwell reports, "had careers that could only be considered ordinary, and a surprising number ended up with careers that even Terman considered failures.... The sociologist Pitirim Sorokin once showed that if Terman had simply put together a randomly selected group of children from the same kinds of family backgrounds as the Termites—and dispensed with IQs altogether—he would have ended up with a group doing almost as many impressive things as his painstakingly selected group of geniuses."[12] Later in life, Terman conceded that intellect and achievement are far from perfectly correlated.

Though Terman's select group was handpicked for high IQ, their adult lives tell us little about the meaning of IQ. However, a 1968 study by Terman's associate, Melita Oden, compared the one hundred most successful and one hundred least successful men in the group. She defined success as gaining occupational positions that required and employed their intellectual minds. The successes were mostly professors, scientists, doctors, and lawyers. The non-successes included electronics technicians, police, carpenters, pool cleaners, and a few average lawyers, doctors, and academics. She found that the hundred successes and the hundred non-successes showed little difference in average IQ. The big differences turned out to be in confidence, persistence, and early parental encouragement.

In spite of these results, the educational establishment has somehow managed to make IQ testing the main sorting device in America's schools and colleges. The SAT tests and GREs that determine who gets into what colleges are still based on the limited set of competencies that Terman's IQ test measured.

The subsequent excess reliance on IQ test was not Terman's fault. When it became evident that his group was not all that select, he tried to find out why. He divided his sample into three groups in accordance with their degree of achievement as adults. The A group included the high achievers, the B group the ones that were just doing satisfactorily, and the C group those who had achieved the least. He found that the only thing that distinguished the As, Bs, and Cs from each other were their family backgrounds. The As came from upper and middle class families, half had fathers who had college degrees, and as children had been exposed to and stimulated by, in Gladwell's term, "an atmosphere of concerted cultivation."[13] On the other hand, the C group came mostly from the lower SEC levels, and almost a third of them had a parent who had dropped out of school before the eighth grade.

Terman's canvassers described the difference in appearance between As and Cs: The former were judged to be more alert, poised, and well-dressed. "You're simply seeing the difference between those schooled by their families to present their best face to the world, and those denied that experience.... The Cs were squandered talent. But they didn't need to be. They lacked something that could have been given to them... a community around them that prepared them properly for the world."[14] Apparently, what parents do for their kids— and the assumptions and expectations that the child becomes imbued with—do matter. And schoolteachers could make the same contribution if they respected individual hopes and dreams more than IQ scores and academic grades.

Terman was still not clear about what his study had proven, so he did another analysis of his termites data. He divided them into two groups: those born between 1903 and 1912 and those born between 1912 and 1917. The Cs were much more likely to have been born in the earlier period. Why? Timing is everything.

Those born between 1915–17 graduated from college after the worst of the Depression was over in the late 1930s, entered the armed service at a young age, and gained the experience and opportunities of going away to war. The Termites born before 1911 graduated from college just before or at the bottom of the Depression, had difficulties getting a job, and then had to disrupt their adult careers for World

War II when they were in their thirties. One could also argue that the earlier group, which fared poorer, experienced their formative years during the privations of World War I, while the later group enjoyed the stimulation and liberty of the "Roaring Twenties" in their formative years.

In any case, the As enjoyed the best parenting environment and the best of times, while the Cs were burdened by the worst family environment and the worst of times—a double dose of good luck versus bad luck. Many individuals in the ill-fated C group were losers in both the birth lottery and the demographic lottery. But both groups demonstrate how culture and chance can trump genetics. And, as a one-time friend once said, "I'd rather be born lucky than smart."

## Rational Thinking Versus a Good Memory

It appears clear that the lives of Terman's Termites were heavily influenced by their family environment, their birth dates, and probably a host of other factors still to be isolated. However, one thing is clear. Their high IQs were not the major determinant in the success of their adult lives. Recent discoveries have confirmed how small a role IQ plays in the grand total of a person's competencies. We now must consider the importance of "emotional intelligence," the role of "people smarts," a practical way of thinking, as well as the varying impact of special skills such as leadership qualities, athletic ability, and musical ability. Gardner makes passing reference to "determination," and Daniel Goleman refers to "deferment of gratification," as part of emotional intelligence, and these are also important success predictors.

These various attributes may be described as some of the "non-IQ" aspects of a person's abilities. They are clearly important in determining success. We do not know the extent to which they are inherited, but we do know that most can be developed or enhanced in childhood. We also know that if they are not developed in childhood, they probably will never be developed. While personality, persistence, and impulse control are partly genetic attributes, it is important for parents to enhance these characteristics in their kids from the very earliest years. Such traits, and learning good habits of living, are more important for the child's future success and happiness than his school achievements.

Stephen Covey's book, *The 7 Habits of Highly Effective People*, develops the importance of such behavioral "tricks" that help make for success. Such rules of conduct and manners have been recognized for years. Dale Carnegie became rich telling people "how to win friends and influence people." Long before that, some of our most eminent Founding Fathers used checklists of such manners to achieve personal improvement. Ben Franklin, Thomas Jefferson, and George Washington were distinguished by their mastery of such graces and the concerted effort they employed to develop them.

Covey's suggested "habits" are very similar to Coach Wooden's Pyramid of Success, which he used to show his players what they should aspire to. And all their admonishments are built on Ben Franklin's foundation of virtuous living. John Wooden's whole life was based on what he had learned from his father. When Wooden graduated from grade school, his father gave him a card that listed "seven suggestions to follow," including: Be true to yourself, help others, make friendship a fine art, pray for guidance, and give thanks every day for your blessings. John's father told him, "Johnny, follow this and you'll do all right."[15]

The famous coach also learned from his dad to live by "The Golden Rule." Wooden was taught that a leader who can't abide by The Golden Rule is like the "rotten Indiana ice in springtime"— undependable and untrustworthy.

Just as Wooden stressed character and integrity, Covey urges children to achieve a unity of purpose, to build a character of total integrity, and live a life of love and service. Parents can help, Covey argues, by giving their kids "wings." And the best way to give them the wings to fly free and securely is to give them foundational roots. They must learn to center their life on correct principles and to "rise above any negative scripting that had been passed down to us."[16] Covey suggests that a clearly stated mission helps a person achieve an independent and principled life—and that the goal is empowering for everyone, especially those from damaged environments.

It seems fair to say that most of the elements of a successful person are not intelligence related. And yet, there does seem to be a range of mental abilities, purely the work of the brain chemistry each of us is given, that contributes to success. We do know that many high IQ people make poor decisions, lack wisdom and judgment, and often straddle the fence for seeing all sides of a question with little ability to make the right decision. And most high IQ people when they do theorize or discuss alternatives do so with clearly marked parameters to the question at hand. However, in real life, most decisions are made under uncertainty with many unknown factors at play, and there is a requirement for a certain type of rationality that is not measured by IQ tests.

Keith E. Stanovich, a professor of human development and applied psychology at the University of Toronto, has addressed this rational decision-making capability that contributes to the success of some people. He begins his book with a review of the Nobel Prize given in 2002 to Daniel Kahneman and Amos Tversky for their work in economics. Their work centered on how people make choices and evaluate alternatives. They found that it is the way human cognition works that makes some of us more or less prone to errors of judgment. But tellingly, such errors of judgment frequently result from an avoidance of the rational processes that should be employed. Errors can be minimized if you train yourself to THINK.

Stanovich's objective was to find out why individuals vary in problem-solving ability. He asserts that there are certain attributes of intelligence that determine a person's rationality, and he finds it unfortunate that none of them are measured on IQ or SAT tests. He consequently advises that the word "intelligence" must be used with a specific understanding quite different from common usage. In the past, we have lumped high IQ, good thinking, and rational decision-making as a composite of what makes a person "smart." But it turns out that the separate elements of a person's overall brainpower must be evaluated separately, because the amount of each segment varies with every person. Obviously, it would be good for a person to have all the useful mental capabilities, but few get them all. It is also obvious that most of Terman's Termites may have possessed only the first one: the algorithmic-level cognitive capacity, which excludes other equally important abilities that many of the Termites sorely lacked.

This separateness of different forms of intelligence was confirmed by Kahneman and Tversky, who demonstrated that there is only a small to medium correlation between IQ test performance and one's capacity for rational decision-making. And yet the rational decision-making skills are vital in allowing people to attain their potential in worldly success, happiness, and well-being. That is why many a working laborer can be happier than the termites who happened to have genius IQ brains but were short on EQ and other cognitive skills.

If we can agree that intelligence is more than the ability to memorize and manipulate mathematical abstractions, then we need not merely argue for the emotional or behavioral skills as a complement to IQ tests. Instead, we can assert that IQ does not reveal the full operation of our brains, because it leaves out the rational thinking requirements for good decision-making. There is no test for RQ (Rationality Quotient), although Stanovich illustrates what one might look like in his book, *What Intelligence Tests Miss*.

Stanovich attributes the poor judgment we see in so many of today's jurists, academicians, expert consultants, and commentators to the fact that they were chosen and elevated due to their IQ rather than their judgment. "The college students who failed laboratory tests of decision-making and probabilistic reasoning are indeed the future jurists who, despite decent cognitive capacities, will reason badly. These students have never been specifically screened for rationality..."[17]

Interestingly, it appears that there are only small differences among the races when measured for practical intelligence or rationality. Robert Sternberg found in his studies that while race and class differences show a big difference in IQ, they are much less indicative of practical intelligence and rationality. Sternberg uses the term "practical intelligence" in much the same way that Stanovich uses the term "rational decision making"—but both are attempts to measure the non-IQ elements that make our brains effective. And it appears that minorities that do poorly on IQ tests are much better matched on the practical intelligence levels. This fact provides further evidence that IQ tests favor those children possessing rich cultural and family backgrounds. These findings also indicate that there is much less difference between the races than those who stress IQ scores would like us to believe.

## Mechanics, Machinists, and the Age of Invention

Most of the individuals who helped lead the industrial revolution had one thing in common. They skipped adolescence and began their work lives in their teens. There were millions of such "inventors" in Western Europe and the U.S. from 1600 to 1900, who created a flood of labor-saving machines. They created the Industrial Revolution that reduced poverty and ushered in a world of plenty for the people of those very few nations involved.

That period of mechanical and electrical invention stood out as unique in human history. For example, consider the earth plow that all farmers around the world required to grow crops. The models in use at the time of the American Revolution utilized the same basic design that was used in the time of Julius Caesar, seventeen hundred years earlier! Then, suddenly, in newly free America, many improvements were made culminating in John Deere's improved steel bladed model. John Deere was the ultimate common man. His father abandoned the family in Rutland, Vermont, when son John was four. The boy helped his remaining family by working with blacksmiths as a youngster, and at seventeen entered an apprenticeship for three years. After that, he started his own smithy and took an interest in innovative farming machinery. Applying a steel blade to existing plow designs may sound simple but it revolutionized farming practices and helped create the cornucopia of American agriculture. None of the educated elites during the prior seventeen hundred years ever thought of it!

Another pioneer that helped invent the modern world was Thomas Alva Edison, born on February 11, 1847, in Milan, Ohio. Edison

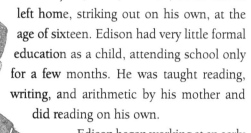

left home, striking out on his own, at the age of sixteen. Edison had very little formal education as a child, attending school only for a few months. He was taught reading, writing, and arithmetic by his mother and did reading on his own.

Edison began working at an early age, as most boys did at the time. At thirteen, he took a job as a newsboy, selling newspapers and candy on the local railroad. He also helped out others at the railroad station and learned how to operate a telegraph. When he was sixteen, he was working as a telegrapher full time. But he did more than learn how to operate

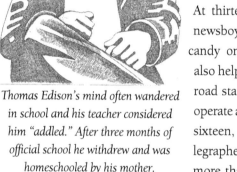

*Thomas Edison's mind often wandered in school and his teacher considered him "addled." After three months of official school he withdrew and was homeschooled by his mother.*

it. By the time he was twenty-one, he had moved to New York to work on inventions related to the telegraph and developed his first successful invention, the Universal Stock Printer. For this and some related inventions, Edison was paid $40,000. This gave the twenty-three-year-old Edison the money he needed to set up his first small laboratory and manufacturing plant. During the next five years, Edison worked in Newark, inventing and manufacturing devices that greatly improved the speed and efficiency of the telegraph.

In 1876, Edison moved his family and staff of assistants to the small village of Menlo Park, twenty-five miles southwest of New York City. The new research and development laboratory was the first of its kind anywhere and became the model for later facilities, such as Bell Laboratories.

Michael Faraday was another "uneducated" youngster from a poor family who helped change the world for the better. Born in England in 1791, he made some of the most significant inventions in scientific history. He developed the first dynamo, which led to all modern generators. His discovery of electromagnetic induction created the worldwide development of electrical machinery, which powered the industrial and electrical era. Typical of many great inventors and scientists, he did it on his own. He was the son of a blacksmith and was apprenticed to a bookbinder at the age of fourteen. He had little formal education but became aware of that era's growing scientific knowledge through self-study and by attending educational lectures in his off hours. When he was twenty-one and his seven-year apprenticeship duties ended, he approached Sir Humphry Davy, a London scientist, and secured an assistantship in Davy's laboratories. Thirteen years later, at the age of thirty-four, he became director of the laboratory.

What all these young scientists and entrepreneurs had in common was that they were not allowed to languish through their teenage years. Instead of letting their minds lie fallow and atrophy, they became actively involved in workday pursuits and put their minds to constructive innovative practices. It has never been established that any form of classroom book-learning can replicate the pragmatic experience that comes from hands-on work.

Samuel Colt was born in Hartford, Connecticut, on July 19, 1814. He attended a local school for a few years and worked in his father's textile mill. He became interested in the mill's machinery and, even as a youngster, took things apart to see how they worked—especially his father's firearms. When he was fifteen years old, he got tired of the work at the mill, so he signed on as a sailor. While at sea, Samuel Colt developed his idea for a pistol with a revolving cylinder. There were a number of pieces of revolving equipment on the boat, from the helmsman's wheel to pulleys and the capstan. One of them reputedly triggered the idea in Colt's observant eye. His resulting invention of the revolving barrel transformed a one-bullet handgun into a multiple-shot device and, as the saying goes, "tamed the West."

In 1835, at age twenty-one and back from the sea voyages, Colt obtained the first patent on his revolver. A year later, he established a factory to manufacture firearms. Colt made many additional inventions and developed the first underwater telegraph cable. Perhaps his most notable accomplishment was the use of interchangeable parts and assembly lines, which accelerated the move to more efficient mass production. Like Edison, Colt's contribution went beyond his inventions, to the manufacturing and research methods introduced. Their creation of innovative manufacturing methods places Edison and Colt in stark contrast to "intellectuals" who merely produce ideas and are little interested in their efficacy or usefulness.

The list of such innovative people includes Sam Morse, Cyrus Eaton, Cyrus McCormick, Robert Fulton, James Watt, Samuel Slater, Eli Whitney, and John Stevens. They were all tinkerers and mechanics, not great academic scholars. McCormick was twenty-two when he came up with his first major invention. Benjamin Franklin, among the most notable, was apprenticed out to work for a printer at age fourteen, with little formal

*James Watt. A thin, weakly child, suffered from migraines all his life. Mostly schooled at home by his mother, he worked on ship's instruments in his father's shop, leaving home when he was 18 to set up his repair shop in Glasgow. Later in life, after repairing the University's model steam engine, he went on to revolutionize the science and engineering of steam engines, combining practical and theoretical scientific know-how to power the Industrial Revolution.*

schooling. He learned everything, as my parents used to say, in "the school of hard knocks."

The extraordinary fact about these individuals that transformed the industrial and financial world was that they were not necessarily great intellects but practical-minded individuals who started their work at very tender ages. Their discoveries were not based on abstractions, theories, or ideologies of the intellect but were mechanical in nature and came from simple observation and improvement of what already existed.

Samuel Smiles has suggested that our engineers and mechanics "may be regarded in some measure as the makers of modern civilization. The problems of political history cannot properly be interpreted without reference to the people themselves—how they lived and how they worked, and what they did to promote the civilization of the nation to which they belonged."[18] Smiles provides an interesting biography of the great engineer Thomas Telford, among the many worthy creators of the Industrial Revolution:

> Thomas Telford was born in an isolated corner of the county of Dumfries, in Scotland, in 1757. One would scarcely have expected to find the birthplace of the Menai Bridge and other great national works in so obscure a corner of the kingdom. Possibly it may already have struck the reader with surprise, that not only were all of the early engineers self-taught in their profession, but they were brought up mostly in remote country places, far from the active life of great towns and cities. But genius is of no locality, and springs alike from the farmhouse, the peasant's hut, or the herd's shieling. Strange, indeed, it is that the men who have built our bridges, docks, lighthouses, canals, and railways, should nearly all have been country-bred boys.[19]

Telford had few advantages. His father was a sheepherder. The family's cottage consisted of four mud walls and a thatched roof, and young Telford was orphaned within a year of his birth. In his childhood, he herded cows and sheep for neighbors and attended a parish school for a few years. "It was not much that he learnt; but in acquiring the arts of reading, writing and figures, he learnt the beginnings of a great deal."[20]

He left school when he was fifteen and apprenticed to a stonemason, working on repairs to local cottages and barns for eight years. He later moved to London and worked on construction jobs. After another ten years of construction work, he was appointed surveyor for the building of the Telford Canal, the first of his many remarkable engineering accomplishments. His is another example of how an early start, gaining practical experience during the teenage years, built the competency for great achievements. Little education was required, for such individuals learned on the job and were tireless in gaining knowledge by self-study and observation.

The teaching establishment will protest that science is too complex today for a child to innovate without advanced education—that the Faradays, the Colts, and the McCormicks are not possible anymore, and that only students with years of preparation can succeed in the computer age. But that is patently false. The computer age and the Internet era were built primarily by young entrepreneurs. David Packard worked initially in a garage to start Hewlett-Packard. Steve Jobs and Bill Gates were self-educated in their chosen field and left school at very young ages to found two of the most successful modern technology giants. And it is clear that current technology rests more on young engineers out of MIT and Cal Tech than on the intellectual soft-scientists graduating from the Ivy League.

The latest findings on how our brains develop indicate that our growth and learning skills are at their highest between the ages of twelve and sixteen. The individuals that manned the Age of Invention were marked by the fact that they were actively involved in the adult workplace during those critical years. They got little formal schooling, were put to work at outside trades before they were fifteen, and made a practice of self-teaching in the fields that attracted their attention.

There is no way of knowing their IQ type intelligence, but it is clear they all worked with their hands more than their minds. They used their minds to watch how mechanical or electrical processes worked and, by tinkering, made them better. Perhaps some form of work-study programs would help provide such useful experience for today's students? Should we not supplement today's sterile school environment, find ways to emulate the valuable apprenticeship experience of history's great inventors, and thereby develop ways to better stimulate the creative imagination of our students?

## SUMMARY

A. There are many components to the aggregate "intelligence" or "competency" of individuals. Both IQ and EQ together fail to indicate all of the components of total competency.

B. I like to think of a "Total Competency Quotient," or TCQ, to allow for all those elements that contribute to success, because it is the combination of numerous aptitudes that count. While many people that succeed in relatively specialized activities such as sales, sports, art, or music may appear to need only a few talents, in order to fully develop that talent, they need a host of contributing traits.

C. Some of the essential elements in all activities are an adventurous spirit, a willingness to defer gratification and invest in the future, thrift and perseverance, self-restraint, and common sense.

D. These important traits may in part constitute one's genetic endowment, but such competencies have been traditionally taught in Western societies to each new generation.

E. Every child has the potential to be great at something. Just a few helpful characteristics may vault him or her into action at the right time—if they are aware of their possibilities and employ the needed work, planning, and persistence for the task.

F. With those unforeseen possibilities in mind, do as one inspirational mother did when she told her child to "hitch your wagon to a star!" The potential of every child is both unimaginable and unpredictable. All you can do is urge them all on.

# Chapter 5
# How the Meaning of Intelligence Has Changed

*"We know people solve problems on IQ tests; we suspect those problems are so detached, or so abstracted from reality, that the ability to solve them can diverge over time from the real-world problem-solving ability called intelligence."*
—Stephen Murdoch

A̲s̲ a̲ s̲t̲u̲d̲e̲n̲t̲ o̲f̲ h̲i̲s̲t̲o̲r̲y̲, I am always impressed by how well-spoken people in ancient times were. If you read the speeches of the great Roman and Greek leaders that lived two thousand and more years ago, you will find that they match or exceed anything to be heard in America today. And the writings from those days, including the Greek dramas and comedies of around 400–500 B.C., are as sophisticated and intellectually stimulating as today's productions. And, even back then, there was a large and appreciative audience that fully understood the pathos and satire presented in their books and theater.

Shakespeare's plays date from about five hundred years ago, and his use of language and metaphor is unparalleled to this day. It is arguable that such ancients set forth a depth of wisdom and exquisite commentary on the human condition that has never been bettered. And yet, there has been extraordinary progress in knowledge, science, communication, and manufacturing. Our technology, food production, transportation, and communication make everything about Greece and Rome appear rustic and primitive. But, wait: Did you notice that all those recent advances have been of a mechanical or material nature? Perhaps we, as individual human beings, have not progressed at all! Is it just our machines and toys that have improved? How can that be?

The answer I have come up with is built on the distinction between hard-science and soft-science in human affairs. The first obeys the laws of the physical world, and scientists, engineers, and mechanics have steadily advanced our technological ability. The same kinds of inventive and practical people that created siege catapults for the Greeks attacking Persians have moved on to machine guns, plastics, airplanes, and computers. In his monumental review of history's "builders," Samuel Smiles writes: "Are not the men who have made the motive power of the country, and immensely increased its productive strength, the men above all others who have tended to make the country what it is? These men were strong-minded, resolute, and ingenious, and were impelled to their special pursuits by the force of their constructive instincts."[1] In that one last sentence, Smiles pays tribute to several qualities of intellect and motivation that would go unrecorded on IQ tests—and yet those are the very qualities that "made the country what it is."

It has been just a case of accumulating know-how, century by century. We know that each generation throughout recorded history has been populated with individuals of about the same cognitive capability. Our progress in material artifacts has been accomplished simply because each new generation of pragmatic "technicians" have had the advantage of learning as youngsters the discoveries of prior generations and thus been able to build further on that base.

The soft sciences are very different. They deal with totally unpredictable things that follow no physical laws. There has been no change in the nature of people in over 20,000 years. They are just as varied and unpredictable as they were when Homer wrote his epic tales of Troy. And by the time of the Romans, or at least by the time of the Renaissance, every conceivable economic and political system had been thoroughly tried.

All around the world, during those past several thousand years, an almost infinite number of cultures rose and fell. Within that polyglot of a stew, innumerable variations of living style, personal beliefs, and habits were employed. Many alternative forms of social and political organizations were designed and perfected. There remains nothing really new to attempt. We can only look back and see which solutions worked best, which cultures helped their people the most, and which lifestyles made people the most successful and contented. My own review of history reveals that progress occurred in those locales where the "engineers" and other practical-minded individuals were given personal liberty and economic freedom—they then did the rest.[2] Soft-scientists and intelligentsias were usually absent until sufficient prosperity was created to support their idle musings.

**Are We Getting Smarter or Dumber??**

The "bottom line" is that humans are no smarter today than they were thousands of years ago. And they have no more initiative, daring, creativity, persistence, or any of the EQ capabilities than our ancient ancestors possessed. Today's engineers and mechanics have the advantage of accumulated knowledge, but the social scientists are no more knowledgeable than their counterparts in ancient Greece and Rome. Indeed, many of today's social scientists, political philosophers, and economists persist in recommending practices that have failed in the past.

In short, soft-science intellectuals have not only offered no new political or social innovations in the past two hundred years, but many have proposed re-adoption of past experiments in government that failed. These facts have a bearing on how we educate our children.

First, students should be made aware that many of today's so-called experts in the soft sciences have an "expertise" that has no foundation in practical experience. They rely on the abstract theories of other armchair experts!

Second, note that the "material" progress that mankind has achieved has always been the work of mechanics, technicians, and scientists, with little to show from the intellectuals, philosophers, or soft-science experts.

Third, we must not assume that just because human cognitive ability has remained relatively constant for millennia that it is not currently declining. Evidence reveals a frightening trend for the future of civilization.

The Flynn expose on rising IQ scores was explained earlier and raises many questions about the direction we are going. If today's people perform much better on IQ tests than their parents did, are we really getting smarter? The large increases in Americans' IQs became obvious, because many tests are used unchanged for years, and the scores have improved year by year on the same test. More than half the test takers score above the prior year's 100-level. Over the past half-century, scores have improved about a third of a point per year. Consequently, a truly average person taking the test that has remained unchanged for ten years will receive an IQ score of 103, three points higher than the original average.

The rise in scores may have something to do with better health and nutrition, but more importantly, today's youth are exposed to a variety of enriching experiences that their forebears did not have. TV, video games, more sophisticated magazines, more educated parents, or more culturally successful families, all provide a stimulating environment that not only exercises the brain, but teaches the children a wider variety of things absent from earlier childhoods. That richer environment makes them better at IQ tests but not necessarily any better at dealing with the problems that face us.

And of course, there is the possibility that teachers throughout school years teach to the test. Today's students are given a number of tests from first grade through high school, and they get to be more proficient test takers. The environmental impact is clear when rural versus urban children's scores are compared. There is thirty-point disparity (Flynn). But are urban children really smarter than rural children?

DNA analysis indicates that all modern human beings that constitute today's family of races were very closely related when they first left Africa and spread out around the earth. The racial and ethnic differences of today must have developed after the movement out of Africa sixty thousand years ago. All humans today share a common language capacity that must have been present at the time of that dispersal. The significance of this biological constancy is that the changes in human behavior and living style that have occurred during the past sixty thousand years have been simply the result of accumulated cultural and technical advances, not from any major cognitive improvement. Colin Renfrew writes: "Modern molecular genetics suggests that, apart from the normal range present in all populations in matters such as IQ, all humans are born equal."[3] And yet he asks why, if people all over the world remained relatively unchanged for sixty thousand years, did it take so long for improved lifestyles to develop? And why did developments vary so much from one region to another?

Michael H. Hart argues that the people that moved north and had to deal with cold harsh weather developed higher IQs and then used those IQs to create societal advances.[4] There is little evidence to substantiate this view, and Hart has to make several contortions to explain the wonders of Greece and Rome (warm climates, calm harbors) versus the backwardness of Vikings and Eskimos (freezing weather, frozen harbors).

Most scholars believe the favorable geography and climate in Eurasia—spread in a broad belt from China to the Mediterranean—allowed a number of civilizations to grow and prosper by simply organizing groups of people and exchanging their many cultural innovations. This accumulation of knowledge enabled area-wide progress, especially in areas where a large number of people were free to explore new applications and innovations.

Under this view, one might fairly say mankind picked itself up by its own bootstraps! And the individuals who did the heavy lifting would have been the ingenious and practical-minded people who tinkered with labor-saving devices that gradually multiplied the productivity and efficiency of human labor. Thus, it may have been the non-IQ parts of human brains that created most of the material progress we enjoy. And that may still be the case today.

Many psychologists who have studied this subject point to a transition from concrete thinking to abstract thinking that has occurred over time and especially during the past one hundred years, as people have had to deal with more complex living situations. This transition is usually described by advocates of IQ testing as a positive change, but then they may well be biased.

Those who still think in practical or concrete ways are reluctant to hypothesize about possibilities, preferring to deal with the known factors they understand. Because such practical minds developed all the labor-saving innovations throughout history, there is reason to question the new emphasis on rewarding abstract thinking.

IQ tests are currently designed to separate "concrete" thinking from "abstract" thinking, with higher scores going to those with a facility for the abstract. Flynn reports that there has been "a profound shift from a merely utilitarian attitude to concrete reality toward assuming it was important to classify it in terms of the more abstract the better; and that the taking of hypothetical situations seriously had freed logic from the concrete to deal with not only hypothetical questions but symbols that had no concrete referents."[5] This trend certainly downplays the importance of "practical" intelligence that we saw in the lives of the engineers and mechanics that powered the Industrial Revolution.

There is no question that the academics who design the tests have made substantial changes in the cognitive skills required to score well on the tests. For example, Flynn cites how fourteen-year-old school children used to be tested (in 1902–1913) on their knowledge of culturally valued information. However, in test between 1997 and 1999, the tests expected only superficial knowledge of such information and tested instead for understanding complex relationships between concepts.[6] This reflects the bias of academics who overestimate the value of their conceptual virtuosity and seek to promote philosophers rather than mechanics.

Current rewards and praise to those with the highest SAT test scores has in fact changed our leadership from practical-minded people to those with an abstract and utopian vision of how they can make things better. Because they get preferred education and all the trappings of civilization, they develop the ability to score well on tests and discuss grand economic and political plans for the future. But it is not clear if that type of abstract thinking has helped in governing the political and social affairs of nations. If we compare today's soft-science elite to those of ancient republics we can only conclude that progress has eluded fifteen centuries of the soft-science intellectuals!

We have every reason to believe that scores should be rising, because the most prosperous half of the population that take those tests are the ones getting more and more schooling and cultural exposure from their well-to-do parents. Our concern should be whether our children are gaining in the non-IQ areas of competency. From what we can read about the people of ancient Greece, Rome, Renaissance Italy, and Shakespeare's England, we are not happier, shrewder, or more able to deal with life and matters of state than those ancient ancestors were. And recent events in Washington and

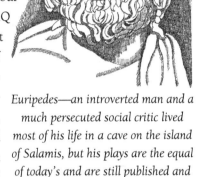

*Euripedes—an introverted man and a much persecuted social critic lived most of his life in a cave on the island of Salamis, but his plays are the equal of today's and are still published and performed 2,400 years after his death.*

Wall Street would indicate that we have too much abstract economic theory and corruption—and not enough common sense and integrity.

## Family Size, Siblings, and Intelligence

Predicting success based on family size has baffled the experts for decades. It has been known since the 1920s that children from large families, that is, with many siblings, have lower IQs than children with few brothers and sisters. As recently as 1989, some experts argued that this was due to their environment; the parents with large families had less time to nurture their kids. After all, studies have shown that the firstborn usually outperforms subsequent siblings, and this could be due simply to getting more direct face-time with its parents.

Richard Lynn disagrees with this theory, because throughout the underdeveloped world, there is no connection between IQ and the number of siblings.[7] The advantage for children in small families occurs primarily in the developed affluent nations. What can explain this disparity?

Further studies have shown that in America's larger families, the children have lower IQs. The actual amount by which the IQ is lower has been calculated by taking the average IQ of the parents compared to the average IQ of the children. After allowing for the hereditability of IQ, Lynn estimates that the part of IQ that is inherited has been declining at almost one point per generation. Since the early nineteenth century, the decline in the IQ of Americans from this "sibling effect" has been about five points.[8]

So what is the cause of this ongoing decline in genetic intelligence that is gradually making Americans as a whole dumber? A few things happened around 1800 that changed families and the dispersion of varying IQ levels. First, there was a reduction in family size. People just started having fewer children, especially the upper and middle SEC. Because IQ is directly related to SEC, when the upper groups raise more children there is a positive movement in a population's average IQs. However, when the lower classes have disproportionately more children, there is a resulting decline.

Historically, over thousands of years, the more competent individuals in a society probably raised more children to adulthood than were reared by the less competent. A survival of the fittest scenario undoubtedly operated to maintain the gene pool and to adapt it to changing circumstances. When the early Mediterranean societies gradually transitioned from hunter-gatherers to an agricultural way of life, different aptitudes were called for. Physical stamina and agility may have played a lesser role as the patience and persistence required for farming activities created new challenges. The subsequent transition to trading and manufacturing cities may have called for a higher degree of innovative and mechanical skills. And success in the past few hundred years may have given an advantage to those with leadership, management, and financial aptitudes. In short, the human genetic pool has adapted and probably improved somewhat over the past tens of thousands of years, although the toll of wars, disease, and random chance may have limited major gains in overall competency.

However, such improvements were extremely gradual, because, as we discuss elsewhere, the impact of advances in shelter and food production, monogamy, and the development of social communities all worked to minimize the most severe dangers that humans faced. Plus, as noted elsewhere, there has been no discernible improvement in today's humans over those who lived two thousand years ago in ancient Greece and Rome. But, the important point is that there has been no observable decline in the human gene pool, at least until recently, when, some commentators fear, everything changed.

In 1800, with more knowledge of birth control, the reduction of family size started in the upper classes and that relationship has continued to this day. The "enlightened" upper classes in America and Europe have cut their family size to about the replacement rate. In Italy, it is below the sustaining level. This process has meant that people in the lower SEC are having relatively more babies and the population is suffering a negative, or Dysgenic, fertility. Richard Lynn attributes this sea change around 1800, at least in part, to the increasing use of contraceptives. Richard Carlyle's and Charles Knowlton's books, published in 1826 and 1877 respectively, gave detailed advice on contraceptive devices and techniques. These books were primarily available only to the upper SEC. By 1900, such knowledge had spread to most of the upper, professional, and middle classes.[9]

By 1950, the awareness of contraception had become widespread and birth rates declined for all groups. However, dysgenic fertility has continued. Richard Lynn attributes this to the fact that less intelligent people use available contraceptives less efficiently and have more accidental pregnancies. There is also the fact that welfare policies have encouraged people to have more children within the lower SEC classes. By subsidizing single moms and their illegitimate offspring, government policies have empowered women to be independent financially without the need to marry. The financial benefits of such an arrangement have induced many potential husbands and wives to comply with the regulations governing the distributions of welfare and food stamp checks and not to marry, but still have more children than they otherwise might have. This fact is confirmed by the ballooning of illegitimate births during the past fifty years.

Since World War II, the rise of the socialist welfare states has changed our demographics, subsidizing the procreation of lower SEC, while at the same time encouraging upper SEC to restrict their number of children to help solve projected global problems of excess population, global warming, and the destruction of the environment. These trends have resulted in an increased reproduction rates among lower SECs compared to higher SECs, and thereby increased the dysgenic or declining competency in Western democracies.

There still are experts suggesting that children raised in small families become smarter than kids in large families because of the extra nurturing they get. However, their reasoning is based on data from only the recent past. Higher IQs were not more prevalent in small families until recently. So it isn't the size of the family that matters; it is the factors that lead some people to have more children than others that are determinant. Couples in the upper economic brackets have deliberately reduced their family size more than have those in lower brackets.

It is the author's belief that those in the lower economic classes are not there due to lower IQ but due to lower EQ and the other behavioral traits that determine success. And they are passing on that reduced pragmatism and initiative to the fastest growing segment of the population. Thus, it is possible that the human race is now influenced by the "survival of the un-fittest." The existence of an excessively compassionate welfare or socialist state turns evolution on its head. Any system that rewards or excessively subsidizes apathy, laziness, inefficiency, or bad behavior will only create more of such anti-social behavior.

**Dumbing Down, Disgenics, and Decline**

The most startling aspect of the trends in IQ scores is its contradictory or two-sided nature. It sounds bizarre, but while IQs have risen, there is reason to believe that actual intelligence has declined! It could be that there is a growing divide in the population. Until 1800, human beings as a whole may have become more competent, meaning "smarter" in various practical and important ways, and they had done so rather continuously for millennia. A certain canny and practical mind was needed to avoid the constant dangers of a primitive world. But in the developed world, widespread affluence and stronger relief systems brought an end to that struggle for survival. The historic process has been reversed as the least successful individuals have now been able to successfully rear more children, while the upper SEC has chosen to voluntarily, even pro-actively, reduce their number of children. This switch in relative birth rates might be expected to cause a decline in the genetically-endowed capability of most populations.

Assume that it is the non-IQ factors that make a person successful, at least to the extent of providing for himself and his family. Then, if the lower SECs have more children than the upper SECs, we would expect the next generation to have less EQ also. The extra number of children in the lower SECs would suffer both genetically and culturally by their less than enriching environment.

Flynn points out that this deteriorating level of intelligence is not directly verifiable, "but is an inference derived from two premises." First, intelligence is to some extent inherited, and two, there is an inverse relationship between intelligence and fertility—that is, the proportionately more children being produced by the lower IQ part of the population. Flynn argues, "Because the two premises are solid, the inference appears to be solid."[10]

For purposes of understanding that initial rise up to 1800 and the subsequent decline, we think of the "intelligence" that favored survival as all the types of intelligence we have discussed—both the algorithmic IQ type as well as the practical kind of intelligence. Because progress to that time had required more practical skills than abstract, the odds are that the higher SECs had plenty of the former. Nevertheless, all such skills helped create an increasingly capable people until some turning point around 1800. At that time, the lower SEC started to out-reproduce the upper SECs, and because they presumably had somewhat less of this combination of cognitive abilities, their relative increase in numbers has resulted in an increasingly less capable people today than two hundred years ago. All this came about because humans reached a point where they had such a firm control over their environment that they overcame the laws of survival of the fittest. With widespread affluence and hunger and disease controlled, the law of the jungle ended. With an ever-expanding safety net, a reverse process took over, and we now have the survival of the un-fittest. In the developed prosperous nations, everyone survives, but the un-fittest have more children.

The distinction between practical wisdom and IQ smarts was indirectly referred to by Jared Diamond when he explained two reasons why Yali, a primitive New Guinea man, was probably more competent than the average European. First, the harsher environment imposed life or death alternatives on Yali's people, who had to be clever to escape the many causes of mortality. Second, the average western household is passively entertained by television, movies, and concerts. In contrast, New Guinea children have little passive entertainment "and instead spend almost all of their waking hours actively doing something such as talking or playing with other children or adults."[11]

*Jared Diamond suggests that a young person in the wilds of New Guinea is in fact more competent than the average American teenager. If given the same cultural advantages might not that youngster equal or surpass an American teenager's academic and vocational success ?*

Diamond adds that good child development requires stimulation and active involvement and that New Guinea children gain this non-genetic advantage, which contributes "to the superior average mental functions displayed by New Guineans."[12] This theory would support the conclusions in this book that all humans are born with the same potential and are then shaped by their culture. But it also indicates that aside from knowing some useful facts to pass an exam, Western men and women may be falling behind Stone Age people in total competency.

The recent decline in genetic endowment in Western democracies is referred to by the experts as dysgenic fertility, to indicate its direct but negative relation to the genes inherited by individuals. But genes may not be the main culprit. The lower SEC may simply provide a less nourishing or motivating environment for their children. Of course, "the lower SEC" represents a broad generalization. There are the "working poor," which David K. Shipley has written about, who maintain the effort to be self-sufficient, and there are those who work little and rely on handouts of one variety or another.

Second and third generation welfare families produce children who have never seen a parent get up early and go to a workplace. Many are never taught the virtue of thrift, persistence, long-term planning, or the need to control their emotions and harness their energies toward a positive goal. Because IQ scores and school grades are raised by a childhood that is stimulated with empowering and motivating values and role models, the different performance as shown by test scores may merely reflect the growing divide in American society.

Richard Lynn suggests that the cultural and environmental factors that are raising IQ scores among the successful segment of the population will gradually decrease and peter out.[13] And he warns that if the decline in intelligence among the largest procreators of the nation is still present when that point is reached, then both practical and IQ types of ability will decline. Flynn concludes, "Insofar as the maintenance of a high level of civilization depends on the intelligence of its population, the quality of U.S. civilization will also deteriorate. It is a curious fact that the evidence pointing to this conclusion has received no mention in contemporary textbooks of psychology and sociology."[14] But that is not really all that surprising, because today's academics are terrified of any idea that smacks of racism or classism. No one in the media wants to advance the idea that rewarding welfare recipients for the number of children born could be one of the unintended adverse consequences that come from most government interference in the economy.

These trends in our population mix provide warnings about the future. And Lynn does not even point to the decline in family structure and the increased rate of illegitimacy, which are two of the major new developments that are destroying the rich environment that nuclear families used to provide.

Few commentators give credit to monogamy as a major element in mankind's advance, but in my opinion, it has been just that. Allowing all males to pass on their genes created a genetic diversity absent when only the strongest males do so. That diversity allowed a proliferation of capabilities and aptitudes to emerge from the mass of humanity. Imagine what our Nobel Laureates would look like, and the prizes they would receive, if our gene pool were established by the most aggressive and powerful. The second major impact of monogamy comes from the fact that all males, once settled into marital bliss, develop a work ethic for a lack of other outlets and become "focused" by the universal and legendary "Honey-do" factor. And thirdly, as common sense tells us, two parents are better than one in directing, controlling, and inspiring growing children into adulthood.

When you combine the degradation of family structure with today's poor schooling system and the low attendance and graduation rates, you can see why there will be a continued division and an overall decline in the ability of America's population. And yet this decline in total cognitive ability is masked by rising IQ scores.

And it is possible that even the tide is not rising. The gains in IQ scores may be meaningless, since they only measure the sophistication and accumulated learning of an increasingly impractical but abstract-thinking population. This conclusion is bolstered by the latest findings that IQ scores are not as significant as they have been considered. They only measure test-taking ability and the areas of the brain needed to hold and manipulate a few conceptual abstractions. If IQ only accounts for 20 percent of a person's success or survivability, the gains in IQ scores do not really represent that big a gain. The danger may not be that those people in the lower SEC that are having all those children are pass-

*Pioneers of monogamy, a few Stone Age couples established the nurturing nuclear family unit that allowed mankind to make the 5,000 year Leap from the Primitive Age to the Present*

ing on low IQs. Worse, they may not be passing on the EQs and other personality traits that make for actually productive citizens. And while that is happening, we are turning over more and more authority to the abstract thinkers who lack the practical abilities that make for progress.

It is not a pretty picture, but it is what the current elites have brought us to. We face national bankruptcy because of the wild spending incurred by Congress. We face a growing population of dependent citizens at the bottom who are incentivized not to work but to procreate! Those who work face a constantly growing burden of taxation and regulation. And we are told that if we hold Tea Party demonstrations to protest the folly and injustice of this system, we are being rude and impolite. It pays to remember that our founders were not afraid to boldly state their case. Sam Adams was not afraid of being called rude. After all, the Liberty Boys tarred and feathered many a Royalist. It is time to recall what was needed to gain our liberty. It is time to put an end to this downward drift.

## Were Our Grandparents Stupid?

The experts who work with intelligence tests have concluded that there has been an IQ gain of about three to six points every decade for more than one hundred years. Part of their documentation is based on data from World War I soldiers in most advanced nations. Figures for Britons indicate that "90% of those born in 1877 fall below the 5th percentile of those born in 1967, which is to say below an IQ of 75."[15] The Dutch military data show Dutch men in 1952 had a mean IQ of 79 when scored against 1982 norms. U.S. data show massive gains from 1932 to 1995 and that the gains began no later than 1918. White Americans gained twenty-five points between 1918 and 1995. That would place the average IQ of Americans in 1918 at 75, or about thirty points lower than ours.[16]

Strict interpretation of that data would indicate Grampa and Gramma were idiots and morons. Now we know that isn't true, so we can only conclude that IQ scores do not reflect in any reasonable way the ability to participate fully in the world around us. Flynn writes: "Going from past generations to the present, one does not see an evolution from widespread retardation to normalcy or from normalcy to widespread giftedness."[17] The current generation is no more competent than the predecessors. History confirms this if we merely look at the extraordinary achievements and mental abilities of predecessors.

The Scots in the 1700s had leapfrogged to the forefront of the world stage in science, engineering, and governmental studies. John Knox had brought Protestantism and free-thinking to Scotland in the sixteenth century. The resulting Presbyterian schools had advanced learning for even the common people. The Englishman Gilbert Burnet visited Scotland in the 1660s and was amazed at the literacy of the common people. "We were amazed to see a poor commonality so capable to argue upon the points of government, and the bounds to be set to the power of princes.... This measure of knowledge was spread even amongst the meanest of them, their cottagers and servants."[18]

And it is hard to imagine that the audiences enjoying the theatrical performances of Euripedes in 450 B.C. Athens or Shakespeare's crowds in Stratford-on-Avon in the sixteenth century were any less literate or sophisticated than modern American theatergoers. And who can doubt that the Lincoln-Douglas debates of 1868 did not far surpass all of today's offerings from Nancy Pelosi and Harry Reid? So much for our ancestors being stupid! It would seem the question should be, "Why are we so much dumber than Grampa?"

**How Malleable Is Intelligence? Developing Talents**

In 1985, Benjamin Bloom wrote a book that claims outstanding achievement is the result of training and coaching, not innate talent.[19] Daniel Coyle's 2009 book, subtitled "Greatness isn't born, It's Grown," amplifies this belief. These are new ideas and indicate a person's capabilities are not fixed at birth but may be significantly shaped and developed by environment. Dr. K. Anders Ericsson reported an interesting story about two Hungarian parents who decided to test the popular assumption that babies are limited by their genes and that especially female babies are precluded from any future in the tasks that require mathematical or spatial thinking. After all, there are few women mathematicians and fewer female architects.

The Polgars also wanted to test established educational theory, so they homeschooled their three daughters and immersed them at a very young age in the intricacies of chess. The three daughters promptly became world-class chess players: All three were ranked among the top ten players in the world in 2000. The youngest became a grandmaster at age fifteen and is now among the best in the world, having defeated almost all the best male players. Apparently, no one ever explained to her the limitations of the gentler sex.

The success of these three young ladies illustrates Bloom's observation that the only predictor of top performance from a child is whether they practiced intensively, were coached by devoted teachers, and had the enthusiastic support of parents throughout their developing childhood. Bloom's study looked at the childhoods of 120 success stories from several fields. He discovered that there was no advance indication of these children's subsequent success. His research showed that there was no correlation between IQ and eventual excellence in endeavors such as music, medicine, chess, and sports. In 2006, many such studies were documented in a handbook edited by Dr. Ericsson. The inescapable conclusion is that experts are always made, not born.

We occasionally hear about individuals who gained their physical superiority by just trying harder. Practice makes perfect. Even in the simplest skills, like riding a bike or driving a nail with a hammer, there is a learning curve. We can't do it at first. But if we keep trying, there is something called muscle memory that takes over. At that point, we just take the hammer in hand or hop on the bike, and our bodies do the rest. And they do it without much conscious concentration. You never forget how to ride a bike, once learned. Some tasks become so easy, the saying goes, that you can do them in your sleep.

The differences between individuals arise only in part from their different genes. Why do some learn to read quicker than others? Is there a gene involved? How does trying harder enhance a person's physical or mental ability? The answer lies in the complex biological processes of our bodies. Certain genes cause our metabolism to operate. Human metabolism and the intricacies of our biology are extremely complicated; we truly have incredible physical blessings. One of the basic biological features of our bodies is the myelin sheaths that surround our muscles and nerve fibers and impact their speed of reaction. The more myelin, the better and faster your brain or muscles react. But that myelin sheathing develops after birth and throughout our lifetimes. And, apparently, it follows the rule of "use it or lose it!" We all know that to get in shape or stay in shape as we age requires regular exercise. Hard physical exercise will keep your muscles "young" and strong. Regular exercise "tones" the muscles. What is much more important lies underneath in the biological and neurological goings on within the body. Exercise also tones the brain.

Daniel Coyle's book, *The Talent Code*, explains how the growth of myelin sheaths around our nerve fibers can add tremendous amounts of capability to the fiber.[20] Most of our physical and mental actions are controlled by electrical impulses sent along chains of nerve fibers. Our brains contain 100 billion such wires called neurons. These neurons are interconnected to each other by synapses. These circuits of wires run to the muscles and control their action. The impulse transmitted dictates the strength and timing of each muscle contraction as well as the content and shape of each thought. With sufficient practice, these circuits "remember" all the impulses and sequencing and timing required to implement a learned skill. That is the "muscle memory" that coaches talk about that allow you to hit a backhand or swing a good wood shot down the fairway without actually thinking about or directing the details of the stroke.

The more we use these circuits the more automatic they become. The memory gets stored and the skill becomes automatic. But a thick myelin sheath around the nerve fiber plays a pivotal role. This layer of white fatty material wraps itself around the fiber and prevents the electrical impulses from leaking out. This white matter and its sup-portive cells account for more than half the brain's mass. In the 1980s, it was discovered that rats, or humans, exposed to a rich environment that encouraged play and experimentation with objects would, within a few months time, add significantly to the amount of synapses and myelin compared to a control group of rats in isolated "boring" environments. There can be thirty to forty layers of myelin accumulate over a nerve if it is exercised sufficiently. Thus both the brain and other muscles have the opportunity to develop and improve in response to empowering environments and exercise. This is another example of how positive nurturing and individual effort can trump genes!

Studies have been done to confirm these findings. Brain scans of concert pianists show a directly proportional relationship between hours of practice and white myelin matter. High IQ correlates with increased density of myelin. "The more the nerve fires, the more myelin wraps around it. The more myelin wraps around it, the faster the signals travel."[21] The increases are huge: The impulse speed can be increased, and the time interval between impulses can be shortened, resulting in information processing capability boosts of three thousand times![22]

Fortunately, myelin wraps when encouraged but does not readily unwrap itself. Once a skill circuit is properly insulated, it remains so unless, through age or disease, it is destroyed. Myelin does grow fastest in children, dependent in part on genes and in part on activity. The growth is not constant but happens in waves, during which times a child is very receptive to learning new skills. Myelin increases until around the age of fifty. Thereafter the amount can increase or decrease depending on activity. That is why learning to play a sport or a musical instrument becomes more difficult with age. And it is why most world-class champions start young. "Their genes do not change as they get older but their ability to build myelin does."[23]

Another factor determining our biological make-up is the extensive hormonal balance within our bodies. The various glands that secrete essential stimuli determine how well our bodies function. Now our hippocampus, pituitary gland, etc., are all initially provided to us at birth. But their future activity within our bodies and throughout our lifetime is determined not only by their original structure but by the changes they undergo as the years go by. As they change, so do our innate abilities, moods, attitudes, and health.

Thus, we can see that not only do genes, our inherited nature, have to share their power with the environment, but their very biological nature is subject to change over our lifetimes. And that change in our biology is caused not only by external forces—our environment—but also by our own willed actions. Thus we are to some extent able to shape or direct, even modify, our original genetic constitutions. An important element of nurturing is to get one's child to understand not his limitations but his extraordinary possibilities.

## The Difference Between the Human and Animal World

One of the harmful concepts that emerged from Darwin's work on evolution was the assertion that human beings are just smart apes. Many intellectuals, being atheists at heart, promulgated this idea, because they believed it undercut the Biblical accounts concerning the Garden of Eden.

However, regardless of one's ideas concerning Genesis, recent discoveries do indicate a fundamental difference between the animal world and the higher nature of human beings. Neuroscientists have found what could be called a Divine Distinction. Daniel Coyle suggests that the fact that humans possess a large quantity of myelin—and have the ability to grow much more—lies at the heart of human supremacy. He observes that monkeys have every neuron type and neurotransmitter we have,

> So why can't they speak and use language like we do? It's because we have 20 percent more myelin. We have the high speed broadband and can process information at lightning speed. Monkeys can get to the level of a three year old, but are stopped there because they are using the equivalent of copper wire.[24]

Coyle elaborates on this uniquely human biology:

> Why are breast fed babies smarter with higher IQs? Because breast milk has more and better fatty acids that build myelin. Why do horses walk at birth and humans take a year? A horse is born with its muscles already myelinated and ready to go. A baby's muscles don't get myelinated for a year and the circuits only get optimized with practice.[25]

This initial disability compared to horses demonstrates the eventual superiority of humans. Horses are preprogrammed with certain skills. Bees are also programmed with specific hive-related behavioral traits that make them remarkable but wholly unadaptable. But human wiring is left open and subject to selective programming as needed. The only way we can have our almost unlimited range of abilities is to have been built on a design that allows continuing development. Coyle's argument goes like this:

What's the best strategy for writing instructions to build a machine that can learn immensely complicated skills? It is not pre-wiring for specific skills. A being wired for specific skills will remain fixed in a stagnant environment forever. Pre-wiring a gifted novelist wouldn't have helped if he was born before language and alphabets permitted writing. A genius at software programming would have been wasted for millennia until the past half-century when computers had been invented.[26]

The human brain is made up of millions of broadband installers that can wrap wires with insulation to make them work better and faster. This follows a simple rule: Whatever circuits are fired most and most urgently are the ones that will develop. These broadband installers work most efficiently in our youth to adapt to the environment, and they work almost automatically, just based on our actions and reactions. This inherent human biology helps explain why the mechanics and engineers who created the Industrial Revolution came from a group of disadvantaged young men who had been apprenticed out at the tender age of twelve to fifteen years of age. Today's schools may be holding back the real potential of their charges by not immersing them in hands-on practical work experience throughout their academic years, the years when their brains are most receptive to learning.

The in-house production of circuitry allows each individual to determine which skills grow. Coyle sees proof in the talent hotbeds he has studied and the 10,000 hours people spend deep-practicing their way to world-class supremacy. He concedes that genes do matter, that there is a basic skill threshold we all are dealt, but talent is not predestined. We have a lot of control over what we develop, and we have more potential than we might ever believe. It is there waiting to be developed.

There was a project called the "staggering babies" study that confirmed the role of myelin development. Several Norwegian and American researchers looked at how babies gradually develop their walking skills. Why do some walk sooner than others? They discovered that the key factor was not height, weight, age, brain development, or any other innate trait, but simply the amount of time they spent trying to walk. Deep practice in any new skill is like the "staggering steps" of a baby, lurching and toppling over. But the longer babies tried, the more they endured the falls, the more myelin they built and the more skill they developed. "To get good, it's helpful to be willing, or even enthusiastic, about being bad. Baby steps are the royal road to skill."[27]

But Coyle does not address why some babies are more adventuresome, more willing to try, and initially more successful than others. Anyone who has watched or helped a baby in its first steps knows the interest, natural inclination, and ability varies greatly. It makes one wonder if there is not a gene for such initiative, daring, and motivation that explains why some babies persist longer and try harder than others. Such initiative and persistence has an obvious connection with personality traits and comprises an important part of a person's total competency. Wouldn't you trade five IQ points for more initiative and persistence?

Unlike animals, humans are endowed with this totally different brain chemistry, a chemistry that allows extraordinary adaptability and continuing development along opportunistic avenues. Bees and ants are programmed for a fixed style of life. Humans have free will—the power to decide what they want to do—and the flexibility to learn how to do it. These powers enabled humans to tame their environment and control their own destiny. That is why neither human nature nor genetic inheritance fully determines what each child will become.

**Genetics and Behavioral Modification**

There is evidence that even seemingly inborn traits can be changed, hopefully improved, by training. In sports, simple practice improves skill, but what about personality traits such as shyness? Is asking someone for a date or introducing oneself to a business prospect a learnable skill? Can you improve your success at "picking up" women (or men) just as you can improve your foul shooting accuracy? A pioneer in behavioral modification, Dr. Albert Ellis, demonstrated that you can do just that.

Dr. Ellis based his life work on his personal experience. As a young man in New York City, he realized he was alone and miserable because of his shyness. A particular result was, in his case, that he could not bring himself to talk with women. But he resolved to do something about it—anything in order to end this handicap. Author Daniel Coyle reports Ellis' efforts: He sat on a park bench near the New York Botanical Garden and started a conversation with every woman who sat down. In one month, he talked to 130 women. Thirty walked away, but the others replied, and he forced himself to chat with them in spite of his ingrained anxiety. The trick to overcoming such anxiety seems to be to linger in the uncomfortable action, to keep forcing yourself to withstand the insecurity, and to "learn" how to perform a task comfortably and repetitively.

Ellis went on to become the second most influential psychologist of the past one hundred years, ahead of Freud (third) and after Carl Rogers, who was first. Ellis challenged Freudian theory of examining childhood experience: "Neurosis is just a high-class word for whining." Daniel Coyle describes a "shyness clinic" in Palo Alto that teaches social skills based on Ellis' principles—that social skills are not inborn but must be developed by practice. There is no need to talk about a person's past and no need to look for a cause. Anyone can start anew—if they will just apply hard work, intensive practice, and self-imposed action.[28]

In the Afterword of this book, I illustrate in bargraphs how such "self-willed" efforts add to one's total competency. It is a separate force for the better, which supplements the benefits gained from the environment and minimizes the "wasted genius" that comes from not reaching one's full potential.

In medical practice, the techniques of behavioral modification have proven that even serious neuroses can be corrected by exposure. For example, an obsession with fears can be overcome by "exposing" the patient to the very things that create the fears. The process appears cruel and subjects the patient to intense agony as they are faced with their worst nightmares. But repetitive exposure forces the mind to deal with the feared thing and gradually the fear lessens. This approach has been successful in helping individuals seriously handicapped by depression, post traumatic stress disorder, obsessive-compulsive disorder, as well as with simple shyness or social awkwardness. In the shyness clinic that Coyle describes, participants start with forcing themselves to do what Ellis did—start simple conversations on the park bench or at the water cooler. Or talk on the phone. As skills develop, they move on to asking for a date. And the shyest people can develop the skills to become an outgoing person, confident, articulate, and at ease with those around them.

Recently a remarkable study indicated that even autism, one of the most severe handicaps that is marked by childhood onset, can be helped by behavioral modification treatment. At the University of Washington, Geraldine Dawson, chief science officer of the advocacy group Autism Speaks, led the study. Children from eighteen months to thirty months were randomly assigned to receive behavior treatment called the Early Start Denver model from therapists and parents, or they were referred to others for less comprehensive care. The therapy focused on social interaction and communication: Therapists or parents would repeatedly hold a toy near a child's face to encourage the child to make eye contact—a common problem in autism. Or they'd reward children when they used words to ask for toys.[29]

After two years, IQ increased an average of almost eighteen points in the specialized group, versus seven points in the others. Almost 30 percent in the specialized group were rediagnosed with a less severe form of autism after two years, versus 5 percent of the others. No children were considered "cured" but the specialized treatment helped greatly.

If the IQ of autistic children can be positively affected by conditioning, there is little reason to believe that a person's IQ is some fixed unchangeable element of his nature. We are more than our genetic endowment. We are what we make of ourselves.

**SUMMARY**

A. Mankind was shaped in its infancy by the exigencies of survival under primitive "Stone Age" conditions. That challenging environment required an individual to possess shrewd common sense and both physical and mental alertness to escape dangers.

B. Those practical competencies helped people develop secure nations and labor-saving machinery. Clearly those non-IQ factors were of primary importance. But once fire, warm clothing, and secure societies were developed, the threats to survival lessened. The idea of "survival of the fittest" as a major determinant of mankind has not played a key role in human affairs for a long time.

C. With the rise of affluent welfare states, with survival needs readily available to all and the differences in birth rates, we may have entered a period of "survival of the unfittest."

D. In the past 150 years, America has been losing its foundational strength, as the cultural practices and beliefs that made the country great have been weakened and even undermined by intellectual ideas that ignore the realities about people, governance, and human motivation.

E. Increasingly, we as a people place too much faith in "experts" and not enough in common sense. The trend to reward bad behavior and penalize good behavior is destroying the ethic of responsibility and self-reliance that built the nation's success.

F. There is the dual danger that our elites at the top are too "smart" with their abstract thinking, and those on the bottom are losing their practical and enterprising competency. This population "divide" has been caused by overemphasis on IQ testing and is resulting in a decline in competency of both those at the top and those at the bottom!

# Chapter 6
## The Determinants of Personal Success

> "We cannot change the cards we are dealt,
> just how we play the hand."
> —Randy Pausch

M ORE THAN ONE HUNDRED years ago, Francis Galton proposed in his "Heredity Genius" that people differ in intelligence and that these variations account for the differences between socioeconomic classes and the relative economic well-being of nations. He attributed the degree of success attained by both individuals and nations to the underlying intelligence of the people involved. Herrnstein and Murray followed up on these studies matching different racial groups in America with their IQs, socioeconomic status, and earnings. Their studies echo many others that show a difference in IQs by race within America and a direct relationship with earning power and socio-economic class. How can this be if IQ reflects only a small part of a person's total competency?

The studies are consistent: Most show whites having about a 10% higher IQ than Hispanics, who in turn had about a 4% higher IQ than blacks. Following that pattern, earnings in the early 1990s were about $27,000, $23,000, and $21,000, respectively for each of the three groups. Studies show that when the numbers are adjusted for IQ, with just calculations for all members in each group having an IQ of 100, their earnings were virtually identical at about $25,200. And surprisingly, they found when those three groups with IQs of 117 were compared as to what percentage were in the top socioeconomic class, blacks had the largest share at 26%, with 16% for Hispanics, and only 10% for whites.[1]

We do know that, in addition to differing levels of intelligence, performance is affected by cultural values. It may well be that the races that have done poorly, such as sub-Saharan Africans, Australian Aborigines, New Zealand Maoris, and American Indians, have been held back by cultures that do not encourage reading, schooling, work, innovation, or long-term planning. B. C. Rosen's 1959 study indicated that such differences appeared between North America's varying racial and ethnic populations. He called these motivational differences— varying levels of desire for achievement and aspiration for upward mobility.[2]

Rosen's studies indicated that Jews, white Protestants, and Greeks had high aspirations that accounted for their educational and occupational achievements. Similarly, reports indicate that Chinese and South Asian immigrants have a stronger achievement motivation than resident whites or blacks. It would appear that motivation might have as big a role in success as IQ scores. It is not known to what degree motivation and persistence are inherited as character traits, but it is believed that they can be cultivated. The question becomes, is IQ the cause of success, or is it the result that arises coincidentally in those with persistence and strong motivation?

### The Realities of Selection Processes and Success

We would like to believe that, in a rational world, each individual would prosper in direct proportion to his merit. A person of high moral character who worked hard and played by the rules should always be a winner, and his opposite would deserve a less favorable outcome. And we would not need a safety net to rescue those who fell behind through no fault of their own. In a free economy, the results should be fair and justice should prevail. But that would be a utopia that can never happen. Of course, all citizens suffer an injustice when corruption in the halls of government tilt the playing field in favor of the well-connected cronies of the governing elite. However, even with a level playing field, bad health, bad timing, and just plain bad luck will prevent fair results for some people.

The severest forms of such obstacles may never be fully remedied, and that is why when families or individuals cannot support themselves, assistance programs are necessary. For the rest of the population that suffer from no significant impairment, we should be able to expect the best. But both the dangers and opportunities facing them should be made evident. Schools could help parents in this area by teaching a few useful subjects—about business careers, finance, healthy lifestyles, home ownership, savings plans, the intricacies of credit and mortgages, and different career paths, so every child is better equipped to carve out a successful niche in life.

During the recent financial meltdown, we heard that many homeowners incredibly had not recognized that when their one-year adjustable mortgages (ARMs) were adjusted (almost invariably upward), they might no longer be able to meet the higher monthly payments! While this smacks of a poor excuse, it would be fitting for school material. Arithmetic might become more relevant and interesting to students if such useful applications were taught. Such skills in financial analysis would help students lead successful lives (that *is* what schools are supposed to do) and prepare their charges for adult life.

It is commonly said that some people make their own luck, by being patient and opportunistic. Others take steps to ensure as much as they can that they will enjoy good health. But there are added obstacles that distort any relationship between success and merit. Some of these are imposed on us by our own institutions and should be corrected. In an earlier chapter, we discussed how the calendar-year format used to select premier youth athletes creates a major distortion in who succeeds and who fails: Almost all the top hockey players were born between January and June. Only 20% were born between July and December.

Now, we know from our understanding of how the human neurotransmitters function and myelin sheaths develop that the favored group given intensive training will develop their full potential while the others will not. If they were all given the same quality and amount of training, the age difference would level out. But without the advanced training, those rejected may never catch up.

This same process works in many spheres. Children encouraged to read and given a wide exposure to activities and cognitively demanding games and tasks will arrive in school with a head start. Some kids play chess and monopoly before entering kindergarten. A child without that family and cultural advantage will be behind before he or she begins. Unless such a disadvantaged child possesses a very fast learning ability, he or she will not readily catch up with the other students. That fact partially explains why IQs vary directly with socioeconomic class. Parents with college degrees create an expectation in their children that they, too, will certainly become college graduates. The upper SECs usually provide a more stimulating environment, better schools, higher aspirations, and more intensive test preparation for their children than the lower SECs do. There are exceptions, but on average, that situation is true, and initial success breeds more success. Being born to an educated middle- to upper-income family is almost as important a success predictor as a hockey player being born in January.

We like to think that everyone is born equal. But are they? My high school classmates were born lucky. There is such a thing as "the birth lottery," and it is not necessarily being born to a rich family. We were born and raised seventeen miles west of Boston in a small rural all-American town that gradually became an affluent suburb. It was at the bottom of the Depression, but we all enjoyed big families with numerous cousins, aunts, and uncles that provided love and a feeling of belonging.

Our high school class of 1950 came along at the tail end of "The Greatest Generation" that developed their maturity during the rigors of World War II. We were all poor, but we always made do and enjoyed the rural small-town America of Tom Sawyer. We read the rags to riches Horatio Alger series and Ben Franklin's stories on thrift and imagination, played sandlot softball, and were rarely ever driven to any athletic or social function by our parents. We all had part-time jobs and learned how to work and how to value the money we earned.

Some of us even inherited schoolbook smarts that made test-taking fun. And to top it all off, by being born in the birth "trough" of 1932–33, even the best schools were scraping the bottom of the barrel when we came to apply for college in 1949. That chance of timing helped get almost everyone in the class into a college program.

Another stroke of luck for that class was that they were born into a culture that emphasized character, honesty, thrift, and family. It took thirty to forty years, but almost everyone moved up from the lowest SEC to the upper middle or highest. Our success depended on luck, timing, parenting, and the culture we were born into, as well as our genetic endowment. When all was said and done, the IQ differences didn't matter all that much.

Some psychologists who have tried to make sense of the IQ versus success issue have suggested that there are IQ "thresholds" that do influence outcomes but that, other than that, the absolute IQ score is meaningless. For example, to be a research scientist in chemistry or biological sciences, one needs a pretty good IQ—that is the requirement of the trade—to remember facts, conceptualize outcomes and possibilities, and make sense of huge amounts of data. Not something for the slowest minds in the classroom!

However, for those who meet the minimal IQ needed for such work—say 110–120—all minds are equal. Indeed, many in the lower range just above the threshold, frequently exceed the accomplishments of the highest IQ scientists. That is because there is so much more than pure IQ involved in any meaningful employment—even for chemistry and physics! Similarly, executives and managers as a class may need, if their tasks are complex, a minimum threshold IQ of 90–100. With that basic capability in hand, the other competencies they bring to the task will determine success. So a 90–100 IQ may well outperform a 120 in many executive posts.

It is especially interesting how this threshold principle applies to affirmative action policies—except that the affirmation should be for all those meeting the required threshold level of qualifications without racial or religious biases. In recent years, many minority students with SAT scores well below a college's normal minimum have been admitted. Studies have found that, although those so admitted may have had trouble keeping up in college grades, in their later life, they achieved success at least as well as the other students that were accepted with much higher SAT and IQ scores. Why is that? Because anyone with the minimum "brains" required to function successfully may outperform higher IQs if they possess more of the other competencies not measured by existing tests.

Unfortunately today, the schoolbook-IQ smarts dominate in schools as a bar to most people's future success. Unless they have that one quality, abstract algorithmic thinking ability, they will play second fiddle to those who do have that dubious distinction. And yet we know that many without top IQ scores can succeed in extraordinary fashion. How many more of them would succeed if they were not relegated to the backbench by low SAT scores?

If IQ and EQ together only account for 40 percent of the determinants of individual success, the emphasis on learning how to more effectively help people and their nations must lie in finding ways to encourage those individuals that have a high degree of the other 60 percent of a person's potential. Why are we wasting so much time on the mere 20 percent contribution of IQ and the 20 percent of EQ??

What this situation tells us is that the availability of concentrated training develops some "lucky" children into superior grownups, whether it is as soccer players, businesspeople, or scholars. That is not democracy at work but artificial barriers and bureaucracy. But tests and birth dates are not the only culprits that hold back many of our youth from lives of accomplishment. There has been a sea change in the cultural expectation for children during the past fifty years. Some combination of affluence and permissiveness has resulted in the deferral of adulthood—a prolonged process of "growing up" that has reduced the chances for great achievement.

## The Maturation Process: Is Adolescence Harmful?

The process of "growing up" should not be an open-ended affair. A child should meet occasional milestones, and there should always be an end in sight. In the many years of going from helpless infants to a reasonably competent young adult, there are a number of developments that must occur before the child may be considered grown up. These developments occur gradually and are accelerated by stimulating environments. Kids should assume responsibility and learn perseverance early and gain social and sexual skills later. But today that calendar of events has been reversed, and the perseverance and responsible citizenship comes, if ever, after the social and sexual skills.

I recently attended a "mitzvah" for one of my granddaughters that demonstrated the importance of celebrating milestones. I came away pleased and astonished that this thirteen-year-old already recognized many of the important values to live by and possessed an outstanding awareness of adult responsibilities. Abby had learned Hebrew; discussed the importance of nature within Christianity, Judaism, and pagan Scandinavia; extolled the virtue of being true to oneself, courageous in one's beliefs, and tolerant of others; explained how her music helped her find happiness and the inspiration to achieve her goals; sang in Latin the Hymn "Give Us Peace;" and detailed the importance of the Jewish Tree of Life. At the closing, after a two-hour performance, she was reverently wrapped in the Tallit. She definitely had earned the honor of having it placed on her shoulders, with these commemorative words:

> The Tallit is a responsibility and a privilege you richly deserve.
>
> A commitment to yourself and your heritage.
>
> Continue to wear it with honor and respect.
>
> Let its presence add to your wisdom,
>
> Guide you to sound judgment,
>
> And experience the gift it bestows.

Abby had spent months studying and preparing for her Mitzvah and had designed much of its unconventional content herself. Her successful presentation before a large audience of family and friends showed she was well on her way to becoming a responsible adult. Her performance would have pleased Jean Piaget, the Swiss psychologist who helped create the first intelligence tests. He understood that parents should be able to see some light at the end of the tunnel—that the day would come when their children would be "on their own." He suggested a schedule: He advised parents that children in their earliest years are not little adults! He advised against trying to reason with young children because rational thinking does not develop until about ten years of age. Consequently in order to properly direct their behavior, parents must employ consistent boundaries and apply simple consequences.

At the ages of eight to twelve, Piaget indicates the child is beginning to apply simple and logical thinking to concrete problems. Although a child at those ages will still have difficulty with abstract or hypothetical thought, he or she is developing what Piaget calls "concrete operational thinking" and is also becoming aware of the opinions of others and the need to negotiate or persuade. Abby's mitzvah performance indicated she was well beyond that twelve-year-old level.

During the first few centuries of American history, a child of twelve to fourteen years was put to work, apprenticed out to learn a trade or skill, and allowed to finish his development while working. This timetable honored Piaget's dictum that a twelve-year-old is ready to do some concrete practical work. Extraordinary men like Andrew Carnegie, J. D. Rockefeller, Michael Farraday, and Ben Franklin got their start in humble full-time apprentice positions before they were fifteen. It is likely that their practical and concrete training, combined with the early start, was more important than their IQs in gaining their eventual achievements.

In the post World War II era, things changed. Parents were more affluent, the family farm had disappeared from most communities, and children were not asked to do much of anything except go to school. Many even expect the four-year college program to run on for a few extra years as their children take time off to "find" themselves! Overindulgent parents have been conditioned to believe they must stimulate, educate, and entertain their kids constantly, by keeping them busy full-time with enrichment classes, museum trips, spelling bees, organized sports, and video-computer games. Ironically, this almost compulsive management of children's time may not represent an improvement in childrearing methodology. Kids have to get ready to manage themselves; they don't really need us every minute and are usually better off on their own. Encouragement, some direction, and a little praise is fine but should be disbursed in moderation. Too many of today's parents believe they must personally enrich each moment with love and learning. In the rest of the world, parents are more apt to see themselves as role models or teachers, not playmates.

And the youth now have spending money, credit cards, and insatiable appetites. America's pop culture was created in large part by media giants in collaboration with advertisers whose sole objective is to seduce the young into buying electronic gadgets, designer clothes, sexually suggestive and titillating entertainment, music recordings, and video games. The rapt attention to Hollywood-type celebrities on TV, video, and printed media has created a particularly juvenile and decadent outlook for teenagers. Some of this is good fun, but much of it is bad, not because celebrity gossip and star-worship is bad in and of itself, but because in excess it distracts children from what is important to their development into adulthood.

When it comes to manipulating electronic devices and gaining sexual expertise, our youth may lead the world, but when it comes to understanding how the world works—how to get a mortgage,

*A prototypical all-American youth, never taught a useful trade, encouraged to entertain abstract thoughts, and provided with too many easy indulgences and expensive toys.*

buy a home, and balance a budget, or how to put up with an eight-hour day—they may trail all others. We have indicated elsewhere how such generalizations must recognize exceptions, and the biggest caveat in this case is to allow for the growing divide between the two Americas. Half the children are "spoiled" by this catering to the teenage culture and the resulting delayed "growing up." The other half are given so little guidance or help that they slide into the gray area of lawlessness, dependency, the underground economy, and victimhood. As for the half that have parents and communities that allow them to defer the assumption of responsibility while catering to their wants, there is the question of how long must adolescence require before they grow up? For the other half, we can only look to cancellation of government programs that reward bad behavior, and then rely on schools to provide the mentoring and guidance their dysfunctional families fail to give them.

Robert Epstein, a Harvard Ph.D., the father of four, and author of twelve books on parenting, adolescence, motivation, and stress management, has an answer. He believes that adolescence should be abolished—that it is an unnecessary part of life we all would be better off without. Teen turmoil, he says, is the result of dated systems and laws enacted a century ago that have broken the formerly smooth and rapid transition from childhood to adulthood. Too many American teens learn everything from their media-dominated peers—the last people on earth that can help them grow up. This process "infantilizes" young people even though they are very competent and could readily assume adult responsibilities.[3]

Epstein lays the groundwork for his theory first at the molecular level: He cites the evidence that "operational thinking" peaks at fifteen years of age. That process involves the degree to which they can think about things symbolically and can use "concommitent variability" to evaluate alternatives. The young teen is capable of experimental and logical-mathematical thinking, of philosophical speculation about theory construction, and even of analyzing his thinking. Those types of reasoning and abstract-thinking powers are what Piaget calls adult thinking. It is gradually acquired in most children up until shortly after puberty, when it peaks, and is more apt to start declining than increasing throughout later adulthood. These processes of growth are accelerated by an enriched environment, so the peak could be reached at eleven to twelve years of age. Unfortunately, many never get to the highest levels, and if they have not by their late teenage years, they probably never will.[4] That is why proper parenting and schooling is so important: The early teen years are critical times of growth, and if wasted, the child can only rarely, if ever, catch up.

In his study of millionaires, Dr. Stanley found that "the earlier a youngster starts developing interest and experience with his or her vocation, the more likely he or she is to become a productive adult." [5] He advises parents not to take low test-scores too seriously. There are plenty of colleges that will accept hard workers regardless of grades. And he can point to his 900 Club, for those who scored below 900 on the SAT. There are many self-made millionaires in the Club, and they attest to the fact that it was persistence and people skills that got them there. The crucial factor is to motivate the youngster to be the very best he or she can be. Then, if they have done their best, never let a child become discouraged by low grades, but instead help find them the niches where they can succeed. And do it early!

The post-teen decline in operational thinking is supported by tests and MRI examinations of the different parts of the brain. The brain volume grows in childhood and is largest at fourteen. The worst news from these new findings is that our brains shrink steadily as we age—by 25 percent or more.[6] A seventy-year-old has the brain size of a three-year-old toddler. It might be relevant to observe that the Supreme Court Justices who are charged with confirming laws about what eighteen- and twenty-one-year-olds can legally do, fall into that "toddler" brain-size category!

Epstein criticizes the many rules and regulations that hold back our youth from reaching adulthood. He mentions the fact that in Mississippi, a fourteen-year-old mother can make major medical decisions for her baby, but she cannot go to the dentist to have a cavity filled without written parental consent! And she can't drive a car, can't hold a full-time job, can't rent an apartment, and in many states is subject to compulsory school-attendance laws. Epstein suggests that "adult competency" can be tested and that many teens would score higher than "the senescent members of the Supreme Court."[7]

Epstein cites the growing biological evidence that different types of experience can modify brain anatomy—especially in people under twenty. Neurons in the brain are considerably more branched in teens who have had enriched environments than those without such advantages. Repeated training on specific tasks will modify and enhance the structure of neurons and the myelin sheaths that empower faster and stronger mental signals. This new science confirms most parents' suspicions that regular attendance at acid rock concerts shrinks the brains of their children, or at least keeps their brains from growing at the exact time that they should be.

Environmental input can build brainpower, and the lack of such positive experiences or cognitive nourishment will stunt a child's thinking ability. While there are certain limits imposed by genetics, reaction to the environment can create variances. For height, the range is small, mostly based on nutrition, but for intelligence, the range is fairly wide, perhaps sixteen to twenty points on a standard IQ test.[8] A rich environment will raise a child to upper parts of that range, whereas a poor environment will confine him or her to the bottom. This factor alone may explain why children from lower SECs have lower IQs than those reared by higher SECs.

Parents must recognize that their expectations are of vital importance. Parents can play a big part in the success of their kids if they look for maturity and growth at young ages. Kids have the biology to excel if the demands and expectations are placed on them. Schools could help in this regard if they changed totally from existing warehousing and conformist systems and adopted the rigorous approach developed by effective coaches like John Wooden and the organizers of charter schools such as KIPP.

Epstein cites this substantial malleability of the brain and thinking ability as reason to reverse the current extension of childhood that caters to the infantile needs of adolescence. In 1944, David Wechsler, the developer of two of the most widely used intelligence tests, wrote that intelligence peaks at about age fifteen. This finding was confirmed by J. C. Raven, creator in 1938 of the Raven's matrices test, another widely used test of intelligence, which indicated that intelligence peaks at an earlier age, about thirteen or fourteen.

Epstein argues that the apparent teenage apathy and lack of rational judgment that we all deplore is caused by four negative cultural forces: [9]

1. Children are not only denied a large range of adult experience, but they are further limited by the narrow and artificial boundaries of the classroom. With the growing lack of discipline in the schools combined with the politically-correct emphasis on socio-ethnic multiculturalism, extreme environmentalism, and moral relativity, their schooling becomes extremely shallow and distorting. And the fact that almost half of our children do not complete high school further limits this possible source of enrichment

2. Drugs and alcohol do impair the growth and development of the brain. Drug abuse may be permanently destroying the potential of many teens.

3. Peer influence creates the wrong role models. In countries where adolescence is nonexistent, budding adults spend the bulk of their time with the type of adults they will eventually become. In America, the teen culture is saturated by attractive, liberated role models from TV, movies, and magazines. Those models are generally promiscuous, superficial, substance-abusing, and irresponsible. Many of our schools and colleges encourage or condone this atmosphere. If there is a "wasteland" in American schools, it is in the junior high schools, where the twelve- to fourteen-year-olds are most infatuated with such

false role models. And yet, those are the years of maximum opportunity for the brain and thinking to develop.

4. Increasing competition: As children progress up the grade levels into high-school courses and college, the competition from peers gets greater. Some of the teens that don't seem smart just aren't good at the types of advanced courses provided. Because the skills required to take advanced placement courses and score high on the SAT tests are used to segregate children on a winner-take-all basis, many high potential children are relegated to second-class citizenry. By being excluded from more elevated disciplines, and being categorized on IQ tests as below average, they become frustrated and lose motivation.

These harmful influences on our children are largely found within the schooling process. Instead of preparing them for adult roles, our extended schooling process may hold them back at the very time when their brains should be maturing the fastest. Epstein writes, "The storm and stress we see during the teen years in modern America are in all likelihood caused by the artificial extension of childhood past puberty. We hold our young people back and isolate them completely from adulthood. Many react in hostile or self-destructive ways."[10] Such isolation within a youthful peer group imposes an immature way of thinking that defers the attainment of psychological maturity. Our problem has been confusing personal liberty with responsibility. Children get the money and permission to participate like grown-ups in social, sexual, and recreational activities without the responsibilities that come from being an adult. We are raising a nation of children.

Evolutionary psychiatrist Dr. Bruce Charlton has confirmed this idea that most of today's adults are acting like children, technically subject to "psychological neoteny," the persistence of childish behavior into adulthood. And he points to academics and other professionals who have been immersed in formal schooling for the longest time as showing the worst signs: "Strikingly immature... unpredictable, unbalanced in priorities, and tending to overreact."[11] Coincidentally, these are the same people who gained graduate degrees by virtue of having the highest IQs and SAT scores.

Earlier societies witnessed maturity at much younger ages than today, with children doing family chores at five years of age and then apprenticed out to learn a trade by the time they were fourteen years of age. Today's markers of maturity such as graduation from college or graduate school, marriage, and parenthood occur over a few decades in a person's twenties and thirties. Dr. Charlton argues that, "For-

> ### Re: Intellectual Hubris
>
> *"From an early age, smart people are reminded of their intelligence, separated from their peers in gifted classes, and presented with opportunities unavailable to others. For those and other reasons, intellectuals tend to have an inflated sense of their own wisdom. It is thus arrogance, and not intelligence, that leads them into trouble. They're so smart, hubris compels them to believe, that they can run everyone else's life."*
>
> —Daniel J. Flynn, *Intellectual Morons*

mal education requires a childlike stance of receptivity," which "counteracts the attainment of psychological maturity" that would normally occur in the late teens or early twenties... "Therefore, in an important psychological sense, some modern people never actually become adults."[12] Their brains miss out on the needed practical experiences to develop during the key formative stage of ten to sixteen years of age.

Being born with algorithmic and abstract-thinking skills, combined with a prolonged childlike environment of college campuses, virtually ensures that such people will have a major disconnect with reality as adults and will lack the pragmatic thinking processes found in the less brilliant students who will have entered the workforce at younger ages. And these latter workers, who will actually assume responsibility for the productive output of the nation, will have to overcome the educational neglect and discouragement they received because they were "just average" students. Worse, they will have to pay for the impractical policies of the abstract thinking elites who get to run the major institutions of the nation!

Today's timetable for the maturation and education of our youth has been drawn out over an unprecedented number of years. During this important formative period, many of our youth get little or no positive stimulation or encouragement, and many get too much pampering and subsidized liberty. Both groups suffer from a lost opportunity to grow into responsible and rational adults. And many of the young, regardless of which group they fall into, are not taught the most important things that are needed for success. There are personal habits of manner and attitude that are neglected in today's youth-oriented culture, which is overly permissive and non-directional when it comes to developing kids. Both the advocates for IQ tests as well as the critics of IQ tests pay little attention to what used to be considered some of the most important characteristics of children: manners, attitude, self-control, the practical arts, thrift, and persistent effort.

Modern children have been denied the helpful habits of such useful virtues. It is old-fashioned to say that manners and work are "character-building," because the whole concept of good character and responsibility are dated. Role models have changed. JFK and Bill Clinton brought Hollywood celebrity lifestyles to the White House, and the children of America had their eyes opened! Cabinet appointees are routinely disqualified for ethical lapses. And too many stay in office after it has been revealed they have ignored the laws and used their position for special personal advantage. Their obvious feet of clay give the lesson that obeying the rules is a sucker's game. If we expect our children to be honest, we must demand the same or more from our elected leaders. And we must make our youth assume responsibilities at a younger age, when their developing cognitive skills can still be most favorably influenced.

It is remarkable that the most famous and prescient French commentator on America predicted that American democracy, great as he thought it was, held dangers for its people. He predicted an eventual drift to a form of despotism different from earlier totalitarian systems; it would be more widespread and milder, it would degrade rather than torment. Sheldon Richman has reported on Tocqueville's foresight:

> He believed that in "an age of education and equality," government power could be more pervasive yet less harsh than in previous times. "I do not expect their leaders to be tyrants," Tocqueville wrote, "but rather school masters." He expected that as people centered on their own lives and families, they would not notice that over them "stands an immense, protective power which is alone responsible for securing their enjoyment and watching over their fate."
>
> What does this government do to its people? Tocqueville says, "it only tries to keep them in perpetual childhood." It does so by providing security and necessities, assuming responsibility for their concerns, managing their work, and more. "It gladly works for their happiness but wants to be the sole agent and judge of it… and little by little robs each citizen of the proper use of his faculties…."[13]

A prime way America's new elites are accomplishing this infantilizing of Americans is through their control of our schools. The politically-correct dogmas taught there shape the minds of the youth into prevailing orthodoxies. And the failure to teach rational thinking processes and simple logic pave the way for a citizenry of docile followers, dependent on what they are told by government controlled media, think tanks, and the educational establishment.

**The 10,000-Hour Rule**

Those of us who have tried to play golf, tennis, or scoop up a fast groundball, understand that some people are more skilled than us, while still others are worse. We also know that lessons and practice can make us more skilled. Neurologists armed with cat scans and MRIs have established in the past few decades that your brain chemistry operates similar to your biceps: The more properly designed exercise they undergo, the bigger and better they get. There are genetic thresholds that may establish limits on just how good you can get, but within those boundaries, it is up to the individual to work toward his maximum or optimum capability. Unfortunately, little is taught in these regards, and most people do not understand the mechanics of making the most of what they have.

Daniel Coyle has explained the mystery of how some people attain an excellent level of performance. He points to three things that will allow anyone to optimize their performance in sports, math, writing, music, or whatever field you choose to work at:

1. Proper training, or deep practice, can increase skill up to ten times faster than unorganized practice. Such workouts are deliberate conscious acts, but to be effective, they need the hot burst of motivation.

2. Motivation or ignition is needed to get one started. Practice is hard work, and proper training requires a high level of commitment. Coyle calls for passion and says it is born out of unconscious desires and can be triggered by certain primal cues. That passion is what separates high achievers from the also-rans.

3. Coaching by an effective teacher: To be effective, a coach must have several strengths to bring out the most from students. They must have years of experience teaching, a sound strategy, and a practiced instinct to locate and understand where the student is, where he may go, and how best to get there.[14]

Such coaches can give just the right kind and amount of information to make their students better. Finally, they need honesty, some theatrics, and lots of love to get across the right messages to their charges. These requirements for skill building are daunting. Many people are not destined to become Olympic champions, but, on a lesser scale, the same practice, motivation, and training are essential to maximize the potential of each student. It is a sad fact that the government-run American school system is dominated by professional educators, unions, and single-interest advocates that render the system almost totally devoid of these kinds of practices. The plague of political correctness, multiculturalism, gender studies, environmentalism, and sex education have reduced much of the school day to a mind-numbing waste of time. It may be fortunate that Blackberries have arrived in time, so the bored students can escape the classroom via text messages that are probably more stimulating than the pedagogy of today's educational establishment.

If there is one positive note from the recent strides in understanding just what our children require to make the most of their abilities, it is the growing awareness that the current emphasis on IQ and SAT scores does a lot of harm. These entrenched yardsticks kill motivation, misdirect resources, and hold back some of the most competent individuals. A better understanding of what determines success and what characteristics indicate potential could unleash a flood of talent that would help the country as well as add to the satisfaction and happiness of the next generation.

### Leadership Talent: The Vital Traits

During the past few decades, Steve Jobs has repeatedly emerged at the head of Apple Computer Company to revive the company's flagging fortunes and bring them to new heights of success. He has been criticized for an aggressive and maverick style that flaunts a large ego, but there can be no denying the success of his company. He has somehow gotten the organization to respond to his vision and to meet the demands he placed on the people of Apple.

In business schools, there are courses on leadership and managerial skills that are designed to teach the mechanics of rational decision-making and the methods of shaping an effective corporate culture. The tone and habits exemplified by a corporation's leaders sets the style for all the employees. Much as the famous coaches like John Wooden and Vince Lombardi brought a team spirit to their sports teams, so corporate executives can inspire, bully, and lead their people to unusual excellence of performance. Clearly these are very important skills, they do not seem to be related to IQ or high SAT scores, and they bring as many benefits to a nation as the discoveries of most physical scientists. Indeed, many of the great scientific discoveries

have come out of the research labs of companies led by such great executives as the Watsons of IBM, Jack Welch of GE, and Bill Gates of Microsoft.

Peter Saville, the founding father of industrial psychology, has spent a lifetime measuring the performance of corporate workplaces. He has defined the attributes of the ultra-talented leaders and suggests they are different from managers. Sports teams and businesses need both—managers to efficiently oversee and direct day-to-day activities and leaders to set the tone and direction as well as to inspire the team to excel—to seek new opportunities, exploit new ways of doing things, and to outperform all competition. In his recent book, *Talent*, he describes the personal qualities that place someone among the elite leaders that drive a team to such high performance:

1. Leadership can be taught but requires some degree of natural talent to build upon. Acting coaches can teach students how to add charisma and charm to their public persona!

2. There may be a genetic factor. Research has shown a correlation with serotonin, a neurotransmitter that effects brain chemistry.

3. Hard work, persistence, and a keen competitive passion drive leaders to try harder than everyone else.

4. Talented leaders demonstrate their superior skill at a young age.

5. Academic achievement does not indicate their future success. In fact, a lively and combative style may have marked them as the ones teachers did not favor.

6. Leaders seek to empower others and gather "teammates," while managers care about detail and are reluctant to delegate power to others.

7. Leaders possess the personal and social skills needed to persuade and encourage others to high performance.

8. Leaders combine a "practical intelligence" and a thorough knowledge of their business that provides excellent decision-making ability, allowing them to think fast and effectively.

9. They may have the human foibles of uncertainty and nervousness, but they know how to control emotions and steer a course through adversity.

10. They measure their own performance, remain flexible, admit when they are wrong, and will change direction until results meet their expectations.

It should be apparent that none of these traits seem to have any link to school-boy smarts. They all include some element of emotional or social skills as well as the rationality of mind that observes results and adjusts action to results. These kinds of minds would never "fall in love" with an ideology that didn't work. They might do so for a short time period, but most would have given up on communist and socialist utopian schemes long before our intellectuals, who still persist in advocating such extensive and damaging government controls. Since great leaders make significant contributions to their country, parents and teachers should not discourage those with such potential by excessive attention to their "merely" average athletic or scholastic achievements.

## What the Parts of the Brain Tell Us—
## Looking Beyond IQ and EQ to TCQ

One of the inadequacies of most books on nature versus nurture is the overspecialization of the commentators. Educators are preoccupied with grades and tests scores. Psychiatrists look at the varying performance elements of sports, music, and the arts. Cultural and social theorists look at the differences between societies and ethnic groups. And many writers are primarily concerned with upholding some favorite social, political, or religious view. However, if we are to synthesize everything we know, we must look at all sides of the question.

A missing link is provided by Daniel G. Amen, M.D., who looks at the way our brains actually function and the impact they have on our lives. His work reveals that the brain, which gives some people the superb algorithmic skills that endear them to teachers and college admission officers, also regulates almost all the other competencies that make up that elusive and amorphous other 80 percent of a person's Total Competency Quotient (TCQ). His book sheds light on what we need to recognize: The brain is a many splendored thing. It has five main lobes, four internal structures, and assorted other parts. Dr. Amen explains why most of these "areas of the brain are most intimately involved with success and failure":[15]

1. Prefrontal cortex, 30 percent of the human brain—Regulates forethought and judgment; helps in decision-making; keeps us on track to achieve goals; manages long-term goal selection; recognizes value systems, right and wrong; and keeps behavior in check.

2. Temporal lobes—Involved with language, reading social cues, short-term memory, processing music and tone of voice, finding the right words in conversation, and providing mood stability; one portion affects temper, aggressive behavior and anger control.

3. Occipital lobes—Visual processing, control of eyes, and transmission of sensory data.

4. Cerebellum—Affects coordination and is involved with motor skills, coordination, posture, and how we walk; also involved with thought control, mental processing speed, and how quickly you can make cognitive, physical, and emotional adjustments.

5. Anterior cingulated gyrus—Helps you feel settled, relaxed, and flexible. Provides cognitive flexibility, improves the acceptance of change, and allows shifts in focus and the recognition of available options.

6. Parietal—Sensory processing and direction sense.

7. Basal ganglia—Integrates feelings, thoughts, and movement; establishes anxiety level, the ability to deal with pressure, tension, and stress; assists in selecting appropriate positive actions and how to react to emergency situations.

8. Deep limbic system—Emotional center; determines the level of optimism and pessimism; filters how you interpret the day's events and affects motivation and drive; involved with social connectedness, bonding, and the quality of moods; affects libido, self-esteem, and the desire and willpower to undertake and complete tasks.
9. Ventral tegmental area—Produces dopamine, and involved with weighing the relative importance of alternate actions.[16]

The basic biological health of each section plays a major role in establishing an individual's capability. Each person inherits one of these sections with a given level of excellence. That genetic legacy is impacted by the environment in utero and throughout life to maintain, improve, or weaken nature's endowment. Dr. Amen's book explains how this works and how to maximize the power of your brain. Because children remain in some ways developing embryos during the more than two decades it takes them to reach adulthood, nurturing the health and growth of their brains is a vital parental and societal responsibility. Steven Pinker's "human nature" and Judith Harris's "peer pressure" help shape the grown adult, but even together they do not come close to matching the importance of the other elements within the brain to determine the future of our children.

Dr. Amen outlines the major ways we have to maximize the soundness of our brain's controlling functions: Proper nutrition, stimulating exercise, practice at controlling emotions, learning to defer gratification, building myelin sheaths in the brain, adequate sleep, avoidance of toxic materials, control over stress, etc. We could add: Family, love, laughter, spirituality, aesthetics, nature, and humor, among other things. All these positive forces can be marshalled to strengthen the brain's functioning. Most people neglect and, worse, abuse that God-given hardware. They would never leave their shiny new convertible out in the rain, but they let their brains go to hell!

One of the most important parts of the brain does not fully develop until our mid-twenties. Because this is the part that checks impulsive behaviors, children cannot be expected to be fully competent in this regard until after they have left the nest. Dr. Amen gives the warning: "At some point our mothers let us go and we are left alone with our impulses. What we do with them is a major determinant of our success or failure in life. Being successful is as much about inhibiting actions as it is about starting or maintaining them."[17]

The ability to control impulsive behavior is the key to success in most endeavors. And apparently, exercising such willpower and restraint builds strength, just as a physical workout builds muscle. Dr. Amen believes that "disciplined behavior increases discipline." And it can start early in life.

> When you allow a child to whine to get their way, you actually teach the child's brain to whine. When you give in to a temper tantrum, you teach the child's brain to have more tantrums... Giving in to bad behavior dis-inhibits behavior and weakens the prefrontal cortex, as the child does not have to exercise any self control. The brain is like a muscle, and the more one uses it, the stronger it gets. The brain, also like muscles, has memory. Giving a child clear, consistent, reasonable consequences for negative behavior, while reinforcing positive behaviors, enhances development in the PFC. So many behavior problems in children are due to erratic or absent parenting... Parents act as a child's PFC until his or her own PFC develops.[18]

If parents do not fill that void, overly-pampered children may never grow up and will be crippled in both their vocational goals and their personal relationships. And if they have been allowed to just "go with the flow," conform to every custom, and conditioned to meet the expectations of controlling parents, they will not develop the independence and self-confidence to be creative thinkers or aggressive innovators. All such functions of the brain must be healthy, practiced, and exercised to develop a child into capable adulthood. That is why I advocate looking at each person's TCQ, or their "Total Competency Quotient." It is the combined power of all those attributes that determine the quality and nature of the adult. And there is evidence that parents and schools can help each child develop and enhance all those competencies and skills.

Many of those who write about IQ and correctly advocate more concern with EQ are stumped by a major conundrum: We know that the ability to do math or to read and write is a function of how smart you are—that is strictly a matter of "intelligence" and is based on some combination of memory and mental processing speed and skill. But it is argued that those other personal qualities such as thrift, prudence, emotional control, and impulse restraint are somehow different; that they are not cognitive abilities but merely "good habits" or "manners." Dr. Amen's book destroys that distinction. The brain does it all. All those other intellectual strengths and weaknesses are 100 percent a function of how well your brain operates—just the same as your arithmetic and reading ability. There is no justification for separating arithmetic virtuosity from self-restraint, humility, long-range planning, and control of one's tempers. Indeed, the arithmetic skills should probably not be ranked near the top of the most essential qualities of a human being.

**TCQ:**
**Total Competency Quotient**

IQ Smarts ...................... 20 %

EQ Skills ........................ 20 %

Other Traits & Beliefs ..... 60 %

**Total Competency ....... 100 %**

## Initiative, Independence, and Imagination

There are many types of supplemental intelligence that are not recognized by IQ and the SAT tests. The omission of such important capabilities represents a major distortion in any scorecard that seeks to select future leaders. The failed history of these tests represents an example of how academics and so-called experts often lead populations in adverse directions. Indeed, it raises the question of whether there should be any attempt to sort people in their youth.

It is unreasonable to pigeonhole people at all, but it becomes barbaric when such classifying from on-high is based on standards that fail to take into account all the traits and cognitive skills that make a person succeed. Human beings are unpredictable, their rate of development varies, and many talents lie dormant until something ignites them. Henry Ford was a bicycle repairman in his forties. No one expected much from him, but his latent genius emerged and changed the world as his assembly lines and mass production made automobiles available to the middle classes. With hindsight, we can say he should have received encouragement equal at least to that granted a classmate that may have already demonstrated a genius for chemistry or mathematics.

It is interesting that all these non-IQ types of emotional and practical intelligence are especially effective in preparing a person for life in a modern complex society, where interpersonal and organizational skills are very important. Such "skills" include self-motivation and the need to work hard under disciplined training to get ahead. However, some of the words that have historically been used to characterize Americans are markedly absent from all the critics' analyses.

The early settlers that built America were not necessarily of above average IQ but they were pious by religion and law abiding by the custom of their English homelands, where common law and the desire for democratic representation were part of their tradition. They were a civilized people, and self-restraint and consideration for others was a common attribute. However, what marked them as different from most people throughout the world was the fact that they demanded freedom—and were willing to assume full personal responsibility for their well-being and for their actions.

Pride in one's self and one's family is a fundamental value for all people. Self-control, empathy, and good personal motivation can occur in most every culture. It was the independence, personal initiative, and self-reliance that marked the early Americans. And most immigrant groups that struggled to get to America for the first few hundred years shared that personal outlook. By their nature, by the fact that they had picked up stakes, abandoned their homeland, and set forth on a perilous journey to a new land, these immigrants self-selected for independence and self-reliance. Those who remained behind self-selected for apathy and a lack of initiative and adventure. If there was a way to test for it, the "I" in IQ should stand for initiative, integrity, innovation, imagination, and independence.

The early Americans may have been pious and law abiding in general, but when it came to personal freedom, they were a riotous and unruly bunch. They staked their lives and sacred honor on independence and freedom, and many preferred to die than to kneel down to the King and his high-and-mighty court of aristocrats. It would be a mistake to ignore that form of emotional intelligence and advance a more orderly idea of self-control, empathy, and corporate organization on men and women. Thus, even Gardner, Goleman, and Sternberg do not address some of the major omissions of IQ tests. There seems to be no end to how much IQ tests miss!

In the millionaire studies that Dr. Thomas J. Stanley conducted, he asked the subjects what were the most important factors explaining their success. The top five factors given were:

1. Integrity: being honest with all people
2. Discipline: applying self-control
3. Social skills: getting along with people
4. A supportive spouse
5. Hard work: more than most people[19]


Note that physical appearance, personality, school grades, and a high IQ were rarely mentioned as explanations for their success. The millionaires' explanations give strong testimony that there are many important traits that may be possessed independent of IQ. And experts are beginning to agree that there is no meaningful correlation between a "general character factor" and the "g" of general intelligence as measured by IQ tests.

Such character traits go beyond the emotional intelligence mentioned by Gardner, Mayer, and Salovey. If Emotional Intelligence is equal to IQ, at 20 % each, there is still another 60 percent of a person's competency to account for. Those attributes could include perseverance, imagination, initiative, trustworthiness, conscientiousness, humor, and kindness. Almost every attribute that shapes an individual is brain based, and a person's ability is made up of how all those parts fit together into one well-oiled machine.

### Relationship Between IQ and Intelligence

Alfred Binet, the French psychologist who designed one of the first IQ tests, did not believe that IQ test scales were useful measures of intelligence. Binet had designed the Binet-Simon intelligence scale as a means to identify students who needed help with their schoolwork. He believed that with extra attention and coaching, most students could catch up with the quicker students and achieve all necessary academic achievements. In effect, he saw his test as an achievement test—to show what the student had learned and what he still needed to work on. It is instructive to realize that such use still makes great sense, but the tangents that subsequent "experts" have taken have twisted the significance of such tests in ways that have done much harm.

In fact, Binet opposed the growing reliance on IQ tests. He correctly said that intelligence was too abstract and complicated a concept to be measurable as one might measure the size of a table. Intelligence is not a measurable fixed entity, he advised, and he opposed "the deplorable verdicts" that came from any belief that an individual's intelligence is a fixed quantity. He believed that intelligence could be increased and the role of tests was to see who needed what type of assistance—and then to measure if the teaching methods solved the problem. Any channeling of children based on such tests he considered a "brutal pessimism... founded on nothing." But that didn't stop many academics from building their careers on a huge expansion of testing, or from claiming that their tests were universally correct and scientifically verified. This brief history demonstrates that, just as good parenting can trump genetics, so too the personal follies and ambitions of some academics can trump all reason and objectivity.

It is only in the past thirty years that the reliability of IQ tests has come into serious question. Steven J. Gould joined the critique in 1996 when he asserted that intelligence tests are based on faulty assumptions and have been used as the basis for scientific racism.[20] He criticized any attempt to treat intelligence as a single entity and reduce its quality to a single number for each individual. And he deplored the use of such numbers to rank people in terms of worthiness. He found it too convenient that results invariably found that disadvantaged groups such as minorities, women, or lower SECs were innately inferior and deserve their status.[21]

We may summarize these recent findings as indicating that IQ is only a small part of a person's total intelligence. An individual's aggregate mental capability goes far beyond the few elements measured by IQ and SAT tests. Because these tests fail to measure many important characteristics of an individual, they give a distorted picture that frequently misleads us when estimating the potential of children.

## SUMMARY

A. Personal success is a concept that has many meanings and is measured differently by most people. Aside from the obvious areas of career achievement and material well-being, there are numerous personal objectives such as being a success at family, Faith, friends, children, and hobbies.

B. Gaining success in one's vocation is largely based on finding a well-suited niche that an individual will be comfortable in and provides the satisfaction that comes from the full employment of his particular talents and skills. Children should be given the freedom and tools to find the niche most appropriate for them.

C. Success, whether in the vocational area or in those intangible areas, is best gained by starting at a young age the process of learning skills and developing the good behavioral habits and personal integrity that give meaning to one's life. Letting your child defer growing up will only cripple his path to maturity.

D. The personal satisfaction of doing a job well can only be gained by a conscious effort to excel at some vocation. I have a friend who works in a lumberyard, helping customers select and load their purchases. The job requires little education or skill but demands full attention, courtesy, knowledge of products available, and how best to select and load them. He is a very contented man, fulfilled by his role in life, which he once explained to me: "The Good Lord put me on earth for one purpose: to carry things from one place to another." He was excellent at his job and got satisfaction from doing it every day of his life.

E. The willingness to strive for a goal depends primarily on how much a person wants it and whether he believes he can do it. "If you believe that your performance is forever limited by your lack of a specific innate gift... then there's no chance at all that you will do the work... But by understanding how a few become great, anyone can become better."[22] Without the positive attitude that you can accomplish a goal, you are beaten before you begin.

F. Most high achievers make use of the same tools—patience, self-restraint, dedication—and some add more enterprise, imagination, and initiative, depending on their personal make-up. They all follow Coach Wooden's mandate to not try to be the best, but to be the best they can be, and always follow the Golden Rule. These rules of self-fulfillment are the best road to happiness, the subject of the next chapter.

# Chapter 7
## Helping Our Children Grow

 *"One of my tasks included teaching members of our team to assume personal responsibility for their success. Ultimately it wasn't up to me. Success or failure was in their hands; it was up to them. This area of responsibility went beyond the basketball court."*

—John Wooden

LENORE SKENAZY, A MOTHER of two boys, got into a lot of hot water recently for giving her kids too much freedom. She let her nine-year-old son ride the New York City subway by himself. In fact, she wrote a column for *The New York Sun* about the incident, and she has become an advocate for children's liberation. She believes children today are coddled too much, overprotected, and that they have lost a proper feeling of self-sufficiency and self-reliance common to earlier generations of Americans.

Her actions were considered newsworthy enough to land her on national TV. Some viewers labeled her "America's worst mom." Undeterred, she wrote a book.[1] She argues that instead of instilling fears in our children, we must encourage them to participate actively in life and resist all efforts to manipulate them. In short, they must be taught to think for themselves—and to grow up!

### America: Home of the Brave

The other side to the story is that this mom endangers kids. After all, aren't we supposed to nurture our children? And doesn't that mean we must protect them? After all, even Sesame Street has changed its message. In 2006, when the old Sesame Street shows were reissued on DVD, they came with a disclaimer that earlier shows "may not meet the needs of today's pre-school child." What formerly was "fun" is now considered "reckless." Crawling through pipes, walking the plank, and crossing streets are now socially outlawed. So who's right? Did the writers at Sesame Street need to issue that warning? Have they forgotten that America stands for the "home of the brave"?

In the "good old days," children wanted to emulate Tom Sawyer and Huckleberry Finn, with exciting adventures like rafting down a river, outwitting others, and standing up for what they believed in. Theirs was an active outdoor life that lent itself to adventure, hardship, and early learning experiences. They made contact with the strange outside world at an early age and grew from that challenging exposure. Tom Sawyer was the embodiment of the democratic humanism and heroism that dates back three thousand years to the Judaic-Greek belief in the sacred nature of man. Whether Western people considered themselves to be a heroic Greek warrior or one of God's chosen ones, each individual was profoundly aware that they had free will and were expected to lead a moral and constructive life, according to the ethical and heroic commandments of their God(s). How different from many of today's individuals, who indulge in frivolous lawsuits based on alleged damage that was actually brought on by their own carelessness.

Today's world is more urban and cultivated, and the experiences that mold our children are more vicarious than real. For that reason, parents should not shield their children from the family and national problems that must be dealt with. It is a clear lesson from history that the sooner children experience life, outside a sheltered cocoon, the more growth will take place inside their hearts and minds—and the better off they will be.

Randy Pausch recently wrote a best-selling book based on his final lecture at Carnegie Tech after he learned he only had a few months to live. As the father of three young children, he was determined not to feel sorry for himself but to make the most of the limited time he had left with his family. His concern was that he would not be there to teach his children all the things he wanted them to learn. He recognized that they were too young to understand the most important lessons—right from wrong, what is important and what isn't, and how to overcome life's severest challenges and disappointments. His lecture was videotaped, and he thought of it as "putting himself in a bottle that would one day wash up on the beach for my children." He lectured about honesty, integrity, gratitude, the joy of life, and other things he held dear.

Randy Pausch was a great believer in childhood dreams. A parent's job is to encourage kids to develop a joy for life and a great urge to follow their dreams. One way parents can help, he wrote, is to help children develop a personal set of tools to help them pursue those dreams. Children have to find their own path to fulfillment, but parents provide the foundation for that quest. Based on Pausch's observations of students who had passed through his classrooms, he came to know that many parents didn't realize the power of their words.[2] What you say and do is noted by your kids, and your actions and words make a bigger impression than you can imagine.

Steve Biddulph urges parents to change the way they interact with others, including their children, so they can work toward positive exchanges rather than negative exchanges. Don't stifle your child; encourage him with purpose and optimism.

Energy is not just about emotional fuel. It is also about what children eat and how much they sleep. Mankind evolved over millennia on simple natural foods and a full night's sleep. While nutrition in recent centuries has improved with the widespread abundance of a great variety of food products, the choices people make from this array of available foods make many of these people more poorly nourished than their ancestors. And a child's score on a test will be lower if he is sleep deprived than if he is well rested. IQ, attention span, and impulse control are all improved by a rested mind. That is another example of how good parenting can help children regardless of their genetics or the cultural influences that surround them. Does it not make sense to direct your children's habits if it will make them calmer, happier, and healthier children who do better at school?

Steve Biddulph gives specific advice in his book. His suggestions center on five points: (1) provide a good breakfast; (2) emphasize the right kind of foods to provide a sustained, day-long release of energy; (3) allow a minimum of junk foods; (4) avoid chemicals, dyes, and preservatives; and (5) make allowances for differences in children.[3]

Steve Biddulph has provided direction to millions of parents on how to make children "happy" and thereby how to turn them into "happy" adults. That should be the goal of good parents as long as "happy" connotes contentment born of self-actualization and healthy family and community involvement. Real happiness does not come from easy indulgences or fancy toys. Biddulph gives depressing statistics demonstrating that a large number of Americans are deeply unhappy, depressed, and in need of therapy and drug-induced sedation, even though they enjoy unprecedented levels of prosperity, safety, and comfort.

Many Americans have been taught to look for fulfillment in shopping malls and are overwhelmed with the need to buy everything they want. And for many, a malaise or unhappiness has been "programmed into them." Since childhood, they have been taught to look on the dark side.[4] Today's media do not help with their mantra that bad news sells. Between parents and media, some kids may have been hypnotized unknowingly, but still effectively, into disliking themselves and their country. This negative programming can often lead to a lifetime of discontent.

Ignore those "experts" who argue that personality is determined at birth; that human nature is a constant unchangeable fact of life, and that parents and mentors have little or no effect. Make sure you avoid "pathological parenting," which can suck the joy out of children. Take advantage of the fact that sufficient nurturing and encouragement can increase a child's love of life. Love them, support them, but don't coddle them. Make them grow into the heroic figures they can be. And even if your effect as a loving parent only contributes an iota of additional joy and self-confidence, is it not worth the effort to contribute that to your son or daughter's well-being?

**Parenting Is Not About YOU But About YOUR CHILD**

Stephen Covey tells a personal story about how he and his wife Sandra dealt with their own son who was failing at school, in sports, and in social situations. At first, they did everything to encourage him, praise his efforts, and apply all the positive mental attitude techniques the books on parenting detail. When others laughed at their son, they protected him. "Leave him alone. Get off his back. He's just learning." But then their son would cry and insist he'd never be any good and that he didn't like sports anyway. The two parents looked on in anguish as his self-esteem plummeted.

But then Stephen and Sandra examined their own feelings and perceptions. "When we honestly examined our deepest feelings, we realized that our perception was that he was basically inadequate." They were more involved with the way *they* perceived the problem than in their concern for their son's welfare. They recognized that "social comparison motives could lead to conditional love and eventually to our son's lessened sense of self-worth."[5] So instead of trying to change him, they accepted him. They relaxed and got out of his way, enjoyed him instead of judging him. They also "cultivated internal sources of security so that our own feelings of worth were not dependent on our children's 'acceptable' behavior." [6]

Most important for the Covey's son was that once they accepted him for whom he was, they stopped protecting him. Once they saw him as fundamentally adequate, they stopped trying "to mold him into an acceptable social mold." Their *unspoken message* was that he was O.K., that he could take care of himself, and that he could be who he wanted to be. That was the kind of support and unconditional love that made him eventually blossom and grow into a successful adult.

Steve Biddulph refers to this same issue—that parents' unstated feelings are picked up on by their children. Biddulph describes "seeds of the mind" as the unthinking ideas that we implant in our children when we make negative statements or reveal disapproving attitudes. "What most people don't realize is that hypnosis is an everyday event. Whenever we use certain patterns of speech, we reach into the unconscious minds of our children and program them, even though we have no such intention."[7] Negative programming of this sort comes from "put-downs" that have a hypnotic effect "that will shape the child's self-image, eventually becoming part of his personality."[8]

The need to promote self-confidence is unfortunately not easy to accomplish and has its dangers as well. Efforts to boost a child's self-esteem by giving lavish and undeserved praise do not work, no matter how well intentioned they may be. Instead, the compliments lower the bar for acceptable performance, reduce motivation, and create complacent kids who harbor feelings of entitlement. By the same principle, overly indulgent parents can ruin their kids. There is much to be learned from great sports coaches, who know just how much praise to be given, when to give it, and how to choose their words for maximum effect.

John Wooden coached UCLA's national championship basketball teams of 1963–1965, and one of his players, Keith Erickson, recognized Wooden's genius for treating each player in just the right way for maximum effect. With Gail Goodrich, he would offer a quiet suggestion, a gentle critique, but with Walt Hazzard, there was no need to mince words: Young Walt needed clear and firm advice, like: "If you do that again, you're out of here."

But on one subject, Wooden treated everyone the same: He expected and demanded that each person be the best they could be. He encouraged progress but never acknowledged perfection. He believed that whatever you have accomplished, you could have accomplished more. Whatever you have done, you could have done it better.[9] He might have winked or given a thumbs-up for an extraordinary move, but he never gushed.

Praise for accomplishments must be based on actual effort and results. And the effect should be carefully considered. The latest fashion in our schools to build self-esteem—by making everyone a "winner"—will create more losers. Just as overindulgent parents prevent children from maturing, today's educational theories are failing to develop skills and character in their students. We will discuss in later sections how a few new schools are employing both the motivational and character-building techniques of the best coaches to help students develop into "the best they can be."

### Encouraging the Compassionate Part of Human Nature

Near the end of his lecture, Pausch reviewed the lessons that he had learned from life, such as how vital it is to focus on other people. It's not just all about you. Man is a social animal, so personal interaction with others along with a genuine concern for their well-being nourishes the spirit of most people. Steve Biddulph makes this same point in his writings,[10] arguing that both parents and children need more than bread and water. He describes the fuel, or energy, that comes from love, recognition, touch, and talking with others. He suggests that every person you meet has an impact on your energy level. They either give you more energy or drain it away. While parenting is a two-way street, your concern as a parent is to charge your kids with positive energy. In return, if you do this correctly, you will get energy back from them.

Randy Pausch used his "letter to his children" to advise them of the non-material aspects of success. He apparently believed that the most valuable things he could pass on to his children concerned their health, contentment, and emotional well-being. There is much more to gaining happiness than a high-paying prestigious job. And some of America's happiest people never spent time in a college.

Pausch's ideas reflect the same emphasis on virtue that drove young Benjamin Franklin to strive for perfection in interpersonal relations. The "Golden Rule" would not have survived for two thousand years without its eternal relevance. John Wooden employed the "Rule" in training his ten UCLA championship teams and emphasized the importance of family, teamwork, and integrity.

It is important to encourage, as Wooden advises, the native spirituality and altruism found in most children. Dr. George E. Vaillant has found after a lifetime of studying groups of individuals throughout their lives that those who deploy the largely involuntary compassion and empathic mechanisms of humor, altruism, and love enjoy far happier lives than those who deploy the less mature and self-centered coping mechanisms. He writes of the need for controlled "adaptation" as we mature. The human brain design has a unique capacity for emotions like love, hope, joy, forgiveness, and compassion, and encouraging those responses in our lives builds both maturity and resilience. Dr. Vaillant asserts that there is a "neurological basis for the compassion that lies at the core of all our great faith traditions.... The fact that the world's surviving great religions... all came up with similar solutions suggests that they discovered an enormously important principle of human nature."[11]

Vaillant explains how the genetic evolution of our limbic spindle cells and mirror cells leading to empathy has taken millions of years and has aided human survival. But he observes that "the cultural evolution of almost universal admiration for compassion in both the New Testament and in Buddhists' Pali Canon has taken only two thousand years."[12] Vaillant contrasts the fifteen-hundred-year-old Benedictine Rule that we must care for the sick to how the "scientifically advanced Nazi Third Reich deliberately killed the chronically ill." He points out that the Nazi order lasted a decade, while after fifteen hundred years, the Benedictine Order is alive and well. Valliant concludes that the compassionate introduction of hospitals "has proven as useful to human survival as a clever brain per se."[13] Thus, the great caregivers, such as the monastic orders and leading women and nurses like Florence Nightingale, Helen Keller, Nellie Bly, and Elizabeth Fry, have played vital roles in the

*Nellie Bly, 1867–1922, cracked the glass ceiling and helped Joseph Pulitzer expose social injustices in America.*

success of Western civilization. Not to mention the missionaries and doctors who, like Albert Schweitzer, have suffered hardship to serve the poor and sick of the world.

Dr. Schweitzer was a religious person, with faith in God. He spoke of the need for "a reverence of life," a reverence and respect that he preached should extend to all living things. "The great experience of my childhood and youth was the influence of the Commandment that we should not kill or torture."[14] Mankind's three-thousand-year-old reliance on the Golden Rule and the Ten Commandments has passed the tests of time. From Abraham to St. Paul to John Wooden, it has served to direct character building traits of Palestinian shepherds, Medieval peasants, seventeenth century settlers in America, and inner city Los Angeles athletes playing for Coach Wooden's teams in March Madness. It is a record of kind and ethical encouragement, with an outstanding and continuing benefit to mankind that is unparalleled in the history of the world. It is important for children to recognize the enduring truth of such long-standing principles, so they can resist the dangerous nonsense about moral relativism that our new elites preach.

**What's Happiness Got To Do with It?**

One of the most revealing indications of the important nourishment that comes from familial love is shown in the writing of, can you believe it, an intellectual's intellectual. George Kennan was a Princeton alumnus, a high-ranking diplomat in the State Department, and much adored by the intelligentsia. He is credited with outlining the Cold War strategy of "containment" of the Soviet threat after World War II, although the more average intellects of Harry S. Truman and Winston Churchill had already done so. But Kennan wrote like an angel and was the darling of what Howie Carr would call the overeducated "beautiful people." He was by nature the stereotypical intellectual— aloof, cold, and devoid of passion and human warmth. But, to give him credit, he sensed what he was missing.

Stopping one afternoon in the streets of St. Petersburg in 1973, near the Embassy where he worked, he saw some ordinary families celebrating the birth of a child. Because the Communists had closed most churches, the parents had been in the Bureau for Registration of Births and had no choice but to celebrate in the alley outside, a poor surrogate for a Church baptism. He describes the scene:

> There they are; the entire family group: grandparents, relatives, father, and, above all, of course, the young wife, bearing the baby on a lace-covered cushion and exhibiting it to be oohed and ahhed at by all comers. The half light of evening is on this little scene; there is a wonderful unselfconsciousness about it, and vividness as in a Renaissance painting. One is aware, standing here among the small band of rubberneckers, that one is witnessing the irrepressible insistence of ordinary people on living as ordinary people have always lived, hoping as people have always hoped, affirming a species of faith in the continuity of personal life, a faith that has nothing to do with reason, and nothing to do with political doctrines but triumphs, in the end, over both.[15]

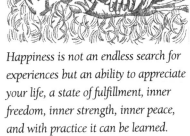

Of course, unfortunately for Kennan, he is on the outside, looking through an impenetrable glass window, to see real people enjoying life. But to his credit, he seems to appreciate the wonders that simple common people are able to savor. Their brains and hearts are still nourished by the essential human ideas and emo-

*Happiness is not an endless search for experiences but an ability to appreciate your life, a state of fulfillment, inner freedom, inner strength, inner peace, and with practice it can be learned.*

—Matthieu Ricard

tions that come from Faith, family, celebrations, and love of country. In President Obama's mind, the fact that "they still cling to their

Faith" may be a put-down, but for a moment, George Kennan saw the Light.

On another occasion, in California, doing research at the Hoover Library, Kennan tried, like many of us, to make sense of the Californian Americans he observed: "These (common) people... ask no questions; they live, seemingly, for the day; they waste no energy or substance on the effort to understand life; they enjoy the physical experience of living; ...If they are wise, surely the rest of us are fools."[16]

There is an obvious moral to Kennan's observations: Make sure your children know how to enjoy and appreciate the simplest and most human pleasures of life. And the best way to teach them is to show them by example.

Gaining this essential human need for the warmth of family and friends is probably more important to your children's future than any of the IQ issues, practical intelligence, or career success that the psychiatrists we have reviewed have been so concerned with. The psychiatrists do assert the personal benefits of a strong family foundation in enabling children to develop and grow in a school and work environment, but the real benefits of such warm and homely nurturing is the resulting happiness and contentment of the individual. Would not every parent want above all other characteristics to see their child just plain happy and content?

## Sensible Career Options

A few years ago, I was working on a construction project in a rural part of New England. My contractors had attended local public schools and then worked at a trade and learned enough to operate as independent contractors. One of them was an electrician who kept his life simple by employing no helpers. He explained that just one employee would require that he maintain extensive employment records, make weekly deposits of withholdings and payroll taxes, report and pay state and federal unemployment taxes, and comply with the host of mandated taxes and reporting requirements that American businessmen must accept to remain legal.

I admired Bob for the simplicity he maintained in his life and the high quality of craftsmanship he brought to his work. I had met many rich professional people and high-powered corporate executives who appeared less content with their life. One day over a coffee break, I was surprised to discover that Bob had a daughter who worked for a major computer software company. Her position required her to travel around the world, troubleshooting for the company's clients and provided her with a six-figure annual salary and a lavish expense account.

I had had some experience with the extensive education that many software programmers must endure, so I asked Bob where his daughter went to college to learn enough for such a position. He looked at me in surprise and told me that after high school, she had just taken a one-year course at an ITT technical school and then gone directly to work at her present company. Apparently she had inherited her dad's ability to keep things simple, and still she found a way to exceed the vocational achievement of many college graduates.

In Chapter 2, we mentioned Nicholas Lemann's book, *The Big Test*, and his three categories of students. He made the point that the "Lifers" and "Talents" can have at least as rewarding a life as the "Mandarins," who, by dint of high test-scores, get into the elite colleges. I'm not sure if Bob's daughter is a lifer or a talent, but she proves Lemann's point. Lemann believes that the "Big Test" is not really worth all the money, effort, and anguish that we give it. Most Americans do not need to be, or want to be, high-powered lawyers or State Department officials. They can be happier working at more mundane jobs, or building their own businesses. In fact, college would be a waste of time for the majority of Americans, who are better off getting on with a vocation at as early an age as possible.

Mike Rowe, executive producer and host of *Dirty Jobs* on the Discovery Channel, has been encouraging young people to look for careers in useful hands-on occupations. Check out his website, MikeRoweWORKS.com. Mike criticizes how schools and many parents push academics and college over useful lifetime vocations. He thinks there are many misconceptions about the practical mechanical arts, too much snob appeal to white-collar occupations, and a phony prestige to having a college diploma. The jobs Mike Rowe is talking about pay higher salaries than many four-year-degree people make.

The National Association of Manufacturers has reported that eighty percent of manufacturers can't find enough qualified workers. Many high school and college graduates do not have the math, science, and technical skills required for today's business environment. However, after one or two years of specialized training, entry-level positions can be very well compensated and are readily available. According to the Department of Labor, eight out of ten apprentices in such technical fields will out-earn their contemporaries who brandish a Bachelor of Arts degree.

Success at many high-paying jobs can be made more certain by merely attending vocational schools, technical colleges, or taking classes part-time while working. If you take paper and pencil to the economics of college, the alternatives are revealing: The top few hundred schools cost about $50,000 per year to attend, for four years. If parents put that money in a trust and told the child to forget college and get a job, the child would be almost guaranteed to have a million dollars in the account when he turned fifty years of age. Or, he would have, right away, an immediate $200,000 to buy his first house. Even if the alternative were a less prestigious school at half the cost—or a state or community college at a quarter or less of the cost—he would have a substantial nest egg instead of a fancier sheepskin. And it isn't an either-or situation anyway. College degrees are becoming more readily available and academically-worthy through computer classes and technical schools, which shortcut the process so they can be earned while working.

### The Value of Family Ties

Steve Biddulph's book, *The Secret of Happy Children*, seeks to advise families on the need to create a positive and happy home for all family members. Getting into the right college and gaining a prestige vocation are goals that have been overstressed by many parents. Such goals often lead to a rat race for achievement and material success. It is right for some but very wrong for others. Both parents and children need more than bread and water. He cites the energy that comes from love, recognition, and friendships.

Developing children need support. Parents used to be the main influence when times were simpler, mothers stayed home, and the home was a place where the children contributed to the chores if not the actual production of food. Today, it is common for both parents to work outside the home, or, in many cases, there is only one parent. The world has become a new and strange place for today's children. It can be scary and confusing, so it is only natural they crave guidance. As they develop, they will watch the world around them and take cues from everything they see. If you don't want what Meg Meeker calls our modern toxic culture to shape them, then you better get to work and shape them yourself. And the results will not only benefit your child but will bring a bonus for yourself. Speaking of the important influence of fathers on daughters, Dr. Meeker writes,

> You are the most important man in her life... if you are willing to guide your daughter, to stand between her and a toxic culture, to take her to a healthier place, your rewards will be unmatched. You will experience the love and adoration that can only come from a daughter. You will feel pride, satisfaction, and joy that you can know nowhere else.[17]

And Dr. Meeker is apparently not in favor of "metro men," the new PC types that are pliant, overly-sensitive, de-sexed, and harmless. She calls out to a different sort of man: "Men, good men: We need you. We—mothers, daughters, and sisters—need your help to raise healthy young women. We need every ounce of masculine courage and wit you own, because fathers, more than anyone else, set the course for a daughter's life."[18] Both fathers and mothers can establish the loving and nurturing "fireside" that helps children grow to maturity, provided they balance the gentle love with "tough love." You will not make your child happy by just doing everything for them. Love comes from the heart. Good training comes from the head.

## Virtue, Independence, and Responsibility

We have so far in this book tried to identify the major factors that determine the eventual "success" of American children. That success has been primarily described in terms of what socioeconomic class the child attains, what his or her income and wealth may amount to, and what social clout they may hold after they reach their ultimate career goals. But there is much more to life that we must teach our children. The satisfaction that comes from a life well-lived is more important to a person's emotional well-being than material success. Much of worldly success comes from taking a long-term view, resisting impulsive behavior, and maintaining self-restraint. Patience and thrift can work wonders financially. But a lifetime of personal prudence can also do wonders for the soul.

"Living a life well" requires a couple things that have little to do with worldly success, academic achievement, or intelligence. Think of an old man or woman on death's door, looking back in the flash of an instant over their entire life. There should be few major regrets at that critical point in one's life. To gain such peace, one needs to have long beforehand committed to conduct one's self in accordance with a principled life of integrity and personal responsibility. Opportunities should be seized, personal improvement should be strived for, responsibilities shouldered, a helping hand extended when called for, harsh and violent words not uttered, friends and family loved and respected; so that in the end, a person can take some measure of pride in what was accomplished.

Such resolution at a young age is not easy to come by. There is a need for extraordinary self-reliance and independence to chart a proper course. There is an unwavering recognition of duty to others essential to maintain a generous and disciplined life. Such virtues may be next to impossible for a spoiled youth. All children would be well advised to read Ben Franklin's writings. Franklin's advice has been well summarized by George L. Rogers, and the second of twelve principles for self-conduct is: "Acquiring the qualities of virtue requires a good plan and consistent effort."[19] Virtues like "Integrity" and "Responsibility" do not come completely naturally or easily. But they can be instilled in your child and nourished if they are taught to make the effort required.

Reb Bradley recently published a book that advises parents to do less for their children. It isn't a matter of caring for them less but of not doing so much that they grow up with an "entitlement" mindset.[20] We have examined how the lessons of hard training can motivate and teach superior skills to aspiring athletes and musicians. Brains and good traits also develop from doing, not from being done for. The rough training camp can be more motivating than a luxurious one. A good coach rations his praise and couches it in just a few carefully chosen words.

Bradley says that our nation's moral decline has not been wholly caused by failed education or poverty but by improper parenting. He warns that any society that is out-of-control must be made up of citizens who lack self-control.[21] Over the past fifty years, parents have softened their parenting, becoming more permissive and accommodating. Children have failed to develop the self-reliance and maturity they need to maintain a functioning society. Many of those children have become today's parents, repeating the indulgences of their parents. They confuse indulgence for love, and as a result, children grow up self-absorbed and with an ingrained sense of entitlement.

The more parents do to soften life for their children, the more those children will grow up with two false notions: One, they will believe that they do not have to live with the consequences of their actions, and two, someone other than themselves should take care of their needs. After a couple generations of such excess compassion, our nation has become full of those who demand to be taken care of and have voted too often for a compliant "mama state." A nation is only as strong and resilient as its people. The more dependent and needy our kids become, the further our nation will fall.

And, America is obviously falling. Just read the headlines and watch the news. There is an awful lot of corrupt, immoral, and nasty behavior going on—and most of it is at the highest levels of our financial and government power centers. Those elites avoid every reform, they design the legislation, and they perpetuate the corruption that is despoiling our country. Many voters have supported the political demagogues who attempt by governmental action to "fix" each person's personal, moral, and economic problems. Similarly vain attempts for progress are sought by spending more, running deficits, so-called reform legislation, and self-esteem affirmation. None of that has worked.

The remedy lies within each individual, and it is the parent's job to drive that point home. Parents have the ability to help shape their children's attitudes and beliefs. It is a brief and limited opportunity, but if parents do it right, they could save our nation! There is just no denying that families—with attentive, common-sense parents—are the backbone of a nation. Unless you, the parent, teach your children to be responsible, no one else will! Our leaders don't want to do that. In fact, political demagogues hate self-reliant responsible citizens, because too many of them would put them out of business!

### You Can't Just Tell Your Kids To Be Responsible

Nearly all parents want their kids to learn to work, to help out, and to take responsibility. So, what's the trick? Can anyone do it? It's easier than you might think.

A good friend of mine spelled it out in a beginning draft of a never-finished book she shared with me on parenting issues. Speaking from experience, she reports that good parenting is simply based on common sense, understanding human nature, and creating incentives for the behavior you want to encourage. It is based on understanding the lessons that children learn from our parenting methods, often the opposite of the lesson the parent intended to teach. She raised her children with a few basic principles in mind, principles that she believed would create the proper incentives. She concludes that, "If the proof's in the pudding, I think I've really got something here." She wrote:

> Many good parents are committed to making sure that their children know that they are loved unconditionally, and that they know their parents will always be there for them. But the parents' fear of undercutting their children's feeling of complete security in their love and devotion often leads them to ignore other responsibilities they have to their children as a parent. The most important lessons parents must teach their children are those that equip them to live a responsible and successful life as independent adults. For parents who are unwilling to teach these lessons—out of fear that the child will resent them for having expectations or out of fear that the child is incapable of meeting the expectations—they are setting up their children to have to learn most of these lessons the hard way. The fact is that these lessons must be learned eventually. The choice is between having children learn them in a protected, supportive environment, from people who care about them or from strangers in a world where the consequences are often larger when mistakes are made.
>
> Perhaps one of the biggest mistakes that many parents make is trying to protect their children from pain and hoping to be able to teach them the lessons of life without the children ever having to experience pain. In effect, this is expecting much more of children than most adults have ever been able to do themselves. People learn how to make good choices by having to live with the consequences of their decisions. Anytime a child is protected from the consequences of his decisions, the opposite lesson is learned: "bad" decisions are no worse than "good" decisions, so why bother learning how to make good ones? Every time this happens, a parent is inadvertently "protecting" their children from the opportunities to learn the important lessons of life.
>
> Many parents hope to teach their children responsibility by example, by being responsible themselves. Unfortunately, this seems to

only teach them that parents are supposed to be responsible and that children don't have to be. In addition, it teaches a lesson that is simply not true—that children shouldn't have to be responsible, because their parents should take care of them, that parents deserve no consideration from their children because the parent's place in life is a self-sacrificing one where they should be happy to give up their own happiness in favor of the comfort of their children. They encourage this belief even further through attempts to assure children that they will always be available to do anything they can for their children, no matter what. A better strategy would be to assure your children that you will be there to help them whenever they *need* it, not just when they *want* it.

Parents do take on a big responsibility when they have children. Infants need almost constant care, because they are truly unable to do almost anything for themselves. Toddlers need a great amount of care, supervision, and assistance, because they are still unable to care for themselves to any large extent. However, at each stage of childhood, children gain greater and greater abilities to take responsibility for themselves, and it is a parent's duty to encourage and expect them to do so. When a parent makes it clear that he is willing to assist the child with those responsibilities that the child is unable to manage himself, but *expects* the child to take on those responsibilities he *is* able to handle, he is teaching the child the important lessons of life and assisting that child in becoming a responsible, capable individual. He is also teaching the child that the only reason he *is* willing to help with those other responsibilities is because he loves the child and the child needs his assistance—not because the child is too lazy or because the parent has nothing better to do or is a ready-made martyr.

This is an important lesson in understanding that parents are people, too, and deserve consideration. It teaches children that it's inconsiderate to expect help with those things that the child is fully capable of doing for himself. (When my kids were young, like age three or four, and we would be out somewhere and they wanted to be carried, if I didn't feel like carrying them, I'd say, "I'm tired, too. Could you maybe carry me for a little while?") For a toddler, this may mean he is responsible for picking up his own toys and showing proper consideration for others. For a five-year-old, it may mean taking responsibility for giving himself a bath instead of expecting the parents to do it, for making his bed in the morning, for making his breakfast and cleaning up his dishes afterwards. For an eight-year-old, it may mean taking on some household jobs like vacuuming, cleaning bathrooms, washing dishes, doing laundry. For a fifteen-year-old, it may mean getting a part-time job to pay for his personal expenses or saving toward college. But each stage brings the child closer to taking full responsibility for himself.

Not only does this build responsibility, it frees the parent from unnecessary work that will then allow the parent more time for more enjoyable time with the child. Even more important, it encourages the child to think of himself as a productive, important part of the household, one who is actually contributing to the household instead of always being on the receiving end. This gives children true self-esteem, not the pseudo-self-esteem talked about so much today. It teaches the child to be competent and to expect competence from himself. It encourages him to take pride in his ability to do things for himself and others, instead of always being dependent and needy.

When my son was eight, he spent the night with two identical twin friends of his. When I picked him up the next day, I asked if he had a good time. He said, "Yes, but their mother sure treats them like babies!" I asked what he meant, and he responded, "When we got up this morning, they sat down at the kitchen table, and she asked what we wanted for breakfast and she made it! I'm sure she thinks we're too stupid to make our own breakfast! Then at lunchtime, they did the same thing!" I was glad, of course, that he reacted like this, as opposed to wondering why *his* mother didn't make him breakfast every morning!

My older daughter had a similar reaction, while listening to a good friend's mother telling us about buying her daughter a brand-new car, shortly after my daughter had purchased her first car (used) with her own money.

In gradually taking more responsibility, children also need to be taught that it is unfair and unacceptable to expect other people to suffer as the consequence of the child's actions or decisions. It is the child's ability to keep this from happening that permits him the right to have freedom of action and to make his own decisions. It is his inability to keep negative consequences of his actions or decisions to himself that restricts his ability to decide things for himself. When my children were young, they had a specific bedtime. This was the time that I wanted to be "off-duty" for the rest of the night, when I could concentrate on getting my work done (I had a home-based business since before my children were born, and I had a pretty demanding work schedule). When they said they weren't tired and didn't want to go to bed, I let them know that bedtime would be abolished as long as I could still be "off-duty." If they stayed up as late as they wanted to, they needed to take care of themselves, not interrupt me if I were busy, not require my attention or assistance, and not make work for me (by messing up the house, for instance). As long as they were willing to take on these responsibilities, they could set their own bedtimes. When they failed to do these things, it was immediately bedtime.

As another example, if we were going for a walk around the neighborhood and I suggested they wear a coat but they didn't want to, I didn't make them wear the coat as long as any negative consequences of the decision were kept to themselves. That means no whining that you're cold, no insistence that we cut the walk short because it's too cold, etc. If they couldn't manage that responsibility, the next time the situation arose, I would be the one to decide who wore coats, not them. In giving them the opportunity to take on as much responsibility as they were able to handle and wanted, I allowed them to make as many of their own decisions as they wanted to make and were capable of making.

I read a very interesting article several years ago that mentioned the resentment that many children feel about having to work for the things they want when they get older—after being raised to believe that these things should be "free." By encouraging children to believe these things should be free, parents encourage feelings of resentment when they must earn their own way and take responsibility for themselves, instead of the more appropriate feelings of independence, competence, and pride. What a tragedy to take from children the ability to feel pride and satisfaction in making their own way in the world!

I have a mere three general principles that I always insisted that my children follow. They are not strange rules that I pulled out of a hat, but rules that govern our society, rules all children will someday have to accept if they plan to stay out of jail. I have no desire to make silly rules about whether my son can grow a beard if he wants to, or whether or not he can dye his hair purple, or whether my daughters should listen to classical music or rap. Those are their personal business, but breaking any of the three rules below, as an adult in our society, would subject them to criminal or civil prosecution. Not insisting on these rules in our household would only delay the necessary acceptance of the rules and encourage them to get into trouble in the future. Here they are: (1) You must respect the property rights of others, including following the rules we set in our home if you want to live here; (2) You must honor your commitments; (3) You must contain the negative consequences of your actions and decisions to yourself, or we will take over the responsibility of making your decisions for you.

My children—now twenty-two, twenty-four, and twenty-six-year-old adults—have told me over and over how much they appreciate the lessons I helped them learned as kids—and how sad it is to watch some of their friends struggle, because they were not so lucky. My older daughter put it this way in her note on this year's Mother's Day card: "Not a day goes by that I don't think of how lucky I am that I had you to help me become the person I am. I couldn't be more thankful." My younger daughter wrote this on her card: "I am very proud of the person I have become, and so much of that is the result of the great mother you have been." Even my son (not the mushy type) wrote this: "I know I can always count on you to help me when I need it, while still teaching me to be self-reliant. That's what makes you such a great mom!"

**Creating Survivors**

Because we cannot see ahead in time or even begin to comprehend the vicissitudes that may face our children, it is essential that we arm them to be prepared for the worst. Like Randy Pausch, all parents can try and bequeath their kids the know-how to survive in a tough world. We must give our children the strength of character and inner resilience to see themselves as "survivors." On the best level, we want them to be able to pick themselves up after failure or rejection and start all over—to try, try, and try again until they succeed. On the worst level, we don't want negative or suicidal thoughts to ever enter their minds.

Ben Sherwood's recent book, *Survivors*, addresses some of these issues, but it is directed primarily to surviving physical disasters. He explains why some people do not survive difficult emergencies. One of those reasons he calls the "Incredulity Response."[22] In emergencies, with the signs of disaster all around them, some people simply don't believe what they are seeing. He cites a case where a ferryboat was sinking in the Baltic Sea and many victims didn't try to get off the sinking ship but were frozen to the spot. In Hurricane Katrina, many endangered residents seemed incapable of acting on their own without direction.

"Brainlock" is another reason Sherwood gives to explain why some people in crisis die. They are so shocked that they forget to think. Under stress, some people freeze both physically and mentally. Closing down the reasoning mind, freezing in place, and panicking are the enemies of survival. Overprotected children may never learn the need for rapid response. That is why participation in sports and mechanical arts, with the need for quick reactions and concerted effort, is customarily advocated as an important part of education.

Giving your child the wherewithal to survive personal and emotional setbacks may be even more important than teaching them physical survival skills. While severe depression is an unusual and very damaging affliction, everyone on occasion gets depressed or suffers from feelings of anxiety, frustration, sadness, and mood swings that impair their ability to function at their best. To avoid or overcome these types of mental hurdles, we all need a set of inner beliefs that will stand the test of time. Religion and a belief in some form of Divine Providence have carried many people through the worst adversity. It is believed by many that parents can also, by their own outlook and behavior, instill more optimism and less pessimism in their family members.

Goleman suggests that although a positive or negative outlook may be inborn temperaments, they can be tempered by experience. "Optimism and hope—like helplessness and despair—can be learned. Underlying both is an outlook psychologists call *self-efficacy*, the belief that one has mastery over the events of one's life and can meet challenges as they come up."[23] In layman's terms, that means that self-confidence and will power can shape how one deals with life. Ignore those genetic determinists who deny free will and the power of personal initiative. Give your children the empowering knowledge that they are "in charge" and capable of great success.

Martin Seligman believes that habits or ways of thinking can be changed, improved, and that individuals can thereby choose the way they think. He suggests parents explain to kids that what they think when something goes wrong actually changes how they feel. "When he suddenly feels sad or angry or afraid or embarrassed, a thought has always triggered the feeling. If he can learn to find that thought, he can change it."[24] What is important in life is not the misfortunes that hit us, but how we defend against them.

> ### Choose To Be An Optimist
> *"Over and above their talent-test scores, we repeatedly find that pessimists drop below their 'potential' and optimists exceed it."*
> —Martin E. P Seligman, Ph.D.,
> *Learned Optimism*

Optimism is in fact one of the successful "mature coping defenses" that Dr. Vaillant found predictive of those who would grow old happily, healthily, and gracefully. It represents a mature defense against the vicissitudes of life and reflects "our capacity to turn lemons into lemonade and not to turn molehills into mountains."[25]

Optimism, it must be noted, is a matter of personal outlook for one's self and one's immediate friends and family. It should never be extended to evaluations of political or business issues that are largely *out* of one's own control. Thus, it is healthy to assume you can apply your free will and, by dint of work and patient determined effort, gain success in what you undertake. However, in matters not under your control, like national economic matters, foreign entanglements, the deficit, Congressional wisdom, the value of educational experts, and the accuracy of the media, pessimism is the preferred and more logical outlook.

John Derbyshire has written a wise book on the value of pessimism that he aptly titled "We Are Doomed."[26] He explains that when it comes to our schools and national leadership, there is no reason to believe the rose-colored "solutions" of utopian liberals and happy-talk conservatives. In those real world settings, things are broken, and the cures are going to be very difficult. Children can master this distinction—positive outlook for what they can accomplish, but healthy skepticism about others—and strong doubt about our elites.

Children with experience dealing with their own problems, under the support and guidance of parents, rather than being "rescued" by parents, are more likely to have the confidence required to believe they can survive and prosper through adversity. Optimism comes from successfully overcoming challenges. And to overcome challenges, they must be faced. Help them develop that confidence at an early age. Self-preservation is supposed to be one of our primal instincts, but overly-coddled children may never learn just how it works.

The best bulwark against defeat is to have a set of guiding principles, a sustaining belief in a few absolute truths. One of the curses of modern liberal intellectual thought is the moral relativism that pervades America's elites. There were some good things about "the good old days," when we were taught that there is Right and Wrong, Good and Evil, Truth and Lies. Honesty and integrity are virtues that allow a person to hold his head high before all comers. Prudence and self-control avoid the dangers of risky behavior and violent confrontations. Common sense is always a wise guide. Such learned behavioral traits are survival keys. That may be why *The Lord's Prayer* includes that tough line about "Lead me not into Temptation." The need for strong willpower has to be taught if your child is to grow up into a mature and respectable adult you can be proud of.

Maturity and wisdom come from a life fully lived, but inner contentment requires that life be lived within moral boundaries. If a person learns to observe those limits—and has been taught the need for guts and grit—he may survive the worst blows life can dish out.

> **Joshua Wooden's
> "Two Sets of Three"**
> 1. Never lie
> 2. Never cheat
> 3. Never steal
>
> * * * * *
>
> 1. Don't whine
> 2. Don't complain
> 3. Don't make excuses

There is no mystery why Coach Wooden based his teachings on fundamental values and ideals, attitudes, and behavior. Or why he stressed the need for intensity while also calling for self-control and emotional discipline. Or why he demanded the Golden Rule—fairness and decency, treating people right—and insisted that character counts. He never forgot his father's directives—"the two sets of three" that define good behavior. And he measured achievement by only one standard: Be the best *you* can be. Don't try to be better than someone else. There is no control over that. Success is the peace of mind that comes from knowing you made the effort to become the best you are capable of becoming. And living by the Golden Rule![27]

### SUMMARY

A. The idea of free will, personal responsibility, and self-reliance were the hallmark of our ancestors. That belief in one's self, that you are the master of your fate, is one of the most important legacies you can give a child.

B. The increased role of government in regulating the conduct and activities of the people has lessened liberty. Bailouts, handouts, subsidies, and special favors for the "insiders" have reduced both the integrity and self-reliance of the American people. In addition, they have unfairly tilted the playing field against ordinary citizens.

C. Children reared to accept the responsibilities that come with free will are able to realize the satisfaction that comes from being self-reliant. Many of the glories of Western literature and music celebrate the acceptance of this struggle and the contentment of having met the challenges meted out. On the other hand, hot-house babies will look to others, accept a victim role, seek mothering from government, and grow old, unhappy, and discontented.

D. The personal ambition that fueled the people of America is being weakened by the radical ideas of America's new elites. Instead of rewarding those who take care of themselves, they reward those who get into trouble because of their own bad behavior. People seem to misremember JFK's famous admonition: It has become "Ask not what you can do for yourself, but find out what your government can do for you."

E. The reasons why the Judeo-Greek-Christian cultures worked so well and led to the extraordinary well-being of the industrialized Western democracies are simple: By encouraging the individual effort of every man, woman, and child, and allowing them the freedom to exercise their common genius, those societies gained the imagination, motivation, and effort of a huge swath of their population. That consolidated effort out produced all other societies that were less open to the aspirations of their common people. How that all works is the subject of the next chapter.

# Chapter 8
# *The Determinants of National Success*

*"The preservation of freedom is
the protective reason for limiting and decentralizing
governmental power. But there is also a constructive
reason. The great advances of civilization, whether in
architecture or painting, in science or literature,
in industry or agriculture, have never come
from centralized government."*
—Milton Friedman, *Capitalism and Freedom*

$M$Y MATERNAL GRANDPARENTS CAME to America from Sweden around 1900 and raised seven children with very modest means. My grandmother took in boarders and did sewing and laundry for local families to augment the family's income. Her husband worked as a liveryman and gardener at Wellesley College. They never received financial help from anyone. But they did have a rule for the children: When they became eighteen, they had to pay room and board if they did not move out. Because they had such limited means, the parents had little choice. They simply could not manage to support seven grown children, let alone send them to college!

It was hard times, but the hardship was, in fact, a blessing in disguise. The kids grew up unspoiled and knew that work was required to prosper. Our children might be better off if today's parents had less to give them. It is difficult to withhold anything from those you love, but they and the country might benefit from exposure to the adversity that forged our grandparents. Children become important to the future of the country only in proportion to the amount of character and self-reliance they bring to their lives.

**What Is a Nation's Most Valuable Resource?**

Good and loving parents will do anything for their children, and that is how it should be and always has been. But in less affluent times, people like my grandparents were forced to make their kids become adults early. And that helped both the kids and the country. When historians have written about the rise and fall of nations, they have often mistakenly emphasized the impact of climate, mineral deposits, geography, rich farmland, and navigable rivers. Those natural resources are a great help to any people attempting to build prosperous living conditions. But to build a comfortable society, you must have enterprising and hard-working men and women. They must be united by a common goal. And once their nation is built, it must have a prudent and self-controlled people in order to maintain the country without squandering its gradually-accumulating wealth.

In a recent book, Alan Beattie proposes to explain the economic history of the world. He states that history was not determined by religion, geology, hydrology, or national culture but by the decisions and choices a country made. This is substantially true, and it correctly contradicts such theories as Jared Diamond's emphasis on natural resources, guns, steel, etc. But Beattie's analysis suffers from a vagueness of how those national choices are made. "Countries" do not make decisions. He says things like "countries were dealt quite different hands but played them differently,"[1] or "America chose a path,"[2] or "America favored squatters; Argentina backed landlords,"[3] or that "America... grasped that building a manufacturing industry would allow it to benefit from better technologies,"[4] or "An economy like America's, with a nimble and productive industrial sector, was well placed."[5]

Simple grammar requires that if a verb shows deliberate action, the subject must be a living thing. Countries and economies—like rocks, guns, and governments—cannot by themselves do anything!

Although Beattie refers occasionally to the fact that Americans were by nature independent, self-reliant, and "shaped their own destiny,"[6] he fails to make it clear that it was strictly the individual initiatives of those early settlers in North America that made the colonies and later the new nation succeed so greatly. And at one point, he writes that a nation's character and culture did not play a role in its progress. And yet it was the culture and institutions that the settlers brought with them that allowed their actions to be so effective.

Instead of saying "America grasped that building a manufacturing industry would (help)" he should have explained that "Some enterprising American citizen could see the need for more efficient means of production so, sensing a social and personal financial benefit to be had, he started a business that provided that means." The distinction is very important, because otherwise a person might think that our great nation just happened, or they might believe that Adam Smith's legendary "invisible hand" created our land of plenty. In fact, that invisible hand, if examined thoughtfully, would be seen as the common man's hand, rough and calloused, perhaps scarred, by years of toil. Many such hands built America, creating spontaneous order and efficient economic activity. We need to raise more constructive and imaginative individuals to keep the ball rolling—and be careful not to tie their hands with excess red tape, taxes, and bureaucratic impediments.

There were three major reasons the American settlers outdid every other people in the world:

1. **Attitude:** Their cultural roots and pioneer character made them more inventive, more enterprising, and more competitive than all others; the kinds of people that chose to brave the Atlantic Ocean to gain a new land may or may not have had good IQs, but they had all the other right stuff—that 80% of "TCQ" that makes for success.

2. **Legal and Financial Mechanisms:** They brought with them 500 years of English economic and political traditions that secured their liberty and equality. This legacy included the legal and financial institutions that had been developed in England to protect their liberty and property, the judicial processes that settled disputes, the contract law that enabled

business dealings, representative assemblies, patent laws, and the natural or common law that protected their Rights.

3. **Economic Freedom:** Once they arrived in America, they enjoyed an open and free economy that allowed all entrants to compete on an equal basis. This empowerment of the people was due to their almost total freedom from elites, aristocracies, regulations, taxation, and big government.

A nation is no better than the sum of its parts—and those parts are the individual human beings within the nation. The effectiveness of those people is enhanced only by a secure, free, and open economy that allows them the opportunity to employ their genius. Those kinds of people come from families that, first, prepare their children to be independent and self-reliant, and second, get them activated and motivated early.

Political and economic conservatives are frequently criticized for wanting to go back to the good days, resisting all change. The truth is that conservatives want to maintain the principles and methods that worked, and they correctly recognize that many changes are for the worse. However, times do change, and the problem is to find ways to use established principles to deal with the new situations. When it comes to raising our children, there are problems that we must deal with:

1. Some of today's most attentive parents are not financially constrained like my grandparents were, so they cannot resist the urge to overindulge their children.

2. Today's schooling drags on too long, with little relevance for some and no relevance for others. This prolonged warehousing in an academic setting precludes any practical training for later life.

3. The prolonged and irrelevant schooling ensures that almost one-half of the students will drop out. Those that drop out often end up in negative environments that prevent their personal growth.

4. The large numbers of children forced into a rigid school format fails to allow for individual differences. This monolithic offering penalizes many who have useful aptitudes that are neglected in favor of those with good test-taking skills.

5. The pampering and sheltering of many kids continues throughout the period from age ten to eighteen, when their brains are most receptive to learning adult skills and gaining vocational experience.

The reality that is facing us is that we are wasting our most valuable resource. Too many children are not being given the necessary environment to grow into whatever their natural and best capacity may be. Others are being shunted aside, ignored, and end up filling an ever-expanding underclass of dependents that must be carried by those who continue to work and pay taxes.

**Inner-Directed Versus Other-Directed People**

The lessons of history make it clear that the gradual decline of successful free nations is due to the gradual growth of an elite class who seek to rule from on high and impose their ideologies to change the country "for the better." They represent a new aristocracy similar in most regards to the landed gentry we escaped from when America was settled and freed from the Lords and Ladies of Old Europe. And this new aristocracy today is populated by those with the least practical minds. They are the anointed ones, the intellectuals, who, as Thomas Sowell has observed, pride themselves because they believe that they have a higher vision, superior to the beliefs and concerns of the population at large.[7] But that vision, which calls for undermining the foundations of America's success, is bringing on the decline of a great nation.

So why do so many people tolerate such a suicidal trajectory? The reason is simple: They have not been taught the lessons of history and are seduced by the fantasies of a visionary secular world. These fantasies are presented to the gullible by political demagogues seeking votes and by radical dreamer-intellectuals, who believe they can create a utopia here on earth. Unfortunately, the mental and emotional weakness of abstract thinkers is to be attracted to such grandiose dreams of "a perfect world," and that enticing goal makes them seductive salesmen to idealistic youth.

Intellectuals love ideologies, theories, and statistical projections, so pursuing a new plan under their control is their dream job. And it pays without getting their hands dirty. Many lesser and more practical minds get hoodwinked into joining such idealistic goals for a couple reasons: For one, they are well-intentioned folk who will subscribe to any charitable purpose, and secondly, most people are sufficiently influenced by peer pressure to follow in a path others provide. They are either too lazy to think for themselves or too concerned about public opinion to risk being different. Such differing traits may be in part genetic, but proper teaching of logic and sound principles can help make a person more rational and "inner directed." It's simply a matter of knowing what is right and what is wrong—and then sticking to your convictions.

> "Ideology serves as a proxy religion for people who view themselves as too smart for traditional religion. And since worshipping a god is an impossible task for the self-obsessed, the intellectual moron worships himself—man—and the ideas that will deliver us all into salvation."
>
> —Daniel J. Flynn

In America today, the elites favor collectivist citizens, because it makes it easier for them to lead. The demand for "political correctness" is being used to reduce the voters' ability to think and speak freely. Academics and the major media have laid down rules on what is the "correct" position on almost every social and political topic. If you violate these primarily semantic rules, you will be in for censure, ridicule, and rejection. The requirements have invaded the work place and classroom to such an extent that it approaches the thought control in George Orwell's book, *1984.* This restraint on our traditional freedom of expression reduces the natural inquisitive search for truth. Such prohibitions can only impair the rationality of a people.

Once so inhibited, we, like trained seals, will bark on command and support the governing elite that seeks to rule America.

## Self-Selection and Historical Migrations

During the past five thousand years of human history, there have been constant migrations of people from one location to another. The American settlers were simply copying what many had done before: looking for a better place. After all, with free will and a little initiative, an individual never had to settle for the climate, social structure, or geography that he happened to be born into. However, for most people, the easier path was to accept the lot in life that was dealt them. There must have been some special quality about those who refused to accept fate and instead took charge of their destinies.

The people that braved the voyage to settle in the American wilderness from 1620 to 1900 may have possessed a more-than-average share of those non-IQ competencies we have referred to. The voluntary migration of people may self-select for certain characteristics, and America's founding families may have been superior in those regards. Whatever that quality was, it was probably not related directly to IQ but to some other portion of their personality or way of thinking about things: in short, some combination of initiative, daring, and pragmatic sense—the kinds of things our schools should be testing for instead of the ability to memorize dates and facts.

After the Protestant Reformation, the people of Western Europe became more robust in their demand for freedom, trade, and wealth. The Dutch revolted against their ruler, the King of Spain, and gained independence in 1581. After the landing of the Mayflower in Plymouth in 1620, there was a flood of millions of the most enterprising and God-fearing Europeans moving primarily in one direction—to the New American wilderness. One can only wonder if these people were not self-selecting—voting with their feet—and bringing a unique gene pool to tame a new land and build a new future.

It was those enterprising pioneers that established the American character and gene pool. When Hollywood made movies about them, they looked for actors like John Wayne, Jimmy Stewart, or Ronald Reagan to portray them. Were those really the kinds of people who settled America? And are they still alive and well in this country? If not, we, as parents, better start making more of them!

## Why IQ Does Not Explain National Success Stories

There have been a number of scholarly works that make the case that IQ differences between races are the explanation for the different degrees of success for both individuals and nations. Thus, they amass fairly convincing statistics that show that the levels of socioeconomic success of individuals within a society varies directly with the IQ and educational achievements of the people involved. Because average IQs of whites and many Asians are higher than blacks, they achieve higher positions and larger incomes than blacks. These theorists can also point to similar statistics that show these results hold true throughout almost every nation in the world, including African and Caribbean countries, with socioeconomic status paralleling IQ.

Most academicians advancing theories that stress the importance of IQ apply the same thinking to past development of different civilizations, suggesting that the world's geographic areas that had the most prosperous growth were the ones inhabited by people with the highest IQs. Thus, the Maori people of New Zealand, the Aborigines of Australia, the Indians of the Western Americas, and the blacks of sub-Saharan Africa were all held back compared to Asians and Europeans by a relatively lower IQ, which presumably held them back from innovating the mechanical, scientific, and organizational efficiencies that were developed in more advanced civilizations.

However, I would suggest those theorists are confusing cause and effect. Since we know IQs are malleable and develop when exposed to stimulating new experiences, the lack of progress for Maoris was not caused by a low IQ but a low level of cultural exposure. If they had had some exposure to the fabled Silk Road and the Hellenistic world of Alexander the Great, their societies, as well as their IQs, could have advanced as much as those of the Europeans.

Professor Colin Renfrew takes the position that everyone born today has virtually the same cognitive potential as the earliest humans that left Africa and spread around the world. Like Eliza Doolittle in *My Fair Lady*, all any of them need is a lot of tutoring from someone like Rex Harrison. During this most recent sixty thousand years, the people in some societies developed cultural and mechanical innovations that created progress in the comfort and affluence of their people. It was the gradual accumulation and application of these systems that explain how various regions of the earth progressed. Renfrew writes,

> Darwinian evolution in the genetic sense no doubt continued, and underlies the rather superficial differences that are observed between different racial groups today—differences in stature, skin color, facial features, and so forth. But the newly emerging behavioral differences between the groups were not genetically determined. They were learned, and they depended upon the transmission of culture.[8]

Sixty thousand years is a trifle in evolutionary matters. And, while that sixty-thousand-year period is largely uncharted, we do know for certain that today's people have not advanced in ability over the Athenians of twenty-five hundred years ago. Pericles could orate at least as well as President Obama, and the Greek scientists and playwrights have never been surpassed.

So, if all humans are equally capable, and have been for thousands of years, why are there such disparities in success? It is a thesis of this book that IQ has not been a key determinant—and in some cases, may have had an inverse effect. Progress for any nation depended on four things:

1. Providing security for the people and their property. Without soldiers, a strong defense, and civic order, no investment can be made or infrastructure accumulated.
2. Establishing governing systems that empowered all their people to actively participate in the nation's affairs. Slave economies

never made great advances but merely maintained their elites in comfort. Free economies with low barriers of entry into commercial activities were needed to create affluence. Feudal societies and the great Asian empires were built on the backs of peasants; their small elites had little reason to innovate, and the peasants were not allowed to.

3. After ordinary people secured the land and allowed everyone to contribute to progress, then and only then could mechanics and scientists accelerate progress. Such conditions occurred only in a few locales and only for a short time before their freedom dissolved.

4. In short, where a group of ordinary people was free to participate in open and competitive business activity, they created affluence. If they also provided security for the region and for the fruits of their toil, affluence and order increased. With security and affluence, the scientific and mechanical "geniuses" accelerated progress by their innovations and discoveries.[9]

This process that created progress in a few isolated areas does not include anything about high IQs. Neither were large bureaucracies, regulatory agencies, or aristocracies required. In fact, the success stories were distinguished by an absence of such negative forces![10] The requirements of national success have always been about ordinary practical people and their mechanical, military, political, and people skills—the 80 percent of their "TCQ" that is not IQ related. Intellectuals only appear in a society after such ordinary souls have created an affluent nation that can support the nonproductive "advisory" roles that such new elites push onto society. Thus, the existence of intellectuals in advanced societies does not mean they created those successful societies; to the contrary, they are more likely to bring on their destruction.

The currently superior condition of Western democracies did not arise from the work of today's upper-class elites. The prosperity of today's Western nations was built one hundred, two hundred, and more years ago, when the elites were quite different from those of today. Indeed, there were few intellectuals in this country when it was built to world supremacy from 1620 to 1880. Ralph Waldo Emerson has been declared America's first intellectual. But it was 1837 when he delivered "The American Scholar" at Harvard's Phi Beta Kappa oration, judged by his contemporary Oliver Wendell Holmes to be the nation's "Intellectual Declaration of Independence."

Prosperous nations have always tended during their mature eras to accumulate an overeducated elite. By virtue of their higher IQs and what Thomas Sowell calls "their verbal virtuosity,"[11] that new elite takes over the administration of what then becomes an increasingly complex society, and they invariably proceed to make the governing structure so much more complex that it eventually crashes. In the final stages of this process, it is not uncommon to see the leading elite enact two-thousand-page laws that no one has read or understands! During the usual centuries-long death spiral, they can exist like parasites, living off the momentum of earlier more pragmatic people. Unless something is done, sooner or later, the abstract thinkers become too big a burden for their country to sustain. Decline quickens, and the once-mighty nation falls into the dustbin of history. That may sound overly dramatic, but it has happened over and over again throughout recorded time, and America is on the brink!

In contrast, it is evident that a different group of people with a different set of intellectual abilities built most of the world's successful nations. One of the mysteries of history is enshrined in "The Radzewicz Riddle," which asks why complex advanced societies with all the educational and cultural amenities usually end up declining, while young start-up republics with few schools, no intellectuals, and no aristocracies or elites, are the ones that have advanced like crazy? The answer, of course, lies in the changes of leadership. The new elites that usurp control in advanced nations do not understand what built the success of the nation and proceed to undermine those foundations. It just may be that the new elites, sporting the highest IQs, the largest brain cavities, and the most abstract thinking, are the cause of such decline![12]

Another possible flaw in the theory that high IQs enabled national success is that most of the studies represent "snapshot" studies of recent societies. As everyone knows, throughout history, societies generally have followed a rise, a plateauing, and then a declining life cycle. It is also known that ethnic groupings and cultural beliefs within nations evolve, and the composition of the socioeconomic elites can therefore be transformed over the three-hundred to five-hundred-year cycles involved. Studies done during the past century only reflect the status of nations during this relatively brief period. The ranking of nations has not changed much during the past century. Western nations have maintained their technological lead—and the related higher affluence, compared to the less-developed world.

The studies, therefore, reflect the situation in advanced nations versus undeveloped nations. The major Western nations, which have the highest socioeconomic success, being advanced nations, would be expected to have the highest college attendance, education levels, and a high number of people in upper economic classes. But the foundations for that success were laid centuries ago by humbler and less educated citizens. No current snapshot can be relied on to indicate the past causes for today's success.

While Northern Europe and America have been the clear winners in providing freedom and affluence to their citizens, there have been other societies that made similar achievements. Sometimes those achievements have been due to copying Western capitalism as in Hong Kong, Singapore, and post-World War II Japan. Those success stories happen to be in populations with high IQs, but what has made them economically successful was their introduction of free-market mechanisms, originally developed in Western Europe. After all, the Mainland Chinese didn't participate in the Industrial Revolution until the past fifty years—and never attained a widespread level of prosperity, in spite of having extensive natural resources, an abundance of hard-working people, an extensive governmental structure, and numerous waterways, canals, and harbors.

Currently, the Chinese are copying the Western capitalist system and reversing thousands of years of backwardness vis-à-vis the Western nations. If their high IQs failed to produce such growth over the past few thousand years, it cannot suddenly be used as an explanation for their recent strides forward. China's recent progress more likely came from the introduction of freer markets and the encouragement of business enterprises. Those related cultural institutions developed in Western democracies over the past thousand years can be readily copied by any nation.

One of the clearest indications that high IQs do not create prosperity comes from a look at the role of small businesses and the entrepreneurs who create them. Dave Thomas was a high-school dropout who helped Col. Sanders with some Kentucky Fried Chicken franchises and then started the Wendy's restaurants. Dave did not have outstanding academic credentials—which is the case with most entrepreneurs, yet they create all the jobs in the country.

*A high school drop-out, Dave Thomas created 40,000 jobs in America. A lonely childhood in an adopted family provided the challenge to overcome hardship and set goals for his future success.*

Col. Sanders started learning how to cook at age five, when his father died, and his working mother relied on him to cook for the family. He dropped out of school in seventh grade and ran away from home soon thereafter to escape his stepfather. He worked as a steamboat pilot, insurance salesman, railroad fireman, farmer, and enlisted in the Army when he was sixteen years old. In his forties, he was operating a service station and cooking chicken to attract customers. This led to a restaurant in his fifties, and eventually to the thousands of

KFC franchised stores throughout the world. Apparently, there is a different mental ingredient for truly innovative business success that is not measured by IQ and SAT tests.

In a survey of millionaires, Thomas J. Stanley reports that less than one in three received a greater percentage of As than either Bs, Cs, Ds, or Fs. Their average GPA was 2.9, just slightly above average. Most of these success stories, more than half of which were self-made millionaires, claimed that a hard-work ethic, leadership skills, recognizing the ability of others, and sound decision-making skills were more important than IQ. Stanley reports that 90% of the variation in leadership performance is not explained by standardized intelligence measures.[13] He dismisses the value of school grades and test scores in predicting business success and concludes that teachers miss the point: First, "teachers are not very good at making predictions of future economic productivity, because they are not economically productive themselves," and, second, "teachers often use the wrong criteria to make these predictions."[14]

Fortunately, many of the average students gain motivation elsewhere, from encouraging parents or from somewhere deep inside themselves. And it's good that they do, because the number one job creator in America comes from their efforts starting new businesses. That is just one more reason why high IQs do not explain national success. It is the various types of practical intelligence that build affluence for all. However, that practical competency is of little value unless unleashed. It has been the advantageous cultural environment in Western Civilization that empowered the common people to outproduce every other nation in the world. That cultural environment had little to do with IQ, guns, climate, geography, or good luck. Success became possible due to free economies that allowed unfettered competition by all willing participants. And when the participants possessed imagination, initiative, independence, and integrity (the real "I" that should be included in IQ), their common genius produced great affluence for all.

## Inflation, Irresponsibility, and Deficits

We know that the big differences in achievement between societies and the people therein over the past couple thousand years were caused by the gradual accumulation of different cultural systems and beliefs. All evidence shows that the original American culture was the best in the world at producing physical security, individual liberty, affluence, and freedom of religion. The political-cultural-religious foundation that underlies the American experiment represents the most successful organizational framework for widespread progress ever witnessed in world history.

Now, four hundred years after the first settlers arrived in the New World, our once-proud Republic has become a populist democracy. Once upon a time, the American people were known for frugality, thrift, saving, investment in the future, and prudence. Those were the virtues pursued by the Americans who built the country. Those attitudes were a testament to the honor and character of a great people. Those were the qualities that were considered good moral behavior. But a growing number of Americans have been seduced by the demagogues that promise them everything and assure them that, as victims, they deserve a handout, a free ride, a boost from their friends in government, and special favors.

Those assistance programs the politicians' promise wind up lessening pride and self-reliance. Those benefits are now referred to as "rights," but they are really crutches and will become chains, as the growing Leviathan of government gradually erodes personal liberty. Qualifying for aid tempts many to become cheats and liars—anything to get something for nothing. We see others taking advantage and accept the unjust nature of many aid programs. Many who work and do not apply for aid end up with less after tax income than some of those on welfare programs. These inequities lead to cynicism. As slow and steady as dry rot in a home's timbers, the temptation of aid from the nanny state destroys American character. And the fault is not so much with the tempted as with those who tempt them—just to gain office, power, and influence for themselves.

There is talk of America becoming a banana republic, a suggestion that our economy will collapse. But the idea of debt has become so ingrained in the American psyche that few worry. Many families have been seduced into letting their own debt grow. Their peace of mind suffers, because they know viscerally that, at some point, it will all come crashing down. The stress this debt-crazy psychology has engendered certainly has reduced the happiness factor. Indeed, the belief that deficits and escalating debts are acceptable is not only destroying the dollar but has added to the decline of American character.

> **On Deficit Spending**
>
> *"History makes it plain that unless restrained, government proliferates to a point where its cost bankrupts the people at the same time it robs them of their freedom."*
>
> —Ronald Reagan

People see their houses skyrocketing in value and think they are rich—attributing their affluence to the government's wise economic guidance. But asset inflation—ultimately, the debasement of the currency—as the principal source of wealth corrodes the character of people. It undermines the traditional bourgeois virtues, making them ridiculous and even reversing them. Prudence becomes imprudence, thrift becomes improvidence, sobriety becomes mean-spiritedness, modesty becomes lack of ambition, self-control becomes betrayal of the inner self, patience becomes sloth, steadiness becomes inflexibility. All that was wisdom becomes foolishness. And circumstances force almost everyone to join in the dance.

The hypocrisy of our elected officials is appalling. As a people, we are often criticized for lavish spending. Our personal consumption of goods (bought with our own hard earned after-tax dollars) is deplored by the elites as harmful to the environment. Our reliance on credit and the large credit card balances we sometimes foolishly accumulate are called a sign of decadence and waste. But if we can manage it, that is our right. After all, unlike the government, when we can't keep the credit current, we get shut off. It is the elected officials that are irresponsible. They allow the government to pile up debt, taking more and more of our income in taxes and creating a huge day of reckoning for us—and, even more likely, for our children. It is that exploding fiscal insanity at the national level that is destroying the nation. The only remedy is a balanced budget, and we need it now, not in the promised "few years" from now.

## Cultural Beliefs and Attitudes vs. Cultural Institutions

When most commentators on the nature-nurture question refer to the "influence of culture," they refer to the attitudes and beliefs of the people. Thus, you will hear that the Protestant work ethic made Northern Europeans and Americans more productive than people in other cultures. And East Asians have often been credited with just trying harder, and that has tended to make them outperform many other ethnic groups. Religion has been cited as a cultural force that can either contribute to constructive activity or conversely encourage inner contemplation and a passive attitude toward the outside world. In this book, we have commented extensively on the habits and ways of thinking that make some individuals more enterprising, innovative, and persistent than others. These factors do make some people succeed more than others, but they are not the whole answer as to why some societies perform better than others.

Culture has another dimension to it besides the personal characteristics and beliefs that individuals bring to their day-to-day life. It is the extraordinary *cultural institutions* that evolved as underpinnings to Western Civilization that allowed its people to flourish. There are a host of immigrants in America of every racial and ethnic background who have afforded themselves of the opportunities here to become affluent. Regardless of their ethnic origin, they all seem to have the personal characteristics needed to engage in the American economic miracle. Of course, they had a degree of extra initiative and ambition, or they wouldn't have made the move to a new country. But why couldn't they have stayed at home and built their native country into an economic powerhouse?

The answer to that question reveals why the West won: It was that the people in a few European nations developed the best legal and financial institutions that allowed success. While these institutions had a genesis in Phoenicia three thousand years ago and in Renaissance cities of Italy and Germany five hundred years ago, they were rarely allowed in the authoritarian empires that ruled most of the world. But a thousand years ago, the English people demanded the Magna Carta from their King and resurrected the ideal of freedom and individual rights that had marked a few ancient Republics. The subsequent thousand years (primarily in Western Europe) witnessed the growth of common law, the rights of citizens, trial by juries, patent laws, limited stock companies, protection of personal and property rights, insurance protection, enforcement of contract law, and many other such orderly systems of applying fair rules and adjudicative solutions to both the personal and business activities of the people. Without those enabling systems, the Industrial Revolution would not have happened. And there are still only a handful of nations that provide those assisting mechanisms to empower the activity of their citizens.

One of the most vital mechanisms is the rather simple Registry of Deeds that records in formal fashion who owns what real estate. Many countries do not have these mechanisms, so individuals have no legal way of owning property, mortgaging their assets, or selling their property. The great Peruvian economist Hernando deSoto writes that we have forgotten the power of the basic financial and legal tools that were developed in the west and that made those nations employing them supreme in the world. He emphasizes that it is not *cultural traits* that make some societies more affluent than others but the *cultural institutions* that make the difference. Without the West's legal and financial mechanisms, most countries languish in economic stagnation. Those cultural mechanisms are the secret weapon that made the West supreme!

Dr. deSoto has documented the problem that holds back the people in the underdeveloped nations. Those people possess talent, enthusiasm, and have large amounts of useless wealth—because they have to operate in an underground illegal market place:

> In Egypt, the wealth that the poor have accumulated is worth fifty-five times as much as the sum of all direct foreign investment ever recorded there. In Haiti, the total assets of the poor are more than one hundred fifty times greater than all foreign investment received since Haiti's independence from France in 1804.[15]

But, all that wealth stagnates because of inadequate legal mechanisms to provide secure title to and free exchange of their owners existing assets. DeSoto observes that it would take the United States, giving foreign aid equal to the Millennial goal of 0.7 percent of our national income, more than 150 years to transfer to the world's poor resources equal to those they already possess.[16] That explains why the trillions of dollars sent abroad from America taxpayers over the past 60 years as financial aid has failed to improve the economic condition of undeveloped nations. Until those countries adopt the enabling legal and financial mechanisms, no amount of aid will reverse their fortunes.

In summary, to be financially successful, individuals need, first, a personal set of empowering beliefs and habits and, second, an environment that provides the legal and financial mechanisms that allow them to safeguard, finance, and readily transfer their assets. America has historically had both of these empowering cultural assets, and we must ensure that our new elites do not weaken them—for they are the foundation of our success.

In passing, it is useful to note that these "cultural institutions" are really simple administrative practices, mechanical procedures if you will, that have meant the difference between national success and failure. The great philosophers did not dream up the Registry of Deeds, or patent law, or the rules of contracts, or limited stock companies. These were all the creations of ordinary businessmen, lawyers, and merchants who saw the need to arrange their business affairs in an orderly secure fashion. The West could have "won" without John Locke or Adam Smith but never without contract and patent law, limited stock companies, and secure private property rights.

## Morality and Ethics: Are They Obsolete?

Human beings are born with an inner conflict between an innate selfishness and a tendency toward generosity born of human empathy. While infants and toddlers often appear to be directed primarily by their selfish natures, they do occasionally express tenderness, gentleness, and concern for others. In the animal kingdom, there is a pecking order seen in most social groupings, and it can be vicious, devoid of the human feelings of empathy and concern for others. Outside of the maternal instinct in animals, there is little concern over others. It is dog-eat-dog. But human beings are not like animals. Humanity's nobleness can be seen in the many acts of charity and relief that arise spontaneously when one individual recognizes the need to extend a helping hand to a fellow human in distress.

The degree of kindness versus selfishness expressed within a society varies. I had a sociology professor in college who pointed to a remote South Pacific island where the people revered trickery and deceit, where the "worst" members were highly regarded, and the "nice" people were looked on as failures! If that were true, it was probably the exception that proved the rule. Most societies value cooperation, trustworthiness, and integrity. This compassionate human characteristic has undoubtedly helped human communities succeed. A society is defined as a social grouping where the participants gather together, give up a degree of freedom (hopefully very little), and expect to benefit in security and productivity (hopefully a lot) from their voluntary association. The whole social enterprise is founded on the benefits that accrue from working together. Pure unleavened selfishness must give way to cooperation and teamwork.

While some advocates of free enterprise suggest that the greatest social good comes from each individual pursuing his self-interest to the maximum, there is a need for rules that limit the most extreme aggressive behavior and unfair tactics. With that caveat, self-interest lightened by sportsmanlike conduct has marked some of the more successful societies. Indeed, some historians have suggested that such moderating of the selfish gene helps explain why some population groups did better than others.

Professor E. L. Jones has argued that the widespread adoption of disaster relief in the Western European nations as early as the seventeenth century helps explain the rise of those nations over many others in the rest of the world.[17] Christianity has been also cited in this regard, because its basic tenets, while extolling the importance of each individual in the eyes of God, teach a kinder, gentler moral code.

Children must be taught the simple logic of balancing the good and the bad. Politicians like to polarize us by saying that Republicans hate the poor and Democrats love the poor. But stop and think! Is either position logical? Almost everyone agrees that a society needs a safety net to assist those who are having trouble. But "loving" them and providing too much for them is just as harmful as providing too little. Ideally, enough assistance is needed to reduce their discomfort but not enough to eliminate their incentive to find a job.

Benchmarks and standards are needed. They should not receive more after-tax income than the working poor! And the aid given should be provided equitably, with safeguards against fraud, not willy-nilly by over fifty different governmental agencies. Further, assistance should be slightly less than essential in order to leave room for private charities to fill the most needy situations. An excess of government aid drives out private charity and breeds resentment among those barely getting by on their own. Such subtlety is not beyond the mental grasp of a fifteen-year-old. But the Washington elite will not simplify and reform the system unless forced to by voters; there is too much patronage that comes from fifty separate government bureaucracies.

These important national issues illustrate why it is important to teach maturing kids to balance their selfish and generous impulses. Part of emotional maturity is based on the development of sound value systems to live by. These value systems will provide a compass for balancing selfishness and generosity. Too much of either can be harmful. Parents can help by giving direction appropriate to the nature of each child. Schools and churches used to help in this area of child development, but their cultural confusion today often makes their guidance of dubious value. It is difficult to teach moderation and morality when everyday we see so many of the nation's elites concentrating almost exclusively on their selfish impulses at the expense of their generous impulses. That is why character counts!

### Is Free Will an Essential Delusion?

Defense lawyers have in recent decades come up with the most ingenious defenses for some of the century's most heinous criminals. An increasingly common defense is to propose that their client is not a criminal but a victim. Their logic relies heavily on the confusion that exists about the relative importance of nature versus nurture. If the evidence against their client is incontrovertible, they will attempt to excuse the criminal conduct by blaming society; if that doesn't work, they will try to assign blame on an allegedly traumatic childhood, bereft of proper nurturing and guidance, and scarred by debilitating neuroses that are allegedly no fault of the individual in question. If the childhood was too good to justify that argument, they fall back on their client's faulty genetic composition: It was really his parents' fault after all, because they bequeathed him faulty genes.

A number of social psychologists have advanced this latter argument—the genetic determinism theory that humans are so controlled by their genetic make-up that they are not responsible for their actions. By these means, they have managed to link a predisposition to violence, sexual excess, paranoia, and instances of temporary insanity to their client's genetic inheritance, thus excusing all bad behavior. Academics have jumped on this bandwagon, creating whole new "sciences" such as evolutionary psychology, psychobiology, and sociobiology. Although much of the work in this field cannot be scientifically established, it has appealed to many minds and has tilted the nature-nurture question in favor of biological determinism and lessened the belief in free will.

These new theories represent a sea change in the basic cultural beliefs of Western Civilization, which was built on the Christian concept of free will, personal responsibility, and self-restraint. Most people manage to control their worst instincts and to suppress their most harmful desires. But some of the supposedly best minds in academia have theorized that our animal instincts are beyond control.

Now we all know from our own experience that we can usually overcome inner drives and impulses. And even if someone fails, his failure does not excuse bad behavior. Actually, the inability to suppress their emotion should be seen as compounding the crime. If it doesn't, we would all have a free pass to break the law whenever desired. This recent distortion of the law suggests that even if free will were a delusion, it is very helpful, even essential, to maintain a civilized society. If we do not recognize free will and demand personal responsibility from every individual, humans are reduced to being just animals, living in a lawless jungle, unrestrained by controlling civil conventions.

It may be that those brains that are dominated by algorithmic abstractions, those clever at conceptual theories, are more attracted to biological determinist arguments than are those people with brains centered on the concrete realities of human behavior. The latter are grounded in the way ordinary people act. They comprehend the simple fact that people need rules of behavior and many will violate them if not punished. The former types of brains can escape that reality by assuming—or conceptualizing—that:

1. People are basically well-intentioned and will always do right unless forced to be bad;
2. Any lapse in conduct is probably, at least in part, society's fault;
3. We should, therefore, "understand" and "excuse" bad behavior, even when it consists of mass murder and extreme violence; and
4. Excusing malefactors will not encourage others to break the law.

Now, that line of thinking obviously uses very faulty reasoning, and if there is a correlation between such thinking and high IQs, it may be very undesirable to be flooding the political, legal, and judicial professions with people predisposed to that type of grand illogic. (No matter how much Katherine Hepburn wanted Bogart to "rise above it," human nature does establish certain inviolable boundaries for social policy.)

Historians have pointed to the strong belief in free will and faith among the pioneer settlers as one of the uniquely American sources of personal strength. The idea of upward mobility through virtue and hard work motivated most of the people who sought the freedom offered in the New World. They wanted to take destiny into their own hands and build successful lives for themselves and their families. And yet some psychologists point to a new situation infecting the land: people who believe they have little control over their lives or that society or genetics have preordained their fate. People who think like that are not prepared to assume the role of mature responsible adult members of the community. They are subject to a condition called "learned helplessness," a sister to the victim mentality.

In looking ahead to picture your child as an adult, would you like to see him as a confident purposeful individual or as an indecisive and hesitant victim? If you want the former, do not let him fall prey to the recent epidemic of "learned helplessness." One of the problems in raising children today is that much of the media and demagogic politicians preach the victim mentality. For one thing, it gets votes, sustains the huge and growing bureaucracy devoted to caring for every citizen's problems, and sells newspapers.

In Chapters 6 and 7, we considered what makes a happy child and a contented adult. Some of the factors are based on the satisfaction that comes from achieving proficiency in some skill and the feeling of being in control, master of one's own destiny, and having resolved by oneself the vicissitudes that inflict every life. By emphasizing the child's responsibility to make hard choices, work hard at mastering necessary skills, and suffer consequences for bad behavior, you can strengthen the idea that he has free will and damn well better use it. What alternative is there? Do you want to encourage him to be a couch potato, a TV zombie, an excuse maker, a sluggard, a slacker, an overweight do-nothing Mr. Oafer? No, but it takes some tough love to reverse the socio-political temptations of today's culture.

## Our Failed Leadership

The failed leadership in America deserves a book to itself, but our interest here is how to teach children useful knowledge and skills for life. Aside from understanding the corruption, crony capitalism, personal ambition, and power hungry nature of our elites, children should understand how to balance a checkbook and stay in the black. Simple arithmetic proves beyond a shadow of a doubt that if a person spends even one cent less than he takes in, he will be free of debt and have a positive net worth. Conversely, if he spends even one cent *more* than he takes in, he will be in debt and have zero net worth.

That simplistic example also applies to governments. However, our government just prints money, issues IOUs, and lets its national debt grow indefinitely. America's national debt has risen from $3.2 trillion in 1990, from $5.6 trillion in 2000, from $7.9 trillion in 2005, to about $14 trillion in 2010. The total debt projected for 2014 is about $18 trillion. The debt now represents about 40 percent of the GDP and is projected to reach 68 percent in 2019.

The extraordinary increase in 2009–2010, under the Obama stimulus plan, dwarfs all prior accumulated debt from the past sixty years.[18] And these are conservative estimates of the actual debt from issued bonds. Unrecognized and rarely considered are the $100 trillion of debt made up of the present value of the unfunded liabilities of the Social Security and Medicare systems. That unfunded but real liability is ten times the current stated federal debt! Those unrecorded liabilities have been mandated and promised by our elected representatives in Congress! Those are political promises that will be broken, but when they are broken, they could break America.

Niall Ferguson calls these numbers "the fatal arithmetic of imperial decline."[19] There have been many deficit hawks that point to the large amount of American bonds held by the Chinese and other governments that could put a call on our treasury. And there is evidence that the annual costs to just service that debt—to pay the interest due the holders—is becoming a larger and larger part of our government's budget. "The federal government's interest payments are forecast by The Congressional Budget Office to rise from 8 percent of revenues in 2009 to 17 percent by 2019, even if rates stay low and growth resumes."[20] That escalating expense dooms the taxpayers to come up with more and more money every year just to pay the interest on our debt! And that's the best scenario: If interest rates rise and the economy stagnates, we'll see our national debt service equal to 20 percent or more of revenues well before 2019.

Ferguson warns that when servicing national debt reaches one-fifth of revenues, potential buyers of a nation's bonds become so skeptical that even-higher rates are needed to sell them, escalating the financial collapse that comes when a nation loses its creditworthiness. This is not complicated economics but simple arithmetic. Anyone with common sense that can add and subtract can grasp the idiocy of borrowing to the point where no more credit will be extended—that is, if they are willing to confront this threat to their future. That is why ordinary Americans without any formal education in economics, or even your fifth-grade child, are more competent in money matters than today's "experts."

A front page story in my newspaper recently illustrated the problem that abstract thinking creates for those who practice the "dismal science" of economics. Dated November 2010, the article suggested that an extension of unemployment benefits would help the economy, because it would boost consumer spending. Now the rationale for that is that economists have for decades collected data and have concluded that when consumer spending is high, the economy is "good." And if such spending has increased over the past month, they conclude that the economy must be strengthening (although if it declines the next month, they will conclude the economy is declining, and so forth). Such "reasoning" is obviously speculative and illogical, but that's how they think, and that is what they call the "science" of economics!

Their statistics may be interesting, but the mystery is why economists assume that there is a cause and effect there that they can manipulate. They theorize that because higher spending by the public in the past seemed to indicate a better economy, they can now create that same type of a better economy if they can somehow raise consumer spending. And their grand conceptual scheme then latches onto the idea that extending unemployment distributions will do just that. It's like thinking that we can turn on heat lamps in our outdoor New Hampshire porch, record the increased temperature, and safely conclude that we have made spring arrive early!

That's a conceptual leap that pragmatic thinkers would not take. If it made any sense at all, we would not just extend the distributions, but we would double them! Or, better yet, give everyone a million dollars! That would really boost consumer spending! It is all quite crazy. But that is how our fearless leaders think—irrationally, abstractly, and without common sense.

> **On Intellectuals**
>
> *"One of the principle lessons of our tragic century (20th), which has seen so many millions of innocent lives sacrificed in schemes to improve the lot of humanity, is—beware intellectuals. Not merely should they be kept well away from the levers of power, they should be objects of particular suspicion when they seek to offer collective advice. Beware committees, conferences, and leagues of intellectuals.*
>
> *"Distrust public statements issued from their serried ranks.*
>
> *"Discount their verdicts..."*
>
> —Paul Johnson, *Intellectuals*

For example, the Princeton Professor Paul Krugman, a Nobel Prize winner in economics, supports the stimulus—sort of a "spend more to reduce the deficit" kind of abstract thinking that is adored by academics. If you can get your kids to suspend disbelief and think like Krugman, it will increase their SAT scores as well as their chances for an Ivy admission. But don't try Krugman's prescription for yourself and your household budget, or you will end up with no house!

Remember in the section above about "Creating Survivors" that the "Incredulity Response" explains why some people perish and others survive. They ignore reality and remain optimistic in the face of sure death! Now, in my day, children were frequently reminded how stupid ostriches are when they reputedly hide their heads in the sand to avoid danger. We were thereby taught with that simple parable about the necessity of facing facts rather than ignoring unpleasant possibilities. But with academic elites like Krugman still peddling Keynesian economics, some people will tend to rely on the *hope* that the deficit doves are correct. As we all know, "hope springs eternal," but our nation's future depends on parent's teaching their children to beware of predictions by all "experts" and their crazy abstract theories.

Many historians who write about the cycles of history emphasize the issues of foreign policy and military spending as causes of declining national fortunes. Thus, Paul Kennedy has argued that the U.S. may be overextending itself militarily and that the costs involved will bankrupt the nation.[21] However, it is not helpful to single out a single budgetary item as the main culprit causing deficits. All federal expenditures have to be considered and their relative importance weighed, until they are balanced within a grand total that is less than revenues.

In fact, Ferguson points out that the costs of the ongoing Middle East "wars" have contributed only in a modest way "to the gathering fiscal storm."[22] It is the aggregate escalation of deficits and debt over extended periods that cause empires to decline. "It begins with debt explosion. It ends with an inexorable reduction in the resources available for the Army, Navy, and Air Force. Which is why voters are right to worry about America's debt crisis."[23] Although we may well question the wisdom of current international interventions and attempts at nation-building, maintaining military supremacy provides the assurance that we remain free and independent.

This past year, with the national health care debate, Americans are beginning to talk about rationing health care. Unfortunately, everything will have to be rationed if we are to balance the federal budget. And that rationing must be based on the essentiality of each expenditure in preserving the freedom, integrity, and strength of the nation. Those priorities must come before special interest groups, the greed of speculators, the egos of politicians, remote environmental threats, and even the needy among us.

If Americans do not come up with a plan to balance the budget, the nation will eventually lose its world standing, its economic power will falter, and we will be relegated, as many prior great civilizations, to the dustbin of history. The present crop of politicians and today's elites in New York and Hollywood will all have died and won't care. All they care about now is staying in power and keeping the gravy train running. They fail to possess the long-range view and prudence common among our ancestors. It is a new way of thinking, fostered by the new elite that dominates Washington, Wall Street, and academia—and their policies will destroy America if not eliminated ASAP.

## SUMMARY

A. There have been a few isolated societies in human history that participated little in human progress. Jared Diamond refers to the Eskimos, a few South Pacific archipelagos, and sub-Saharan Africa as examples of people that were held back by climate or geography. However, those are the exceptions. Among the dozen or so major civilizations of the past four thousand years, progress was primarily a function of how they were organized politically, spiritually, and economically. That is obviously true, because in all other respects the people themselves were equal, and each society enjoyed good climates, geography, access to transportation, and large organized populations. Yet they fared very differently.

B. The autocratic empires and stultifying faiths and philosophies of most of those societies held their people in a stagnant time warp. Their elites lived in opulence and resisted change; the peasants were enslaved and were not allowed to effect change.

C. Only in a few regions around the Mediterranean Sea and, eventually, Western Europe did people gain economic freedom, and this enabling feature reached its zenith in America. The resulting success was based on the spirit and independence of the people, the absence or limited role of an aristocracy, and the minimum impact of government regulation, allowing free enterprise to flourish.

D. The people in other regions of the world could have kept up if they had the empowering legal and economic institutions that were developed in the west. Every ethnic and racial group had the innate ability to succeed—but few were allowed the legal and economic tools that were developed in the freer Western nations.

E. Today in America, there is a new and growing aristocracy of people who would rule from the top. Their actions are expanding the role of government, reducing individual freedom, and bankrupting the nation. They seek to justify the need for their programs by crippling the free economic system and the self-reliance of the people. Their reason for being is only justified if they can make our economy and heritage fail.

F. The collectivist and dependent mindset created in a nation's people by socialist policy does even more harm than the faulty economic mechanics of a socialist system.

G. Ordinary free people built the nation. That progress happened under past policies. The new "experts," intelligentsia, and demagogues who preach the socialist state are destroying the country by subverting the principles that created our success.

H. It is possible that the nature of our new elites is being determined by the excessive role given to those with an affinity to abstract thinking and ideological passions. The special advantages directed toward such "intellect" and the neglect of more practical minds is deforming and damaging the human capital of America.

## Chapter 9
## *School Reform To Truly Leave No Child Behind*

 *"On average, private secular and religious schools pay teachers 10 to 40 percent less than do public schools, yet by any standard of measurement they do a superior job with students."*
—Martin L. Gross, *Conspiracy of Ignorance*

THE JOB OF EDUCATING America's children is much too important to be left in the hands of the experts. For too long, ordinary American parents have been led to believe that trained educators know best and that the task is too complex for the average parent to understand. However, American progress has always been built on the common-sense notion that you always distrust the expert, and there is no better place for such skepticism than in the case of today's public school system.

### Do Experts Possess Any Expertise?

The fallibility of experts was demonstrated in 1976, when wine experts were asked to make a blind tasting of twenty French and California wines. The tale is described in a *Harvard Business Review* article to show how common assumptions are often false. The test took place in a Parisian wine shop, and all nine judges were established French wine experts. The results were extraordinary: The California wines won the highest scores.

The article's authors emphasize that two assumptions were shattered that day: One was the widespread belief that French wine was superior to American wine, and the other was the equally erroneous belief that expert wine-tasting judges actually possessed some useful knowledge. The authors go on to assert that "current research has revealed many other fields where there is no scientific evidence that supposed expertise leads to superior performance." [1] In particular, they tell how psychotherapists with advanced degrees are not reliably more successful in treating patients than beginning therapists with just three months of training.

The same authors suggest a few guidelines to use to determine whether or not you are dealing with a genuine expert:

1. An expert's advice must lead to enhanced performance that is consistently superior to that gained from alternative solutions.

2. The expert's recommendations or actions must produce concrete results. It is not enough for the surgeon to perform the operation with perfect skill if the patient dies!

3. Do not rely on anecdotal examples or hearsay. True expertise is evidenced by repeated measurable success and consistently higher performance.

4. Do not rely on expert explanations. "Some supposed experts are superior only when it comes to explaining why they made errors."

5. Expertise can be subjected to scientific testing. If it cannot be replicated and measured, it is unreliable and of no use. [2]

It is no wonder if, as you read the above five tests, you started thinking about how today's education experts fail on each of those indications of expertise. While there are some very good schools, the underlying fact is that over the past fifty or even two hundred years, there has been no real advance in the efficiency or quality of the product. When it comes to results, why can't most sixth-graders read? Why are achievement scores declining? And does not the real expertise of our teachers associations reside primarily in their powers of explanation for their failures?

**Can an Elementary School Ignite Passion in Students?**

Parents have to cope with the subtleties of motivating their kids every day, and their children often become deaf to their words. But what about the schools, music groups, and sports teams that occupy most of the daytime hours for most children? Are they observing the best practices for teaching and motivating their students? Does all the recent attention to minority status, gender, sexual orientation, and multiculturalism help or hurt students' growth? Does the emphasis on IQ and SAT tests send the right message to kids? And do those tests fairly separate students onto different pathways that are best for the kids? Is the violence and lack of discipline in many schools a positive aspect of the learning experience? Do teachers' tenure and union oversight make the level of instruction better? Do the architecturally-perfect and elaborate public school buildings erected at great cost to cities and towns help the kids learn more or become more motivated?

The answer to all those questions is most likely "no." If that is so, we can understand why America's schools are failing so many youths and hurting their chances for a better life. And if the schools are failing the children, the schools are also failing their parents. Worst of all, the schools are failing the country. How did this disaster come to pass?

Most people believe that universal free public education was a boon to those nations that provided it. Common knowledge tells us that literacy soared and the rudimentary Three Rs advanced the children's abilities to deal with the evolving modern world. But that theory is, in fact, one of those assumptions, like the wine-tasters' expertise mentioned earlier, that

*Under the gun! Teachers and students at work.*

is open to question. Recall the creators of the Industrial Revolution referred to in Chapter 4. Few had much of any schooling. What they did have were parents who taught them the basics, parish schools, and tutors. And most of them received only a couple years of such "education." But that basic education along with self-study and early apprenticeships produced almost all the scientists, technicians, doctors, and engineers that built England and America to world supremacy. Can we truthfully say that the public school system has improved the capability of its students?

The history of the education system in America has been summarized by Sheldon Richman to reveal the contrary side to this question. A section of his argument is reproduced below. It effectively supports the need for an open and competitive schools system and underscores the general decline in effectiveness that accompanies most government run activities:

> Why were the public schools ever established? Did the private sector fail to set up schools or set up too few of them? Were large segments of society barred from obtaining education? Was the education of poor quality? The answer to the last three questions is no. The public schools were not established to make up for any deficiency in people's ability to learn to read, write, do arithmetic, and acquire knowledge of other subjects. The government schools were set up for another purpose entirely.
>
> As Jack High and Jerome Ellig have written, "Private education was widely demanded in the late 18th and 19th centuries in Great Britain and America. The private supply of education was highly responsive to that demand, with the consequence that large numbers of children from all classes of society received several years of education."
>
> High and Ellig show that the government's involvement in education "displaced private education, sometimes deliberately stifling it [and] altered the kind of education that was offered, mainly to the detriment of the poorer working classes." In colonial times through the early Republic period, when private schools were the rule, a great many

people were educated, despite the relatively low living standards of the day. As the historian Robert Seybolt wrote:

> In the hands of private schoolmasters the curriculum expanded rapidly. Their schools were commercial ventures, and, consequently, competition was keen.... Popular demands, and the element of competition, forced them not only to add new courses of instruction, but constantly to improve their methods and technique of instruction.

Schooling in that early period was plentiful, innovative, and well within the reach of the common people. What effect did it have? High and Ellig note that 80 percent of New Yorkers leaving wills could sign their names. Other data show that from 1650 to 1795, male literacy climbed from 60 to 90 percent; female literacy went from 30 to 45 percent. Between 1800 and 1840, literacy in the North rose from 75 percent to between 91 and 97 percent. And in the South during the same span, the rate grew from 50–60 percent to 81 percent. Indeed, Senator Edward M. Kennedy's office issued a paper not long ago stating that the literacy rate in Massachusetts has never been as high as it was before compulsory schooling was instituted. Before 1850, when Massachusetts became the first state in the United States to force children to go to school, literacy was at 98 percent. When Kennedy's office released the paper, it was 91 percent.

According to Carl F. Kaestle, "Literacy was quite general in the middle reaches of society and above. The best generalization possible is that New York, like other American towns of the Revolutionary period, had a high literacy rate relative to other places in the world, and that literacy did not depend primarily upon the schools."

Another indication of the high rate of literacy is book sales. Thomas Paine's pamphlet *Common Sense* sold 120,000 copies in a colonial population of 3 million (counting the 20 percent who were slaves)—the equivalent of 10 million copies today. In 1818, when the United States had a population of under 20 million, Noah Webster's *Spelling Book* sold over 5 million copies. Walter Scott's novels sold that many copies between 1813 and 1823, which would be the equivalent of selling 60 million copies in the United States today. *The Last of the Mohicans* by James Fenimore Cooper sold millions of copies. John Taylor Gatto notes that Scott's and Cooper's books were not easy reading. European visitors to early nineteenth-century America—such as Alexis de Tocqueville and Pierre du Pont de Nemours—marveled at how well educated the people were.

High and Ellig sum up the experience of the 18th and 19th centuries by noting that "the available evidence strongly indicates that Americans of the period took an active interest in education....The private supply was extensive, not only in the number of children served but in the spectrum of social classes involved."

Thus, the rise of public, or government, schools was not a response to any inability on the part of society to provide for the education of its children. As Joel Spring has written, "The primary result of common school reform in the middle of the nineteenth century was not the education of increasing percentages of children, but the creation of new forms of school organization." It should be obvious that the school systems were not set up merely to serve the poor. As Milton Friedman has noted, if the only motive were to help people who could not afford education, advocates of government involvement would have simply proposed tuition subsidies. After all, when proponents of government activism wanted to use the state to subsidize the purchase of food, they did not propose that government build a system of state grocery stores. They instead created food stamps. So the question is: Why are there public schools rather than "school stamps"?

We may break down the reasons into two broad categories, the macro and the micro. The aim of the public schools at the macro, or social, level was the creation of a homogeneous, national, Protestant culture: the Americanization and Protestantization of the disparate groups that made up the United States. At the micro, or individual, level the aim was the creation of the Good Citizen, someone who trusted and deferred to government in all areas it claimed as its own.

Obviously, the two levels are linked, because a certain culture cannot be brought about without remaking the individuals who comprise it.

Throughout history, rulers and court intellectuals have aspired to use the educational system to shape their nations. The model was set out by Plato in *The Republic* and was constructed most faithfully in Soviet Russia, Fascist Italy, and Nazi Germany. But one need not look only to extreme cases to find such uses of the educational system. One can see how irresistible a vehicle the schools would be to any social engineer. They represent a unique opportunity to mold future citizens early in life, to instill in them the proper reverence for the ruling culture, and to prepare them to be obedient and obeisant taxpayers and soldiers. Unsurprisingly, rulers and intellectuals jumped at the chance to make the schools a mill for the creation of Good Citizens. That motivation has been part of every effort to establish government schools.[3]

The over-arching reason public schooling has stagnated for the past century is that it is a government monopoly that has been further burdened by the dictates of a strong union. Between government mandates and the orthodoxy of union influence, the entire educational establishment has failed to innovate or improve. Almost every other activity in our country has become more efficient, more effective, and less costly in real dollars. But the public education system has failed in all three of those measures of performance.

Reading, writing, and arithmetic are still essentials, but the schools are doing a poor job even at that basic function. And in all the other functions that they have assumed, it is fair to ask, "Are they doing more harm than good?" As Americans, we understand that improvement is always possible, and in America today, there is more room for improvement in our school systems than anywhere—that is, other than in the wisdom, conduct, and morals of our governing officials.

**The Promise of New Methods of Schooling**

There is not one recipe for building excellent schools, but key ingredients in most of them include motivating the students, encouraging a hard-work ethic, and stressing the importance of being courteous and helpful to others. There are some schools and parents that have managed to provide just what it takes to be effective in spite of the deteriorating culture that surrounds all of our children. Dan Coyle gives an excellent example of what some charter schools have done. He describes the KIPP Method and its great success in bringing inner-city children to above-average achievement levels. Case studies of such schools that *have* worked provide better direction than can be found in theories of what *might* work.

> "The best guide to making a super school is not a plan of what might be done but an analysis of what has already been done"
>
> —Jay Mathews

In 1993, two second-year teachers in their early twenties became disgusted with their work. It is significant that they were not education majors but had volunteered to teach for two years in the Houston public school system. Coyle reports, "They'd tried to innovate but had found their efforts blocked by incompetent bureaucracy, unhelpful parents, misbehaving students, hidebound regulations, and the other blunt cogs of the most efficient frustration-machine ever invented: The American inner-city public school system."[4] So they decided to open their own school.

By luck, Texas had just passed laws funding charter schools. They were given a single room in a corner of the Garcia Elementary, put up a slogan, "work hard, be nice," and tried everything to motivate the students. The school operated on long days, uniforms, a clear system of punishment and reward, times tables were taught to rap, and each student was given a goal—to enter college after high school. One-half of the entering class had failed their achievement exams but at the end of the year, 90 percent passed. They opened more schools, and by 1999, the KIPP academies in Houston and New York were scoring higher on standardized tests than any other public schools in their districts. By 2008, there were sixty-six KIPP schools serving sixteen thousand students across the country. They produce students who get some of the highest scores in their cities, and 80 percent of graduates go to college.[5]

Richard E. Nisbett has also examined the results of KIPP schools and finds that their success is remarkable. He concludes that "poor minority children—at any rate, those whose parents care enough to get them into KIPP schools—can perform academically at levels as high as those of middle- class whites. The next step will be to find out whether children whose parents are not so concerned about their children's education can also benefit from KIPP-type programs."[6] This comment reveals the widespread understanding that kids' performance in school is largely determined by their home environment. They will not learn much if they have not been brought up to value education. It's more about motivation and attitude than IQ.

Most independent schools follow a known educational theory such as Montessori, but the KIPP program was developed by its two founders for the inner-city kids that arrive with little preparation and little hope. They were born into a zip code that predetermines that most will fail. But at KIPP schools, right from the start, they are told they are going to college and that they will be successful—but they have to work very hard and be very nice to their teachers and classmates. Both Nisbett and Coyle explain in detail many of the devices the teachers use to kindle the eager participation of their charges.

The "no excuses" group of charter schools, which includes KIPP, have achieved success in raising the performance of minority students in inner cities. The KIPP group has a written list of principles—The Five Pillars—which may give an idea of why they succeed while many charter schools do not. The Five Pillars are:

1. The teachers let the students know they have high expectations for them.

2. They expand the learning time by extending the school day and school year.

3. They use tests to monitor results and show who needs more attention.
4. They create a team spirit, a family atmosphere where every student has to "be nice." There is no bullying or disrespect allowed toward anyone.
5. The principals must have "the power to lead."

The KIPP officials place a lot of responsibility on their leaders: "Sometimes they would delay opening a school if they could not find a school leader who showed the teaching ability, love of children, people skills, and toughness they thought was necessary."[7] Charter schools have the latitude to innovate, hire and fire teachers, utilize technology in the classroom, select any instructional material they desire, and, in short, run the school. Regular public schools cannot do anything without following the regulations and contracts with unions and the mandates of politicized departments of education and accrediting boards. That freedom from top-down regulation allows the KIPP principal and teachers *to teach!*

It is clear that existing public schools and the teachers who studied in teachers colleges, as well as their supervisors trained in prevailing educational theory, could never pull it off. KIPP builds character, demands total effort and perfect behavior, has a clear goal, and offers intensive instruction in the basics. The teachers constantly remind the students to exercise their brains: The harder they work them, the smarter they get. No one seems to care about IQ. The KIPP system's innovative approach to public schooling takes all comers— kids with little hope, average IQs, and poor prospects—and helps them make themselves into winners.

KIPP teachers believe in the work of Martin Seligman and Angela Duckworth, who studied the behavior and achievement of hundreds of eighth-graders. They found that self-discipline was twice as accurate as IQ in predicting student's academic achievement.[8] And they found that character is simply a skill, waiting to be ignited, developed, and perfected by practice.

## A Free Market in Education

There are many other experimental and charter schools, along with traditional Catholic schools, managing to far outperform the public schools. That opportunity has been fostered by the Milton and Rose Friedman Foundation for Educational Choice. The plan behind this growing movement is based on the Friedmans' advocacy of free markets versus government controls. Unfortunately, the teachers' unions are actually taking some of these charter schools to court to close them down. The entrenched educational establishment is fully committed to holding back progress.

But the undeniable advantages of school choice are making headway. A recent Friedman Foundation newsletter tells of developments in Chicago:

> Parents in Chicago's worst performing and most overcrowded elementary schools might soon know real school choice. Legislation introduced by state senator James Meeks (D–Chicago) would give school vouchers to more than thirty thousand families whose only current option is a failing or overcrowded public school.... Once thought a non-starter in Illinois, school choice has gained steam since Meeks committed to championing the idea last winter. Long considered "a Republican idea," to use his words, school choice became attractive to Meeks after other reforms lost traction in the legislature or, if passed, failed to have a meaningful impact.[9]

Schools are no different from other organizations. Central top-down engineering, accompanied by regulations and restrictions, will always inhibit quality and innovation. A decentralized and loosely-controlled system will deliver new and better ways to achieve the organization's goals. And there is little risk. There is so much to be learned by children that one can hardly go wrong academically. The difference between good schooling and bad may not be so much in the academics, but in the nurturing, motivating, igniting, and training involved in deep prolonged effort and discipline.

Today's public schools operate within a rigid bureaucracy, offering a primarily mandated curriculum, and are controlled by their union leaders and the politicians in power, not by the parents. A true free market in education would bring an abundance of educational options, from which parents could choose based on their child's needs. Gone would be the days when the school board needs to decide if evolution or creationism (or both) should be taught. If you want that to be part of your child's curriculum, you would choose a school that offers it. There would be church-run schools, non-profit-run schools, and for-profit schools. The schools parents preferred would be successful; those they didn't would go out of business.

If school taxes were abolished, most people could afford a good school for their children. Others might have to depend on scholarships or charity. But until school taxes are abolished, why not give the parents control of their education dollars? If parents were free to take their "education funds" to the school of their choice, there would be no doubt that all Americans could afford schools—better schools—for their children.

Consider this proposal that attempted (and failed) to make the Michigan ballot in 2008:

The Personal Education Account Initiative would have changed the way Michigan funds education by creating personal education accounts for each student, managed by their parents or guardians. The personal education account (PEA) would have been based on the principles of the G.I. Bill, offering education dollars directly to the students, to be spent at a school of their choosing. The PEA initiative would have maintained the current method of state funding, but the education funds—the same annual per-pupil funding normally given to the school districts—would have been instead deposited into a PEA for each child age four to eighteen years. Parents and guardians would be free to choose the school to send their children to and what bank or credit union their PEA will be deposited to. Parents would have been free to look at their local school, other schools in their area, as well as specialty schools that might better suit their child's particular talents, needs, or style.

Under the proposal, no public school could charge more than the per-pupil rate provided to each child, but they would be free to charge less to attract more students. Prudent spending would have been rewarded, because the savings would not expire at the end of the year. Unlike a voucher system, where savings from frugal spending go back to the state, wise spending of PEAs by parents would, under this proposal, become savings, which would stay in the account and be added to the next year's per-pupil funding. When the child graduated from high school, annual deposits to the PEA would end, but all funds remaining in the account, due to the choices made over the previous years by the parents, would have been available to spend at any college or university within the State of Michigan over the next twelve years. After twelve years, remaining funds would have been deposited back into the school aid fund. In the event of the death of a child, any balance in their PEA would be transferred to the child's next-of-kin's PEA or, if no next-of-kin existed, to the school aid fund.

These are the kind of proposals that the education establishment can't stand—but they would go a long way toward improving education in America.

Even though the Michigan proposal failed to make the ballot, some experiments with opening up a free market in education have been tried—and very successfully. In 1972, School District 4 in East Harlem ranked last among New York City's school districts in reading and math. Ninety-five percent of the district's students were minorities; over half were from families headed by a single female; almost 80 percent qualified for free-lunch programs. But District 4 had educational leaders willing to try a new way. According to John E. Chubb and Terry M. Moe in their book, *Politics, Markets, & America's Schools*:[10]

> Beginning in 1974, they oversaw the creation of an expanding number of alternative schools built around distinctive themes, philosophies, and programs.... The district encouraged teachers with innova-

tive ideas to put forward their own proposals, and with the district's involvement and consent, form their own schools. Teachers were only too happy to take advantage of the opportunities, and schools sprouted up like mushrooms. To make this proliferation possible, district officials also rejected the traditional notion that each school must have its own building. In East Harlem, schools were henceforth to be associated with programs, not buildings....

These schools have been granted very substantial autonomy.... District officials assist parents through orientation sessions, information on each school, lessons in decisionmaking, and meetings with school representatives. But the schools control their own admissions—they set their own criteria and make their own decisions about who to accept and reject. More generally, the schools are largely (but not entirely) free to make their own decisions about programs, methods, structure, and virtually everything else pertaining to the kind of education they provide.... Teachers, parents, and students are all encouraged to think of themselves as their school's "owners" and to take the responsibility—and the pride and involvement—that real ownership entails.

The district has pursued innovation and diversity, and that is what it has achieved. The names of some of its junior high schools helps illustrate just how spectacular the variety can be when the supply is liberated: the Academy of Environmental Science, the Creative Learning Community, the East Harlem Career Academy, the East Harlem Maritime School, the East Harlem School for Health and Bio-Medical Studies, the Jose Feliciano Performing Arts School, Music 13, the Isaac Newton School for Math and Science....

While schools have control over their own admissions, their distinctiveness and their sheer need for students—the district puts them out of business if they fail to attract enough clients—has meant that schools and students tend to match up quite well on their own. In recent years, 60% of students have received their first choices, 30% their second choices, and 5% their third choices.

On virtually every relevant dimension, the East Harlem reforms have been a tremendous success. There are lots of schools, emphasizing everything from music to science. Teachers are enthusiastic about their work and largely in control of their own schools. They are empowered, professional, and satisfied—all achieved through the natural dynamics of the system, not through the artificiality of bureaucratic rules. School organizations are small and informal, built around team cooperation and cohesiveness of mission. Parents are active, well-informed, and take pride in "their" schools.

Meanwhile, student achievement is way up. While only 15.9% of the district's students were reading at or above grade level in 1973, 62.6% were doing so by 1987.

**The Homeschooling Option**

Millions of American parents elect to homeschool their children for some or all of their twelve years of pre-college training. By providing an intensive adult-oriented, success-seeking atmosphere, they have, in the simplicity of their homes, outperformed the professional educators in their multi-million-dollar public school monuments. One of the biggest burdens for American families is the real estate tax on their homes. About half that cost is the cost of public schools, a government and union-dominated monopoly that spends $5–$30 thousand a year to educate each child. And still, one-half of the students can't pass basic arithmetic, reading, and writing skills tests. The national figures are available. Homeschooled children win a disproportionately large number of Merit scholarships, score higher on the SAT tests, and get a better education than their public school peers.

The fact that the educational establishment hides from is that schooling a first to twelfth-grader is not rocket science. The need for trained teachers, nationally-approved curricula, and elaborate buildings is just so much crap! My wife and I homeschooled our seventh-grader by buying $250 worth of books, computer software, and supplies and giving them to the child with instructions to work through all the material. Using only four to five hours a day, with an hour of assistance and review from the parents, the child did fine. Achievement tests at the beginning and end of the year showed she had advanced one-and-a-half years of schooling, about normal for a child from a higher SEC family in the Northeastern suburbs. In addition to the $250 of books and CDs, she had an inexpensive computer and a card table set in a corner of the playroom! Legend has it that Abe Lincoln went one better: He had ten classic books and a candle in a corner of his log cabin, where he learned most everything he needed to know.

Other homeschoolers operate on an even smaller budget than my wife and I did. Homeschooling gives parents the flexibility to use whatever methods they find useful, to use a formal curriculum or not, and to focus on teaching their children the things they think they need to know. Some—often called unschoolers—do virtually no "formal schooling" but help their children learn the lessons they need to learn through everyday living. In virtually all cases, homeschooled children get a better education than is available in the public schools. At the very minimum, they have teachers who truly care about them and their education, which is a great start.

**Back to Basics**

Since basic literacy and arithmetic skills are attainable by all but the slowest learners, achievement tests are desirable—not only to find the students that need special help but also to determine the teachers' proficiency. There is no excuse for a school system to fail at teaching sufficient basic skills to pass simple tests on vocabulary, reading, writing, and arithmetic. Emphasis should be on practical everyday requirements of literacy and calculation. We have seen how many new charter schools are succeeding regardless of the IQ or racial or socio-economic origin of their students. Everything they will be taught hinges on the foundation stones that the Three Rs provide. And perhaps some of the 50 percent that drop out without graduating would stay in school if they were taught reading and doing sums before they were asked to read Shakespeare and do algebra.

Steven R. Quartz supports the research that indicates that "complex environments... initiate a cascade of growth changes that result in more complex brain circuits."[11] In studies with animals, he finds that for the enriched environment to be effective, the subject has to actively deal with and explore the environment, "not simply passively watch it." These two explanations about how intelligence and skills develop echo Daniel Coyle's call for building thicker myelin circuits through "deep practice." The code to increasing talent is a matter of hours of practice combined with concentration and motivation. In his book, *The Talent Code*, Coyle reveals the secrets of training "hot beds," where budding world sports champions hone their skills. A common denominator for these locales is great experienced teachers, 10,000 hours of practice, Spartan facilities, and igniting and sustaining motivation. Those who stick to such well-directed and repetitious training will gradually improve and refine their competitive talent.

Dr. Quartz applies these findings to the elementary classroom and to the problem of teaching reading skills in particular. Many educators scoff at teaching the Three Rs, and that may explain why 40 percent of American students are below their grade-level in reading achievement. But reading ability is basic to all school subjects. It is a strong predictor of educational success and is a teachable skill. Getting it right is more important to every child's future than learning about feminism, gender studies, multiculturalism, slavery in the American south 150 years ago, or the bombing of Nagasaki. Those topics, which make up too much of today's schooling, are mandated by the educational elites to undermine support for American history.

Quartz points out that reading skills are frequently deficient among even those who score average or above on IQ tests. Certainly there must be a major reform of our school system so those children will not be left behind. He suggests that such students aren't stupid; they just don't hear well! Deficits in the speed of auditory and visual processing present in some children may explain this reading and language impairment.

Researchers have found that this processing speed varies among individuals and correlates with literacy skills. So how do we improve the brain's processing speed of auditory and visual stimuli? An individual brain's processing speed is probably inborn. Does that support the determinists' view that genetics determines a person's fate? Or can an enriched environment trump genes?

Quartz reports that Michael Merzenich of the University of California, a pioneer in brain plasticity, trained monkeys to discriminate subtle differences in rapid sequences of sounds. As their skill improved, the timing of neural responses in the animals' brains changed. Subsequent research on humans showed that practice led to improvement in the ability to recognize brief stimuli.[12] Since speech sounds involve changes at a rate of a hundredth of a second, a child that needs a tenth of a second will be handicapped.

In 1996, Merzenich teamed with Paula Tallal, an expert in the brain and reading at Rutgers University, to develop a computer-based training program to improve children's auditory processing. They constructed computer games in which success depended on recognizing changes in computer-modified sounds, and as the children adapted, the sounds were programmed to become more rapid. The subjects played on these exercises one hundred minutes a day, five days a week, for four to eight weeks. They achieved meaningful gains in auditory processing rates.

The next year, the two developed a similar game to enhance reading skills called "FastForWard." Quartz reported in his 2002 book that approximately 100,000 children have taken the program since 1997, many of them improving their reading from one to four grade-levels. The program apparently changes the brain structure in the speech processing area. As Quartz writes: "The cornerstone of IQ, that the essence of intelligence is raw, unmodifiable mental horsepower, does not stand up to scrutiny in light of contemporary brain science."[13]

So much for biological determinism! The lesson is that children, especially young children in the earliest grades, have the potential to vastly increase their academic skills if provided the right tools and experience. In today's schools, many have been identified as slow learners by the third or fourth grade, and after that, both the child and teacher proceed as if the child has little academic future. This false perception, when it incorrectly denies a child's potential, will lessen his or her confidence and willingness to face challenges. Low expectations become self-fulfilling prophecies. And that is a lose-lose proposition, not only for the child but for a nation that needs everyone to become all they can be.

An individual's ability to learn the Three Rs, or traditional "school book stuff," is readily apparent to teachers and parents. It is not difficult to rank any child with respect to his relative ability to master these basic subjects. However, the educational establishment has, for many students, abandoned any pretense of achieving a minimum proficiency in these subjects. They scoff at the Three Rs as old-fashioned and talk about the importance of teaching "more." Fine, but they should start with a mastery of the basics. And at least for the Three Rs, they should not protest against teaching to the test.

**The Need for Realism in Education Reform**

A word of caution is called for at this point. Much of the material in this book suggests how our failed school system and our children can be "saved," but to some extent, it all suffers from what John Derbyshire calls "happy-talk." Most successful charter schools rely on a student body selected by "choice and commitment." That is, their application process discourages families "unlikely to cooperate"[14] with the school's techniques. That is not an argument against charter schools but evidence that, when all is said and done, families matter.

It is arguable that eliminating policies that encourage or condone illegitimacy and single-parent families would do more for educating our youth than any academic reforms or teaching improvements.

Children from homes that lack positive encouragement, show a disdain for education, or fail to teach self-restraint and a work ethic, will probably not do well in any school. But children whose families want a better future for their children do deserve the chance to gain access to the best schools they can find. Family motivation is the key!

Many educators suggest that assigning the "best" teachers to inner cities, spending more money, or reducing class size will solve our problems. But they won't, if the students aren't interested or their families discourage them. Some reformers point to more early intervention to offset the bad influence of dysfunctional homes. Head Start has been a landmark program since it was created in 1965. Over twenty million children have been given such early schooling. We have spent over $60 billion on the program, but there is little benefit ever been shown from that effort.[15] It is sobering to recognize that most reforms of the past half-century have failed.

American schools spend about $8 billion a year to reward teachers who get a master's degree, even though there is evidence that getting the degree does nothing to improve student achievement. (This is probably because the degrees are usually in education pedagogy—not the actual subject being taught). We spend billions funding salary schedules based on a seniority system, even though studies show that, after five years, seniority does not improve student achievement. We've spent billions to reduce class size, even though there is no strong evidence that smaller classes in high school improves student performance.[16] Those three "reforms"—higher pay for masters degrees, automatic "step increases" in pay for seniority, and smaller class sizes—are actually of benefit only to the teachers, the union members who get paid more and work less as a result of such policies.

Children and their families have to want to learn and behave to become educated. That desire to learn is much more important than class size. Many families fail in this regard. No amount of government intervention will change that. In fact, most such interventions reward the families that fail to provide decent environments for their children!

Only the risk of suffering the consequences for bad behavior can create appropriate motivation. That is the stark fact of human nature we must not forget in all our rosy prescriptions.

Almost all the studies that have attempted to correlate adult success with childhood environment find that "family background" is the single most determining factor. Although a child's genetic coding may place parameters as to what types of future outcomes are attainable, it is the family environment that determines whether the child will succeed or fail within those possible parameters.

Derbyshire takes direct aim at the idea that, given the opportunity, any child can do anything and can learn to do it well. We have stressed in this book the huge potential each person possesses and how, with good training and self control, great strides and success can be achievable. But there are limits, and those should be realistically evaluated. Most children will not benefit from college. Most children are best suited for only a small percentage of all possible vocational outcomes. But they can be the best that they can be at something, and helping them see those most available avenues is the job of parents and teachers. It is a mistake for high schools to make it a goal to maximize the percentage of their graduates going to college. What they should be doing is maximizing the probability of success for those graduates who will not benefit from college.

## The Problem with the Educational Establishment

On June 16, 2009, the U.S. Department of Education released the results of a study of the first federal initiative to spend taxpayer dollars on private school tuition. It found that students in the Washington voucher program overall did no better on reading and math tests for the second year in a row than their public school counterparts. Both groups took widely used standardized math and reading tests. These findings are similar to the results found by the educational establishment in other studies. They supposedly "prove" that schools are limited in what they can accomplish with students from disadvantaged backgrounds.

This conclusion, they argue, is in line with the landmark Coleman report, which found in 1964 that the quality of schools attended by black and white students has little influence on the difference in average achievement between the two. What is far more predictive of how a student will do in school is the socioeconomic background of his family. Now, family environment does influence a child's readiness for school, but it is not the whole story. Schools can help. Many charter schools have worked. The studies that conclude that some alternative programs don't work does not mean that *all* alternative schools will not work. The establishment data and conclusions are really just a means to avoid change. There are many independent and charter schools that have been able to take children from the poorest neighborhoods and gain successful outcomes, provided they were completely free of the failed methods imposed on most schools by the educational establishment.

The stubbornness with which the establishment denies the success of many charter schools, alternative schools, and homeschools indicates the hurdles we face in getting improvement from the government/union-run monopoly that controls the public school system.

There is little reason to believe that the people who dominate the present school systems will make meaningful reform. Professional educators have implemented dozens of "new and improved" teaching methods over the past hundred years, with little progress gained. Is it possible the teachers colleges and the educational establishment are as inept as most government-run operations?

A major problem that also increases costs dramatically is the increasing number of "support personnel." Most schools have gradually accumulated bureaucracies of "expert" administrators, who remain far removed from the classroom. Such support personnel used to account for 5–10 percent of a school's staff, but they now approach or exceed 50 percent of the employees. And that 50 percent never even see a student!

The fault is not with the teachers. Most teachers are dedicated and seek to do a good job. The problem comes from the leadership. The

NEA and AFT, which pose as professional groups with an "expertise" in education, are little different from the UAW and Teamsters. They are unions, with little interest in raising the quality of education. Although they are responsible for the education of 88 percent of American schoolchildren, their real interest is in maintaining the status quo and making the job of its teachers easier and higher paid—and maintaining a politicized elite at the top controlling the purse strings.

Ironically, the officers of the National Education Association may want to keep the status quo in education, but they seek change in every other social and political venue. They have lobbied state legislatures to gain great power. Each school district is required, at taxpayer expense, to collect union dues from every teacher by payroll withholding. No teacher can refuse and keep their teaching certification. These dues exceed $1 billion a year and may be used to support any political party or position, regardless of the individual teacher's wishes.[17] According to the Federal Election Commission, 98 percent of the money spent by the teachers' political action committees went to Democrats. Teachers' union representatives made up 11 percent of the delegates to the Democratic National Convention—more than the entire delegation from California.[18] These same unions have brought lawsuits to the courts to oppose most reforms and to close independent charter schools. Wherever there is a successful charter school that is succeeding with minority students, the unions use legal bullying to try to close them down. Any successful reform is a threat to their dominance and power.

The teachers' unions have done nothing to improve the education or experience requirements for teacher certification. They continue to support the very inferior training and standards of America's teaching colleges—a degree which is required to teach in public schools. Martin Gross writes that, "Even the late head of the American Federation of Teachers, Albert Shanker, expressed his disdain: 'By and large we are getting people who wouldn't be admitted to college in other countries,' he confessed."[19] Quite differently, in the very reputable private school, Choate, none of the 172 faculty members has an undergraduate degree in education and, of the 104 with Masters Degrees, only four have the degree in education.[20] Since they want quality teachers, they expect their teachers to have degrees in the subjects they teach!

Public schools are also influenced, often for the worse, by the U.S. Department of Education and the fifty state Boards of Education. These appointed supervisory Committees have broad powers over school curricula, and they designate "approved" textbooks. They are highly politicized bodies, and their dictates have replaced sensible, balanced content in the social studies courses with revisionist dogma. In March 2010, the Texas Board of Education voted 10–5 to enact new teaching standards for history and social studies that, among other things, dropped Thomas Jefferson from a history section devoted to great political thinkers. In that case, it was the conservatives that wanted the omission. In other cases, the radical left imposes coverage of their favored issues. The need for proper instruction in economics, history, and political science loses out and lies buried under these ideological battles. It can only be hoped that until these administrative bodies are eliminated, principals and schoolteachers will find a way to avoid the mandates imposed on their efforts to truly educate their students.

If we are to believe that winners are developed, not born, then parenting and schooling become very important. Even the most disadvantaged inner-city kids of minority parents can be taught to achieve college credentials way beyond normal expectations. These demonstrated facts indicate the need for more independent schools. Without competition and innovation, our schools will lag far behind their potential. So-called reforms from the NEA or the Boards of Education will not help and have never helped. Being government-run operations, they cannot solve the problems, for, as President Reagan wisely opined, they *are* the problem.

**SUMMARY**

A. The American public school system needs a total overhaul. Piecemeal "reforms" have not and will not create the needed changes. Top-down mandates from Departments of Education should be eliminated.

B. The system must be decentralized with a removal of the tight control from unions and government regulation. We must move away from present teacher certification and the reliance on teachers colleges to staff our schools. Principals must regain the power to lead, to hire and fire, and to introduce innovative methods of instruction.

C. Alternative schools must be designed and "marketed" to those disenchanted children who drop out. Work-study options could be good for many students. Experimental Charter schools must be encouraged. Parents must be given the free choice of where to send their kids.

D. The efficiencies of computer courses and lectures, home study, and online techniques must be added to the regular classroom sessions. If there is any place that screams out for a new disruptive technological breakthrough, it is our system of educating our youth.

E. The motivation and discipline that distinguishes the few successful schools must be spread across all systems. To accomplish such far-reaching changes, we must set aside education theory and look to and copy the systems that have actually improved student performance.

F. The changes and innovations will have to come from the bottom up. Every school district should be allowed to seek new solutions free of government and union dictates.

# Chapter 10
# How Culture & Family Trump Race & Genes

*"Families and societies fail in the absence of self-restraint. Fathers who instill it are in a very real sense the trustees of civilization, and they hold its future in their hands."*
—Reuven Bar-Levav, M.D., *Every Family Needs a CEO*

In America, we, as individuals, have been taught that the sky is the limit. There is supposed to be upward mobility for all. If not this generation, your children will have the opportunity to rise and be anyone they want to be. It just takes work. So the traditional storyline goes. The limiting factor in a free economy is not the system or the class structure so much as each individuals' perceptions of themselves and what is possible. That is why the politicians are against self-reliance and independence. People with those values will not vote for the socialist agenda and expanded government programs.

Demagogues seeking political power prey on our self-confidence and our faith in God and country. They do much harm by convincing people that the system is stacked against them and that there is no use trying. They preach pessimism to induce a negative defeatist attitude that will allow them, and big government, to take over the country. It would be far better for the demagogues to make sure the system is fair and that opportunity is equal for all. But demagogues feed on misery, and that is why they spread it around as much as they can. Their preachings explain why so many American children have lost the confidence to even try. The self-serving habits of politicians have infected most of the Washington insiders. If we're going to change Washington, we have to change the people we send to Washington. It's that simple.

In early American history, the people were spread out, independent, and self-reliant. There were no intellectuals or "experts." There were few schools, almost no central government, few regulations, and no aristocracy. They had chosen to leave their homes and travel across the ocean to find a new life and freedom. There had been a self-selection of sorts, even though these immigrants came from different ethnic and national groups. While they were predominantly Christian, they represented many different faiths including Catholics, Puritans, Jews, Quakers, Huegenots, Dutch Reform, and the other Protestant faiths. And they formed new faiths, such as Christian Science and Mormons. They represented all socioeconomic classes, all sizes, and all types of personalities. But they must have all possessed a robust and optimistic attitude to have been moved to so drastically upset their lives and start over in the New World. Certainly, they did not feel shackled by either the bonds of society or the limits of genetic inheritance. They were simply prepared to do whatever needed doing to carve out a new life. They must have experienced great personal growth in grappling with the demands they encountered, for such momentous action stimulates the body and soul.

There are several conclusions to draw from the research we have looked at in the preceding pages concerning personal growth. One is that the factors that have made Americans the envy of the world are based on our cultural institutions, our personal attitudes, and our motivational fuel. Two of those three supporting characteristics happen to make up most of the "other 60%" of our total combined competency. They are the foundation blocks that have traditionally distinguished the American Character. But these enabling "parts" can

**Total Competency**

IQ - 20%

EQ ---------- 20%

Cultural Beliefs - 15%

Motivational Energy ---- 15%

Personal Attitudes & Traits ---- 30%

**TCQ—100%**

also be found among the people of almost every other society, so what makes Americans so special?

The positive attitude and imaginative initiative that appear so uniquely "American" only do so because America alone has had the open and free society that allowed its people to express those ennobling characteristics. That enabling environment is based on the legal and financial institutions that have been such an important part of the American scene. In sections of this book, we have referred to these as the "mechanical" conventions such as our Bill of Rights, deeds, mortgages, the court and jury system, corporate entities, due process, insurance systems, the law of contracts, and so forth. I call them "mechanisms" because they do not rest on theory or ideology but simply on the mechanical functioning of a free enterprise system—the economic ordering most in tune with human nature, individual happiness, and our basic search for the good life.

The "cultural beliefs" can be found in the Bill of Rights, a uniquely American document that seeks to protect the personal dignity, equality, and respect of each individual. The Founding Fathers wrote the Constitution and added the Bill of Rights to ensure that autocratic forces could not deny us liberty and property. Our religious heritage and the almost universal respect for the Ten Commandments complements the secular Rights of Man. When you add the idea of playing by the rules, a level playing field, and open competition, you have covered most of the cultural beliefs that made America supreme.

"Motivational Energy" varies greatly among people and while such initiative or ambition is important for the nation as a whole, it is useful to accept the fact that it is not a universal attribute of mankind. Many self-help books make the mistake of assuming that with a little advice any person can do anything. Professor Ericsson warns us that, "The journey to truly superior performance is neither for the faint of heart nor for the impatient. The development of genuine expertise requires struggle, sacrifice, and honest, often painful self-assessment. There are no shortcuts."[1]

Little is known about what "ignites" an unusually strong drive to achieve or why it happens to some and not to others.[2] The point is for parents to support their children's effort to be good at something—anything—as a sufficient goal and not to put their own ambitions or social needs ahead of their children's needs. A child should believe that he can do anything so he isn't held back by a negative outlook, but he should have the option to set her or his own goals.

Much of this book has been devoted to the sound "personal traits" that parents hope to see in their children. They are represented by integrity, persistence, initiative, altruism, self-control, self-reliance, long-range thinking, practical decision-making, and an adult adaptation or maturity that can face adversity with confidence and optimism. They are the bedrock for all other personal characteristics and, though in part inherited, can be shaped and nurtured by wise mentors.

Our national success has come from the work of all the Americans throughout the past few hundred years applying their total competency to build successful lives for their families and country. Americans are almost totally made up of immigrants and their children and grandchildren who sought out their new homeland for the freedom and opportunity it offered. That may have marked them as possessing special initiative and drive but, as generations succeed generations, that unique strength of the people can gradually weaken. That weakening of our character is accelerated by the academics and demagogues who constantly denigrate American traditions, patriotism, and family values.

Meanwhile, other nations have found ways to emulate our success. The leaders of Singapore and Dubai have reduced regulation and unleashed the power of an open and free economy—igniting an explosion of economic activity and demonstrating for all to see that their people, like all people, have about the same TCQ as Americans. By simply copying our economic and financial systems, they can compete with the best and maybe even overtake us.

If America is to remain that "shining city on the hill," we must remain true to the heritage that got us here. Elevating abstract thinkers with high IQs is not the way to go. They are disfiguring our beautiful America, taking away our sweet liberty, and trying to shackle the bravest among us under a growing bureaucracy of central planners. Good parents will teach their children to be wise, apply common sense, and rid us of the new intellectual and collectivist elite that is taking over our institutions. After all, it was those institutions, along with a self-reliant attitude, that made for success.

We may have lost a lot of self-reliance and optimism during the past four hundred years. But for each and every American, the mistake when facing up to personal inadequacy is to believe that you were "born that way" and that there can be no hope to change that genetic blueprint. In fact, we are all born almost a blank slate and must learn and practice the many skills that see us through life. That may be why self-discipline is such an important skill—because it leads you to work hard and practice all the useful skills that mark a successful person. And that knowledge—that one is master of his or her fate—provides the confidence and the mental attitude to create constructive change.

The strength to maintain confidence in the face of adversity—to pick yourself up after defeat and keep trying—is a matter of character, something that parents can instill in their children. It can be critically important even for the strongest soul. Hulk Hogan tells of his own experience, when, in spite of his great success, he was down and almost out. In his book, *My Life Outside the Ring,* he tells how he pulled himself up out of despair in 2008. One of his motivations came from reading an inspiring book that reminded him that each of us is responsible for attracting everything that happens in our lives—that we have the power to be as happy or sad as we want to be. Modern science confirms this fact. Our bodies never stop growing; our brains keep remaking themselves. We can make ourselves stronger, smarter, and wiser—if we work at it. No one can do it for us, for it must come from within.

# *Afterword*

A FEW SIMPLE DIAGRAMS MAY SERVE to illustrate some of the major concepts advanced in this book. When my friend, Mitch Estaphan, introduces his students to the nature-nurture debate, he uses two circles to demonstrate the effect of environment on a person's development. Across both circles he draws a line at approximately the midpoint and explains that the area below the line represents the ability one is born with, and the area above the line represents that person's potential. At birth, there is no second line above the first to show how much capability has been added to the child's original genetic blueprint. But, at age twenty-five, there is a second line above the first, representing the individual's aggregate capability as increased by parenting, schooling, the culture, and life experiences.

Mitch draws in such a second line in one circle that is just slightly above the base line to show how little growth there can be if a child grows up in a poor environment, without exposure to enabling and ennobling ideas and experiences. In the other circle, he draws a line well above the base line showing the higher total competency that results from a good environment. And it is that simple. We have seen throughout this book how a person's total adult competency grows from the acculturation and nurturing received. Even SAT scores go up with training and concerted practice. So do all the other competencies that make up the mature adult, and the amount of those increases are directly proportional to the quality of the individual's training and experience.

Mitch's circles inspired me to draw a few diagrams to demonstrate similar points about the nature of intelligence and how it develops. **Figure 1** (on the following page) shows in a bar graph format five segments of an adult's competency. The blank white area at the bottom represents the genetic blueprint at birth that dictates for most children what they are born with, let's say a range somewhere between the 30-60 percentile of overall capability. In the illustration, the genetic given is set for this hypothetical average individual at the middle—or at a 50 percent level, in comparison to the population at large.

The shaded area above that shows the added capability that comes from environmental impacts as that child grows. Such impacts come from parents, schools, hobbies, sports, church, gangs, etc. and add approximately 10 to 30 percent to the child's capability—depending on how constructive to personal growth that exposure proves to be.

The next higher area (with the diagonal lines) represents the growth that comes from self-education and self-willed improvement. Thus, if a child actually tries to emulate idealized mentors who provide positive role models—and tries to learn and follow simple

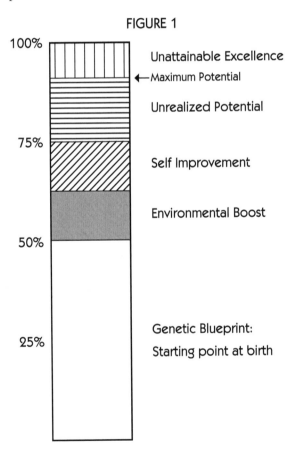

FIGURE 1

rules of good behavior and manners and develops good work habits, people skills, and initiative—then that child will gain additional maturity and capability from such efforts. Now, this area is influenced in part by the environment, in that a good environment will provide good role models and the long-term outlook that encourages a child to outline his objectives and the means of attaining them.

However, I show this "self-willed" area of growth separately from the general environmental influence, because anyone from any environment can, by the exercise of free will and true grit, make such gains. It is a mistake to lead any child to believe that some outside forces—culture, schools, parents—bear the entire responsibility for making him grow! It is essential the child recognize the need for his active effort and involvement.

It would be much easier, however, for the child to strive for such gains if schools taught them that one can in fact pull themselves up "by their own bootstraps." That old-fashioned expression has become virtually outlawed by our academic and big government experts, because it fails to excuse bad behavior. They prefer to create grand programs that will somehow "make" children grow up, rather than encourage individuals to be responsible for themselves. Demagogues like dependent citizens who are unable to take care of themselves. If everyone lifted themselves up on their own, the politicians would be out of business!

If we skip to the top segment of **Figure 1**, the area with vertical lines indicates the unattainable area of an individual's growth. That limit will vary by individual, with perhaps Abe Lincoln and Thomas Jefferson getting very close to the "perfect" top line, but, for the rest of us, obviously, there is a lower point above which no one can expect to surpass. Some come close, some are way down on the scale, but the line at the bottom of that area represents the maximum attainable growth of an individual. What's of crucial importance is that everyone has the potential to rise to that personal optimum point. As John Wooden admonishes us all, it isn't about being the best, it's about being the best you can be.

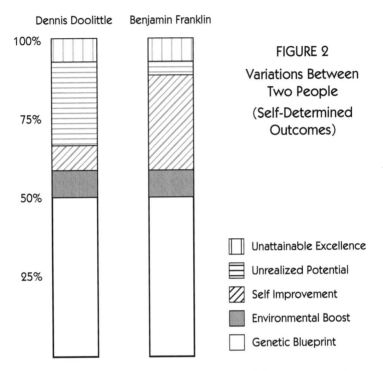

Dennis Doolittle    Benjamin Franklin

FIGURE 2

Variations Between
Two People
(Self-Determined
Outcomes)

Unattainable Excellence

Unrealized Potential

Self Improvement

Environmental Boost

Genetic Blueprint

The segment with horizontal lines, second from the top, shows the potential not attained. The line above that area marks the maximum possible; the line below marks the attainment realized. The difference represents potential not gained. It is the wasted genius that comes from not doing a better job in the two areas where growth can be gained: the positive environment and the encouragement of individual motivation. Coach John Wooden was aware of all this when he told a player, who had just performed very well, "That was good, but next time you might do it better." Wooden's teachings are exemplified in the adage that "potential" just means something you haven't done yet. The purpose of good parenting and good schools is to help children minimize that portion of their potential never realized.

**Figure 2** shows these same three sources of capability for two different individuals. Both have the same genetic base and gain the same amount from their environment. But Dennis Doolittle on the left does not apply himself very vigorously to personal growth, so his wasted genius, his potential unrealized, consumes a lot of space. Quite differently, Ben Franklin's presumed graph on the right side shows that he followed his axioms and rules for proper behavior rather seriously and reduced his unattained genius to a minuscule segment. He gained great recognition for his contributions to society, as well as the comforts of a life well lived.

In **Figures 1 and 2**, we have treated a person's competency as a monolithic unit that can be increased by both the environment and self-help. **Figures 3 and 4** illustrate the constituent parts of that competency, with IQ being just one of those parts, shown in the column to the left. For simplicity, the other four areas of competency are labeled EQ, (P)ersistence, (In)itiative, and (Im)pulse control.

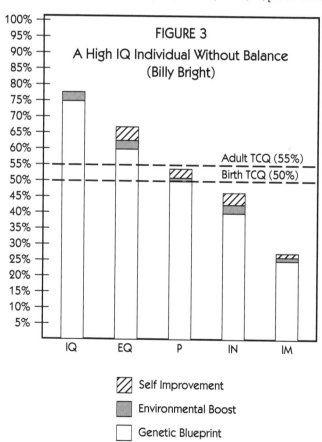

Somewhere in those latter three columns, we would look for common sense, practical mechanical smarts, logic, imagination, good decision-making ability, and the numerous attributes cited in earlier chapters that make a person successful.

It should be a challenge for future investigators to more precisely identify and measure the capabilities suggested by those three right hand columns. However, until that is done, we do know from recent neurological studies that all of the many competencies we have discussed are the product of various segments of the brain, just as memorization and algorithmic skills are, and that therefore there should be no "extra" importance or distinction given to one form of ability over another. This conclusion is buttressed by the fact that we have seen sound evidence that many of those other capabilities are better predictors of success in life than is gotten from measures of IQ alone.

**Figure 3** charts the hypothetical growth of Billy Bright, a boy with a high IQ but merely average levels of ability in the areas of people skills, impulse control, persistence, common sense, and other important character traits. At birth, his raw overall score for combined competency is 50 percent, the mathematical average of his five capabilities, which is represented by the blank area at the bottom of each column. **Figure 3** also shows that by the time he reaches adulthood, he will have gained 10 percent more in each category, achieving an adult TCQ of 55 percent. Thus, in spite of a high IQ, he probably will not turn out to be a major achiever. Perhaps if he had studied Benjamin Franklin's *Almanac* instead of multiculturalism, he would have raised those right-hand columns enough to get a better score, rather than be doomed to relative mediocrity.

The equally hypothetical character denoted in **Figure 4**, Annie Able, has a much lower IQ and a lower overall TCQ at birth (46 percent) than Billy Bright. However, in spite of a lower IQ, she applies herself to self-betterment and may have enjoyed a more diverse environment. While raising her IQ a mere 10 percent, she raises her other skills by 25 percent or more and attains an overall adult TCQ of

60 percent, well above the adult level attained by Billy, even though his IQ remains well above hers.

Unfortunately, under present educational policy, Billy would get preferential nurturing and would be advanced to better schools and occupations. That biased process is an example of the Matthew Effect that we saw operating with the Canadian hockey players—where an improperly selected group gained an edge over equally or more worthy individuals. The comparison between Billy and Annie also illustrates that the individual with the lower IQ can, in fact, be as competent (or more competent) than another sporting a higher IQ.

**Figures 3 and 4** also provide an insight into what different individuals should look to in choosing vocational interests. For ex-

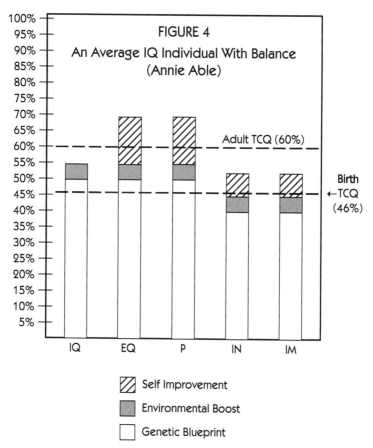

FIGURE 4

An Average IQ Individual With Balance
(Annie Able)

ample, the high-IQ person may make a good scientists, accountant, or engineer. The high-EQ person may be excellent at activities requiring sales or leadership skills. And a person with a lot of persistence may be suited to become an inventor or entrepreneur. But significantly, the diagrams also indicate what fields a person will *not* be good at. Regardless of their high IQs and EQs, we should beware of people with low common sense, poor decision-making skills, and/or a love of abstract ideologies, carefully separating them from authoritarian positions so that their arrogant impulses are not given the opportunity to usurp excess power over the rest of us.

A record of self-restraint, logical decision-making, common sense, and good character are the qualities to be looked for in choosing elected officials. No amount of IQ intelligence or polished speaking ability trumps common sense, character, and love of country. Indeed, we have recently witnessed how the most brilliant talkers and thinkers, the elites advanced to leadership posts in Washington and Wall Street, those same elites claiming to be more knowledgeable than the common people, brought on the major financial debacle that wiped out the savings of millions of Americans—and they then proceeded to claim they could fix it all by adding trillions of dollars to our national debt and spending our way out of recession! If that multi-trillion dollar fiasco doesn't convince you of the dangers coming from very "bright" abstract minds, then nothing will!

The format of **Figures 3 and 4** may be used by any reader interested in a little self-analysis. Just mark out the five columns on a piece of paper and raise each of them to the levels you think you were born with—that is, your innate abilities in each area. If your EQ people skills are average, mark the midpoint of the chart. Then show how much you have raised each of the five skills, distinguishing between how much your environment contributed and how much your own willed efforts may have added. Finally, consider what your maximum might have been, and how much unexploited potential you may still have to work on. It could be a lesson in humility, which is one

of the valuable traits suggested as belonging in the three right-hand columns. Any gain there would raise your TCQ score.

# Acknowledgments

THIS BOOK HAS BEEN an adventure: a search for conclusions on a subject that has been much debated and never resolved. There are many people who have shared this effort. They will recognize their own ideas within the pages of this book. It could not have been completed without their help. Special thanks must go to my parents and extended family, who taught me to avoid flights of fancy and to keep both feet firmly planted on the ground. Their honest and simple impact throughout my childhood provides testimony that parental influence has the power to shape the child.

Thanks must also be awarded to the examining professor at a Harvard graduate school who, after my dismal Doctoral Oral Exam, told me I just didn't have sufficient conceptualizing skills to deal effectively with abstractions. Taking that as a compliment, I abandoned postgraduate studies and entered the realm of business and politics. There are countless individuals that have subsequently contributed to my education, while I worked with middling success as an elected politician, an appointed officeholder, a faculty member, a businessman, an investor, carpenter, an accountant, auditor and business consultant, board member, landlord, professional trustee, farmer, sailor, and aspiring joke-teller. Such active involvements, dealing constantly with the vicissitudes of reality, have protected me from the lure of abstractions and ideologies.

I also acknowledge a debt to my many great teachers. It is unfortunate that today's academics have fallen so far beneath the titans of yesterday who instructed and inspired their students with an impartial and scholarly erudition, unmindful of restrictions imposed by political correctness. Those teachers gave us the gift that keeps on giving—a hunger for truth and understanding, free of fanatical ideology—and sowed in our minds a life-long love of learning.

My family and friends deserve special mention, because they have either supported or tolerated my quasi-intellectual efforts. Their solid confidence and honest comments provided both sufficient encouragement and an accurate compass to see it through to the end. My wife, Catherine, and our nine children and fifteen grandchildren have been a motivating force—especially when they demonstrate that their success in life may have been in spite of my efforts rather than because of them.

Probably the biggest debt is due to the hundreds of writers who have ploughed this ground before me. Most authors, in their acknowledgments, list all the eminent scholars who they have worked with, but then magnanimously suggest that all errors are theirs alone. I cannot wholly share that sentiment because I have actually relied on the dozens of authors cited herein. If they are wrong, I may be, too, but I doubt it. There are just too many writers who have indicated that the mind is a many splendored thing, amenable to good development, and subject to the power of free will; that progress comes strictly from individual human action; that freedom demands personal responsibility; and that intellectuals are a net burden on mature nations. They all may stop short of the obvious conclusions to be drawn, but their piecemeal decimation of the academics and intelligentsias leaves little room for confusion.

All I have done is connect the dots. That is why I owe so much to Julian Simon, Daniel Goleman, Jared Diamond, James Flynn, Hernando de Soto, Malcolm Gladwell, Mancur Olson, Thomas Sowell, Steve Biddulph, Reb Bradley, Benjamin Bloom, Robert Conquest, Keith Stanovich, Paul and Barbara Tieger, Richard Lynn, David McCullough, Robert Epstein, Theodore Dalrymple, Steven Quartz, Thomas Stanley, George Vaillant, John Wooden, Sheldon Richman, Steven Pinker, Geoff Colvin, Paul Johnson, Stephen Murdock, Daniel Coyle, Richard Nisbett, Eric Voegelin, Ludwig Von Mises, and all the other commentators cited in this book. It is their exhaustive, scholarly, and insightful writings that provided the foundation for this new theory of individual growth and achievement as well as an understanding of the sources of historical progression.

Finally, I want to thank Kathleen Wikstrom, former president of Laissez Faire Books, for her wise and thoughtful advice and counsel on all sections of the book. In addition, my gratitude goes to my daughter, Amy Greene, for her insights on psychological counseling and parenting; Professor Mitchell Estaphan, a devoted investigator into the workings of the human mind; and my other four daughters and three daughters-in-law for their inspiring love of teaching, counseling, and their great concern for children. There are others who have shared their reactions to early drafts of *Wasted Genius*, and all have helped maintain my enthusiasm for the project. It is not for the faint of heart to endorse a book that shatters a number of academic icons and challenges traditional orthodoxies. Thanks are due to all the editors who have red-lined the material and reduced my occasionally erroneous, exaggerated, and outrageous prose to tolerable levels.

Bruce Greene deserves special recognition for the illustrations depicting some of the common people, heroes, and other respected characters from the pages of history. His unique renderings emphasize for me the unusual and varied nature of the uncommon commoners who made the march of human progress successful. Such practical and hard-working individuals repeatedly emerged from the masses and applied their varied talents when needed to advance the well-being of mankind.

# Notes

## Chapter 1

[1] Judith R. Harris, *The Nurture Assumption,* 2nd Ed. (New York: The Free Press, 1998)

[2] Steven R. Quartz, *Liars, Lovers, and Heroes* (New York: Quill, HarperCollins, 2003), 125

[3] John Derbyshire, *We Are Doomed*, (New York: Crown Forum, 2009), 144

[4] Ibid., 144

[5] Ibid., 156

[6] Paul D. Tieger & Barbara Barron-Tieger, *Nurture by Nature* (New York: Little, Brown & Company, 1997), 13

[7] Steven Pinker, *The Blank Slate* (New York: Penguin Books), x

[8] Ibid., 2

[9] Ibid., 161

[10] Paul D. Tieger & Barbara Barron-Tieger, op. cit.

[11] K. Anders Ericsson, *The Making of an Expert* (*Harvard Business Review*, Managing for the Long Term, July–August 2007)

## Chapter 2

[1] Daniel Goleman, *Emotional Intelligence: Why It Can Matter More Than IQ*, 10th Anniversary Edition (New York: Bantam Books, 2006), 34

[2] Stephen Murdoch, *IQ: A Smart History of a Failed Idea* (Hoboken: John Wiley & Sons, Inc., 2007)

[3] James R. Flynn, *What is Intelligence?* (Cambridge, UK: Cambridge University Press, 2009)

## Chapter 3

[1] Nicholas Lemann, *The Big Test* (New York: Farrar, Straus & Giroux, 1st ed., 2000)

[2] Theodore Dalrymple, *Our Culture, What's Left of It: The Mandarins and the Masses*, (Chicago: Ivan R. Dee, 2005)

[3] Malcolm Gladwell, *The Story of Success* (New York: Little, Brown and Company, 2008), 22

[4] Benjamin Bloom, *Developing Talent in Young People* (New York: Ballantine Books, 1985), 42

[5] *Commentary*, January 2005, 84

[6] Daniel Coyle, *The Talent Code: Greatness Isn't Born, It's Grown* (New York: Bantam Books, 2009), 18

[7] Ibid.

8 Stephen R. Covey, *The 7 Habits of Highly Effective People: Powerful Lessons in Personal Change* (New York: A Fireside Book, Simon & Schuster, 1989), 106

9 John Wooden and Steve Jamison, *The Essential Wooden: A Lifetime of Lessons on Leaders and Leadership* (New York: McGraw-Hill, 2007), 7

10 George E. Vaillant, *Adaptation to Life* (Cambridge, MA: Harvard University Press, 1977), 363–366

11 Hulk Hogan, *My Life Outside the Ring* (New York: St. Martin's Press, 2009)

12 Coyle, op. cit., 108

13 Coyle, op. cit., 135

14 From website: Thinkexist; http:thinkexist.com/quotes'like'my_method_is_different-

## Chapter 4

1 John Mayer and Peter Salovey, *Emotional Intelligence* (Port Chester, NY: Dude Publishing, 2004)

2 Daniel Goleman, op. cit., 44

3 Ibid., 44

4 Ibid.

5 Robert Sternberg, *Wisdom, Intelligence and Creativity Synthesized* (Cambridge, UK: Cambridge University Press, 2007)

6 Goleman, op. cit., 25

7 Ibid., 26

8 Ibid., 27

9 Sternberg, op. cit.

10 Ibid.

11 Gladwell, op. cit., 4

12 Ibid., 90

13 Ibid., 5

14 Ibid., 112

15 Wooden and Jamison, op. cit.

16 Covey, op. cit., 316

17 Keith E. Stanovitch, *What Intelligence Tests Miss: The Psychology of Rational Thought* (New Haven: Yale University Press, 2009), 6

18 Samuel Smiles, *Lives of the Engineers* (London: The Folio Society, 2006), xvii

19 Ibid., 199

20 Ibid., 200

# Chapter 5

[1] Smiles, op. cit., xvii

[2] Bill Greene, *Common Genius: How Ordinary People Create Prosperous Societies and How Intellectuals Make Them Collapse* (Little Rock: Laissez Faire Books, 2007)

[3] Colin Renfrew, *Prehistory: The Making of the Modern Mind* (New York: The Modern Library, 2008), 28

[4] Michael H. Hart, *Understanding Human History* ( August, GA: Washington Summit Publishers, 2007)

[5] Flynn, op. cit., 181

[6] Ibid., 181–2

[7] Richard Lynn, *The Global Bell Curve* (Augusta, GA: Washington Summit Publishers, 2008)

[8] Ulric Neisser, Ed., *The Rising Curve*; "The Decline of Genotypic Intelligence," by Richard Lynn (Washington, D.C.: American Psychological Association, 1998), 358

[9] Ibid., 342

[10] Flynn, op. cit., 30

[11] Jared Diamond, *Guns, Germs and Steel* (New York: W. W. Norton & Company, 1999), 21

[12] Ibid., 21

[13] Neisser, Ed., op. cit., 359

[14] Ibid., 359

[15] Neisser, Ed., op. cit., "IQ Gains Over Time," by James R. Flynn, 33

[16] Ibid., 33–36

[17] Ibid., 61

[18] Arthur Herman, *How the Scots Invented the Modern World*, (New York: Three Rivers Press, 2001), 21–2

[19] Bloom, op. cit., 4–5

[20] Coyle, op. cit., 14

[21] Ibid., 40

[22] Ibid., 41, 15

[23] Ibid., 45

[24] Ibid., 67

[25] Ibid., 67–8

[26] Ibid., 71

[27] Ibid., 94

[28] Ibid., 212

[29] Sally J. Rogers and Geraldine Dawson, *Early Start Denver Model for Young Children with Autism* (New York: The Guilford Press, 2009)

## Chapter 6

[1] Lynn, op. cit., 11

[2] Ibid., 295

[3] Robert Epstein, *The Case Against Adolescence* (Sanger, CA: Quill Driver Books-Word Dancer Press, 2007)

[4] Ibid., 165

[5] Thomas J. Stanley, *The Millionaire Mind* (Kansas City: Andrews McMeel Publishing, LLC, 2001), 121

[6] Epstein, op. cit., 201

[7] Ibid., 193

[8] Ibid., 178

[9] Ibid., 172

[10] Ibid., 142–3

[11] Bruce Charlton, Discovery Channel News, 6-23-06

[12] Quote from Michael Crichton, *Next* (New York: Harper, 2006), 284–5

[13] Sheldon Richman, *Tethered Citizens* ( Fairfax, VA: Future of Freedom Foundation, 2001), 11

[14] Coyle, op. cit.

[15] Daniel G. Amen, M. D., *Magnificent Mind at any Age* (New York: Harmony Books, 2008), 48

[16] Ibid., 52–63

[17] Ibid., 157

[18] Ibid., 166

[19] Stanley, op. cit., 11

[20] Steven J. Gould, *The Mis-Measurement of Men*, (New York: W. W. Norton, 1996)

[21] Ibid., 23

[22] Geoff Colvin, *Talent Is Overrated* (New York: Penguin Group, 2008), 206


## Chapter 7

[1] Lenore Skenazi, *Free-Range Kids: Giving Our Children the Freedom We Had Without Going Nuts* (San Francisco: Jossey-Bass, 2009)

[2] Randy Pausch and Jeffrey Zaslow, *The Last Lecture* (New York: Hyperion, 2008),198

[3] Steve Biddulph, *The Secret of Happy Children* (New York: Marlowe & Company, 2002) Bay Books Sydney 1984), 142–3

[4] Ibid., 4–5

[5] Covey, op. cit., 19

[6] Ibid., 20

[7] Biddulph, op. cit., 5

[8] Ibid., 5

[9] Wooden and Jamison, op. cit., 129

[10] Biddulph, op. cit., 2

[11] George E. Vaillant, *Spiritual Evolution* (New York: Broadway Books, 2008), 162

[12] Ibid., 160

[13] Ibid., 160

[14] Charles R. Joy, *The Animal World of Albert Schweitzer* (Hopewell, NJ: The Ecco Press, 1950), 45

[15] George Kennan, *Sketches From a Life* (New York: Pantheon Books, 1989), 248–9

[16] Ibid., 170

[17] Meg Meeker, *Strong Fathers, Strong Daughters* (New York: Ballantine Books, 2006), 7.

[18] Ibid.

[19] George L. Rogers, *The Art of Virtue*, 3rd Ed. (Midvale, UT: Choice Skills Publ., 1996), 13

[20] Reb Bradley, *Born Liberal Raised Right* (WND Books: Los Angeles, 2008)

[21] Ibid.

[22] Ben Sherwood, *The Survivors Club* (New York: Grand Central Publishing, 2010), 10

[23] Goleman, op. cit., 89

[24] Martin E. P. Seligman, *Learned Optimism: How to Change Your Mind and Your Life* (New York: Vintage Books, 2006), 236–7

[25] George E. Vaillant, *Aging Well: Surprising Guideposts to a Happier Life* (New York: Little, Brown and Company), 206

[26] Derbyshire, op. cit.

[27] Wooden and Jamison, op. cit., 15

## Chapter 8

[1] Alan Beattie, *False Economy* (New York: Riverhead Books, 2010), 9

[2] Ibid., 11

[3] Ibid., 12

[4] Ibid., 17

[5] Ibid., 22

[6] Ibid., 4

[7] Thomas Sowell, *Intellectuals and Society* (New York: Basic Books, 2009), 197

[8] Renfrew, op. cit., 82

[9] Greene, op. cit., 13

[10] Ibid., 13

[11] Sowell, op. cit., 37

[12] Greene, op. cit., 13

[13] Stanley, op. cit., 38, 97

[14] Ibid., 105

[15] Hernando deSoto, *The Mystery of Capital* (New York: Basic Books, 2000), 5

[16] Ibid., 5

[17] E. L. Jones, *The European Miracle*, (Cambridge, UK: Cambridge University Press, 1987), 39

[18] Niall Ferguson, "An Empire at Risk," *Newsweek*, November 28, 2009

[19] Ibid.

[20] Ibid.

[21] Paul Kennedy, *The Rise and Fall of Great Powers* (New York: Vintage, 1989)

[22] Ferguson, op. cit.

[23] Ibid.

## Chapter 9

[1] K. Anders Ericsson, op. cit., 2

[2] Ibid.

[3] Sheldon Richman, *Separating School and State* (Fairfax VA: Future of Freedom Foundation, 1994), 37–40

[4] Coyle, op. cit., 49

[5] Ibid.

[6] Richard E. Nisbett, *Intelligence and How to Get It* (New York: W. W. Norton & Company, 2009), 141

[7] Karl Weber, Ed., *Waiting For Superman*; "What *Really* Makes a Super School?" by Jay Mathews (New York: Public Affairs, 2010), 180

[8] Martin E. P. Seligman, *What You Can Change and What You Can't* (New York: Vantage, 2007)

[9] Colin Hitt, "Illinois Moves Closer to Passing School Choice Bill," *The School Choice Advocate*, June 2010, 5-

[10] John E. Chubb and Terry M. Moe, *Politics, Markets, & America's Schools* (Washington, D.C.: Brookings Institution Press, 1990)

[11] Steven R. Quartz, *Liars, Lovers, and Heroes* (New York: Quill, HarperCollins, 2003), 45

[12] Quartz, op. cit., 237

[13] Ibid., 46

[14] Derbyshire, op. cit., 99

[15] Ibid., 100

[16] Weber, Ed., op. cit.; "Educating America's Young People for the Global Economy," by Bill and Melinda Gates, 209

[17] Martin L. Gross, *The Conspiracy of Ignorance* (New York: Harper, 2000), 215

[18] Ibid., 217

[19] Ibid., 212

[20] Ibid., 55

## Chapter 10

[1] Ericsson, op. cit.

[2] Colvin, op. cit., 195–199

# Bibliography

Daniel G. Amen, M. D., *Magnificent Mind at any Age* (New York: Harmony Books, 2008)

Alan Beattie, *False Economy* (New York: Riverhead Books, 2010)

Walter Berns, *Making Patriots* (Chicago: The University of Chicago Press, 2001)

Steve Biddulph, *The Secret of Happy Children* (New York: Marlowe & Company, 2002) Bay Books, Sydney, 1984

Benjamin S. Bloom, Ed., *Developing Talent in Young People* (New York: Ballantine Books, 1985)

Reb Bradley, *Born Liberal Raised Right* (Los Angeles: WND Books, 2008)

John E. Chubb and Terry M. Moe, *Politics, Markets, & America's Schools* (Washington, D.C.: Brookings Institution Press, 1990)

Bruce Charlton, Discovery Channel News, 6-23-06

Gregory Cochran & Henry Harpending, *The 10,000 Year Explosion* (New York: Basic Books, 2009)

Geoff Colvin, *Talent is Overrated* (New York: Penguin Books, 2008)

Peter W. Cookson, Jr., and Kristina Berger, *Expect Miracles* (New York: Westview Press, 2002)

Stephen R. Covey, *The 7 Habits of Highly Effective People* (New York: A Fireside Book, Simon & Schuster, 1998)

Daniel Coyle, *The Talent Code: Greatness Isn't Born, It's Grown. Here's How*, Bantam Books, NY, 2009)

Michael Crichton, *Next* (New York: Harper, 2006)

John Derbyshire, *We Are Doomed* (New York: Crown Forum, 2009)

Hernando deSoto, *The Mystery of Capital* (New York: Basic Books, 2000)

Jared Diamond, *Guns, Germs and Steel* (New York: W. W. Norton & Company, 1999)

Theodore Dalrymple, *Our Culture, What's Left of It: The Mandarins and the Masses*, (Chicago: Ivan R. Dee, 2005)

Theodore Dalrymple, *Not With a Bang But a Whimper: The Politics and Culture of Decline* (Chicago: Ivan R. Dee, 2008)

Robert Epstein, *The Case Against Adolescence* (Sanger, CA: Quill Driver Books, 2007)

K. Anders Ericsson, Michael J. Prietula, and Edward T. Cokely, "The Making of an Expert," *Harvard Business Review*, July–August, 2007

Niall Ferguson, "An Empire at Risk," *Newsweek*, November 28, 2009

James R. Flynn, *What Is Intelligence?* (Cambridge, UK: Cambridge University Press, 2009)

Jerry Fodor and Massimo Piattelli-Palmarini, *What Darwin Got Wrong* (New York: Farrar, Straus and Giroux, 2010)

Malcolm Gladwell, *Outliers: The Story of Success* (New York: Little, Brown and Company, 2008)

Daniel Goleman, *Emotional Intelligence: Why It Can Matter More Than IQ*, 10th Anniversary Edition (New York: Bantam Books, 2006)

Steven J. Gould, *The Mis-Measure of Men* (New York: W. W. Norton, 1996)

Steven J. Gould, *Ever Since Darwin* (New York: W. W. Norton & Company, 1977)

Bill Greene, *Common Genius: How Ordinary People Create Prosperous Societies and How Intellectuals Make Them Collapse* (Little Rock: Laissez Faire Books, 2007)

Martin L. Gross, *The Conspiracy of Ignorance* (New York: HarperCollins Publishers, 1999)

Martin L. Gross, *National Suicide* (New York: Berkley Books, 2009)

Judith R. Harris, *The Nurture Assumption*, 2nd Ed. (New York: The Free Press, 1998)

Michael H. Hart, *Understanding Human History* (Augusta, GA: Washington Summit Publishers, 2007)

Arthur Herman, *How the Scots Invented the Modern World* (New York: Three Rivers Press, 2001)

Colin Hitt, "Illinois Moves Closer to Passing School Choice Bill," *The School Choice Advocate*, June, 2010

Hulk Hogan, *My Life Outside the Ring* (New York: St. Martin's Press, 2009)

Paul Johnson, *Intellectuals* (New York: Harper Perennial, 1990)

E. L. Jones, The European Miracle, 2nd Ed. (New York: Cambridge University Press, 1987)

Charles R. Joy, *The Animal World of Albert Schweitzer* (Hopewell, NJ: The Ecco Press, 1950)

George F. Kennan, *Sketches From A Life* (New York: Pantheon Books, 1989)

Paul Kennedy, *The Rise and Fall of Great Powers* (New York: Vintage, 1989)

Nicholas Lemann, *The Big Test* (New York: Farrar, Straus & Giroux, 1st ed., 2000)

Richard Lynn, *The Global Bell Curve* (Augusta GA: Washington Summit Publishers, 2008)

John Mayer and Peter Salovey, *Emotional Intelligence* (Port Chester, NY: Dude Publishing, 2004)

Meg Meeker, *Strong Fathers, Strong Daughters* (New York: Ballantine Books, 2006)

Ludwig von Mises, *Human Action*, 4th rev ed. (Irvington-on-Hudson, NY: The Foundation for Economic Education, Inc., 1949)

Stephen Murdoch, *IQ: A Smart History of a Failed Idea* (Hoboken: John Wiley & Sons, Inc., 2007)

Ulric Neisser, Ed., *The Rising Curve* (Washington, D. C.: American Psychological Association, 1998)

    James R. Flynn, "IQ Gains Over Time"

    Richard Lynn, "The Decline of Genotypic Intelligence"

Richard E. Nisbett, *Intelligence and How to Get IT* (New York: W. W. Norton & Company, 2009)

Randy Pausch and Jeffrey Zaslow, *The Last Lecture* (New York: Hyperion, 2008)

Steven Pinker, *The Blank Slate: The Modern Denial of Human Nature* (New York: Penguin Books, 2003)

Steven R. Quartz, *Liars, Lovers, and Heroes: What the New Brain Science Reveals About How We Become Who We Are* (New York: HarperCollins Publishers, First Quill edition, 2003)

Colin Renfrew, *Prehistory: The Making of the Modern Mind* (New York: The Modern Library, 2008)

Sheldon Richman, *Tethered Citizens* (Fairfax, VA: Future of Freedom Foundation, 2001)

Sheldon Richman, *Separating School and State* (Fairfax, VA: Future of Freedom Foundation, 1994)

George L. Rogers, *The Art of Virtue*, 3rd Ed. (Midvale, UT: Choice Skills Publ., 1996)

Lyle H. Rossiter, Jr., *The Liberal Mind* (St. Charles, IL: Free World Books, LLC, 2006)

Martin E. P. Seligman, *What You Can Change and What You Can't* (New York: Vantage, 2007)

Martin E. P Seligman, Ph. D., *Learned Optimism: How to Change Your Mind and Your Life* (New York: Vintage Books, 2006)

Ben Sherwood, *The Survivors Club* (New York: Grand Central Publishing, 2010)

Dean Keith Simonton, *Origins of Genius* (Oxford: Oxford University Press, 1999)

Lenore Skenazi, *Free-Range Kids: Giving Our Children the Freedom We Had Without Going Nuts* (San Francisco: Jossey-Bass, 2009)

Samuel Smiles, *Lives of the Engineers* (London: The Folio Society, 2006)

Thomas Sowell, *Intellectuals and Society* (New York: Basic Books, 2009)

Thomas J. Stanley, *The Millionaire Mind* (Kansas City: Andrews McMeel Publishing, LLC, 2001)

Keith E. Stanovitch, *What Intelligence Tests Miss: The Psychology of Rational Thought* (New Haven: Yale University Press, 2009)

Robert J. Sternberg, *Wisdom, Intelligence and Creativity Synthesized* (Cambridge, UK: Cambridge University Press, 2007)

Charles J. Sykes, *Dumbing Down Our Kids* (New York: St. Martin's Griffin, 1995)

Paul D. Tieger & Barbara Barron-Tieger, *Nurture by Nature* (New York: Little, Brown & Company, 1997)

Harry C. Triandis, *Individualism and Collectivism* (Boulder, CO: Westview Press, 1995)

Harry C. Triandis, *Culture and Social Behavior* (New York: McGraw-Hill, Inc., 1994)

George E. Vaillant, *Adaptation to Life* (Cambridge MA: Harvard University Press, 1977)

George E. Vaillant, *Spiritual Evolution* (New York: Broadway Books, 2008)

George E. Vaillant, *Aging Well: Surprising Guideposts to a Happier Life* (New York: Little, Brown and Company)

Karl Weber, Ed., *Waiting For Superman* (New York: Public Affairs, 2010)

    Jay Mathews, "What *Really* Makes a Super School?"

    Bill and Melinda Gates, "Educating America's Young People for the Global Economy"

John Wooden and Steve Jamison, *The Essential Wooden: A Lifetime of Lessons on Leaders and Leadership* (New York: McGraw-Hill, 2007)

Neil Clark Warren, *Finding Contentment* (Nashville: Thomas Nelson Publishers, 1997)

# Index

# Also by Bill Greene...

**COMMON GENIUS**
Guts, Grit & Common Sense

How Ordinary People Create Prosperous Societies and How Intellectuals Make Them Collapse

by Bill Greene

"Mr. Greene shows how history progresses through the spontaneous creativity of ordinary free individuals, and not through top-down design by experts or intellectuals. A fascinating and clearly written book that challenges the conventional wisdom of our society's cult of expertise. It is likely to be controversial among our cultural elites."

—Joseph F. Johnston, Jr., author *The Limits of Government*

**Common Genius** looks at major trends of the past 3,000 years of world history, revealing why some societies prospered while others remained mired in poverty. Join the author in his quest to find the causes of history's sublime spectacle—the march of mankind forward from poverty to prosperity.

- ➤ See how "great men" and "great events" did more harm than good.
- ➤ Find out which religions and philosophies helped and which hurt.
- ➤ Discover the lessons of history and how they apply to today's issues.
- ➤ Learn 10 "tipping points" that determined which nations advanced.
- ➤ Explore why foreign aid has failed to help Third World Nations.

"Bill Greene has written a provocative book that celebrates the common sense of the people who built the West, and disparages the dangerous and faulty theories of the academics who want to tear down this civilization."

—Ricardo Duchesne, professor, University of New Brunswick